# This Book Belongs To:

AF486771

PART 1 ~ Practice tracing, writing and coloring the letters of the alphabet . . . The ABC'S.

PART 2 ~ Learn to read, write and spell 405, 1-9 letter Sight Words.

PART 3 ~ Learn and practice CVC Phonics skills with 150 CVC words.

PART 4 ~ Congratulations! You are awarded the . . . "CERTIFICATE OF ACHIEVEMENT".

Learning is Fun!

Sight Words instruction increases a child's familiarity with the high frequency words he/she will encounter most often, while CVC Phonics is a method for learning to read in general, by practicing the blending of individual sounds.

With combining the two, this FUN workbook with many activities, games and puzzles will help your child develop their reading, writing, spelling and vocabulary skills while learning and practicing Sight Words and CVC Phonics Words.

CATERPILLAR KIDZ PRESS

## ~ PART 1 ~
## Let us begin by recapping the letters of the ALPHABET

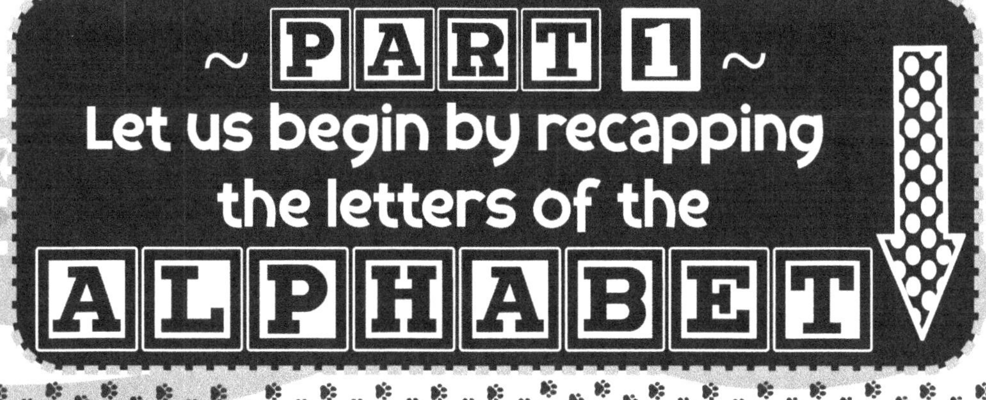

# WANT FREE FUN ACTIVITIES ?

Email me at
CATERPILLAR.KIDZ.PRESS@GMAIL.COM
and I will email you some fun activities!
Please choose ① from the following themes:
Unicorns, Princesses, Mermaids,
Dinosaurs, Robots, Space or Cute Animals.
Then, enter your chosen theme in
the subject line of the email.
TALK TO YOU SOON!

And,
Thank You!
CATERPILLAR KIDZ PRESS

## Trace the letter

A    A    A    A

a    a    a    a

## Color the letters

A a

## Write the letter

A

a

## Find them

d   L   E   g   a

C   v   y   A   R

a   f   T   t   A

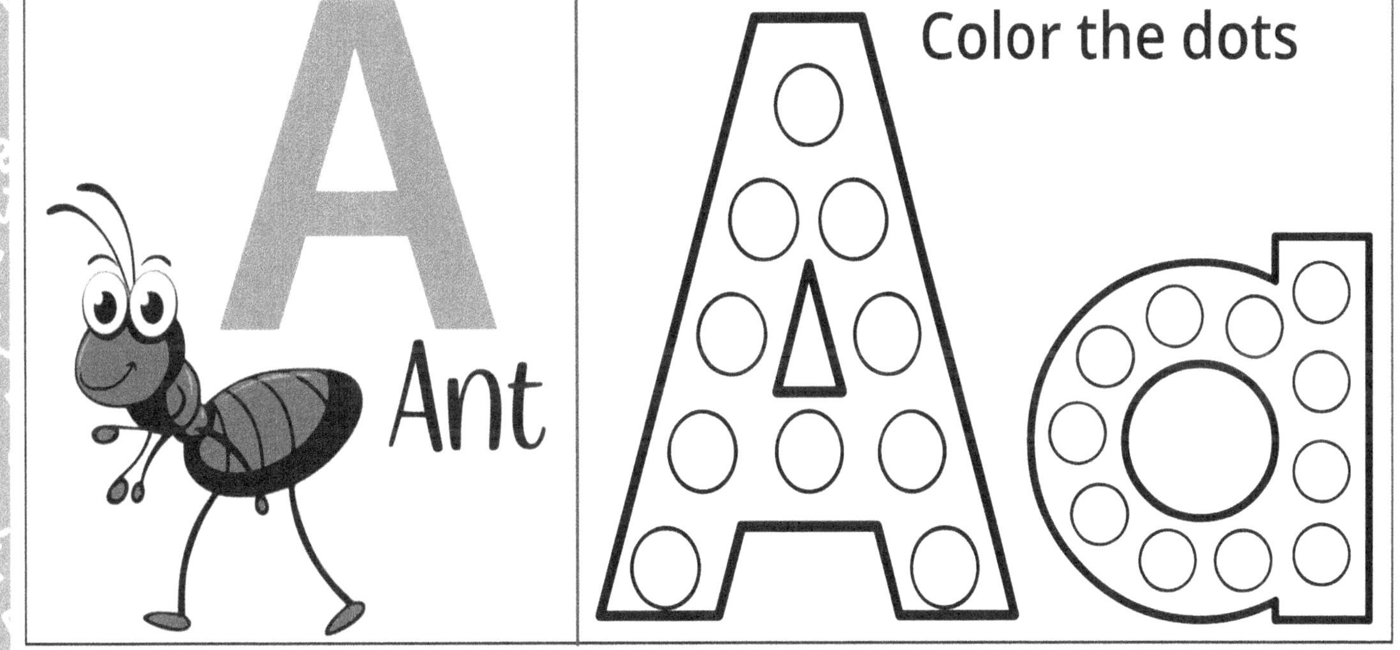

A Ant

Color the dots

A a

## Trace the letter

B B B B

b b b b

## Color the letters

B b

## Write the letter

B

b

## Find them

| | | | | |
|---|---|---|---|---|
| d | L | E | g | A |
| B | b | y | A | R |
| a | f | T | t | b |

B

Bee

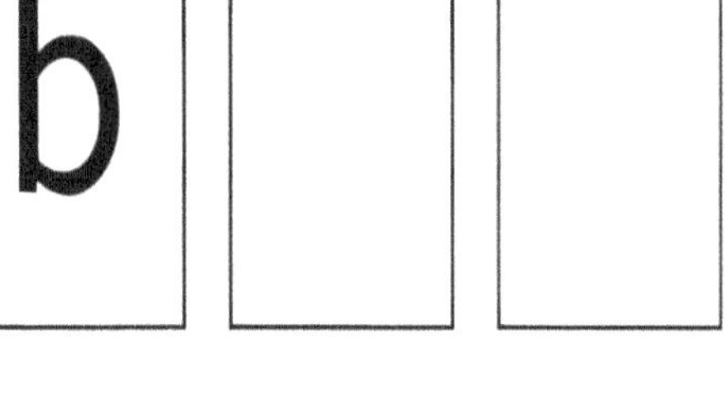

Color the dots

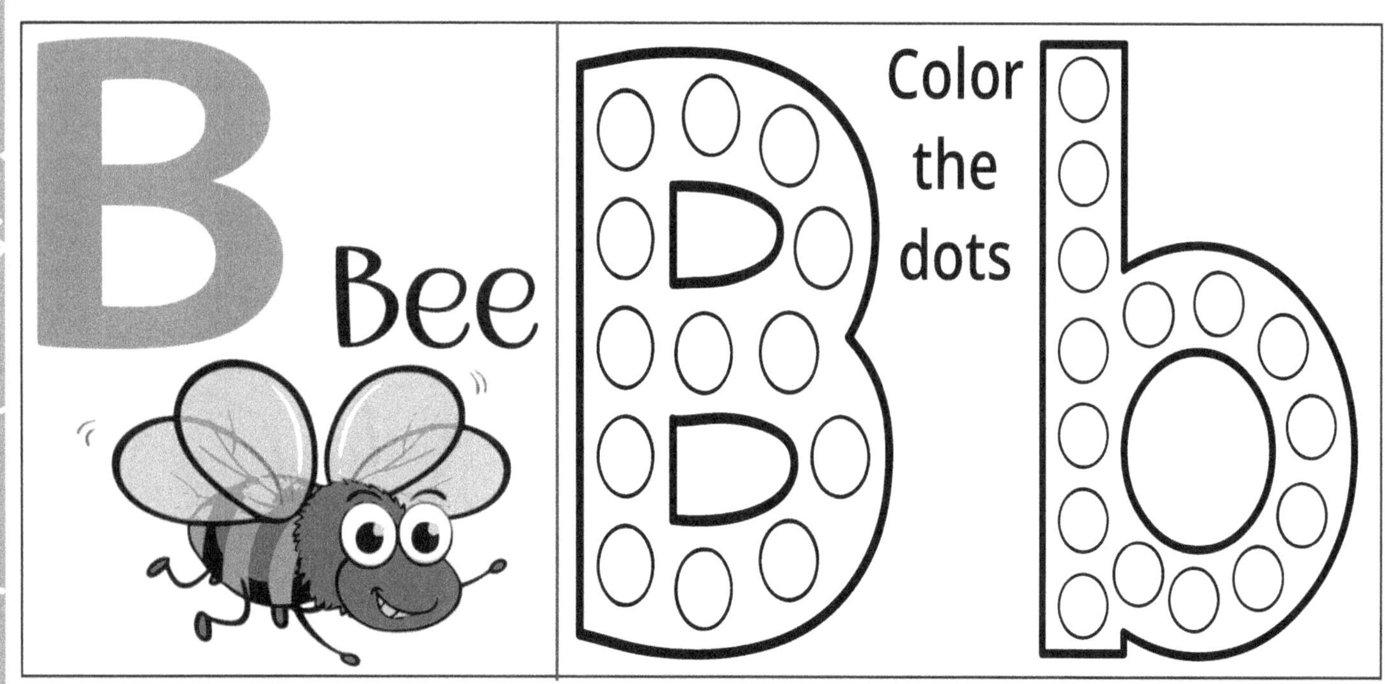

## Trace the letter

C C C C

c c c c

## Color the letters

C c

## Write the letter

C

c

## Find them

| | | | | |
|---|---|---|---|---|
| d | L | E | c | A |
| C | v | y | A | R |
| a | f | T | c | A |

C

Cat

## Color the dots

C c

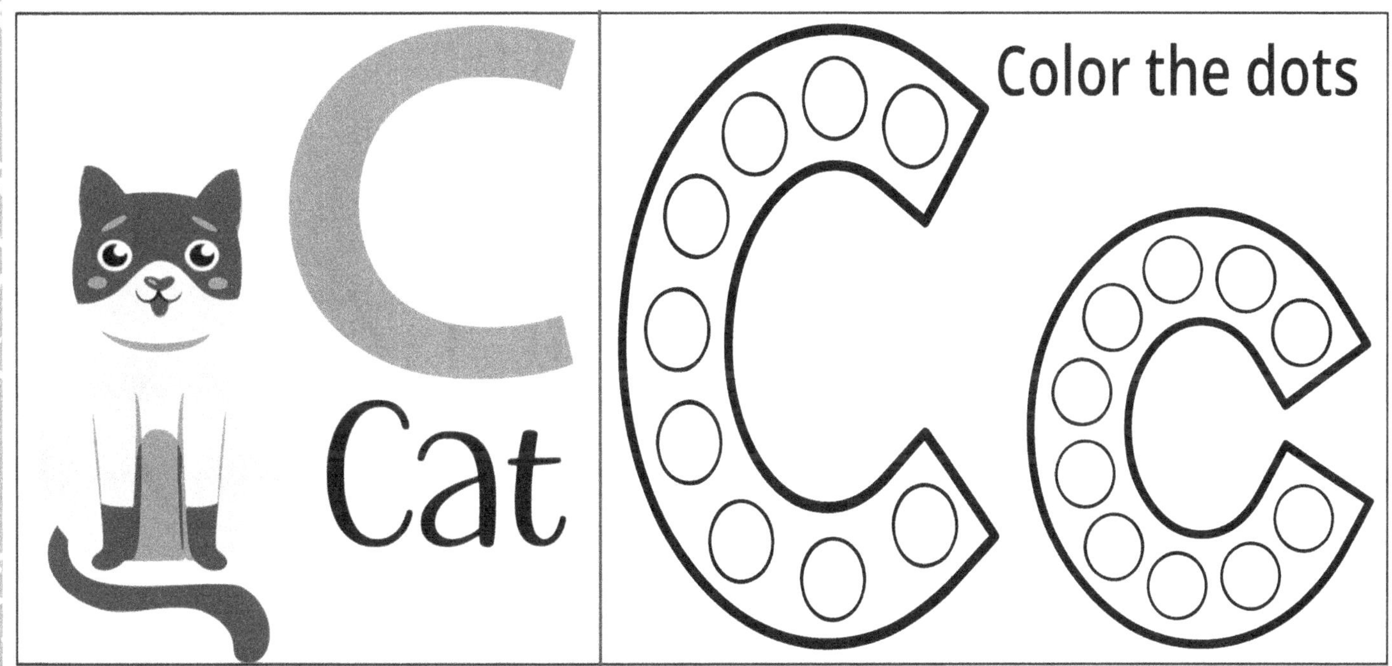

## Trace the letter

D D D D

d d d d

## Color the letters

D d

## Write the letter

| | | | |
|---|---|---|---|
| D | | | |
| d | | | |

## Find them

| | | | | |
|---|---|---|---|---|
| d | D | E | g | D |
| C | d | y | A | R |
| a | f | T | t | A |

D

Dog

## Color the dots

D d

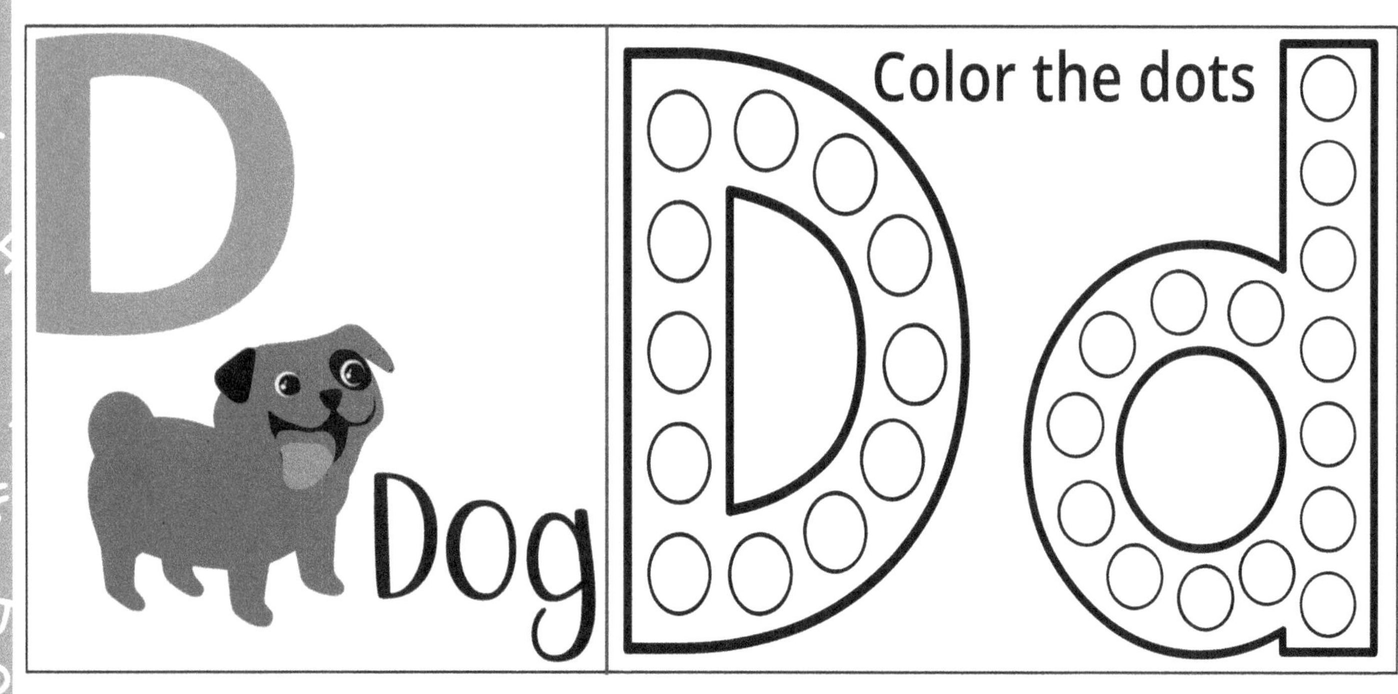

# Trace the letter

E  E  E  E

e  e  e  e

# Color the letters

Ee

# Write the letter

E

e

# Find them

d  L  E  g  A

C  e  y  A  e

E  f  T  t  A

E

Eagle

# Color the dots

## Trace the letter

F F F F

f f f f

## Color the letters

F f

## Write the letter

| | | | |
|---|---|---|---|
| F | | | |
| f | | | |

## Find them

| | | | | |
|---|---|---|---|---|
| d | L | f | g | A |
| C | v | f | A | f |
| F | f | T | t | A |

F

Frog

Color the dots

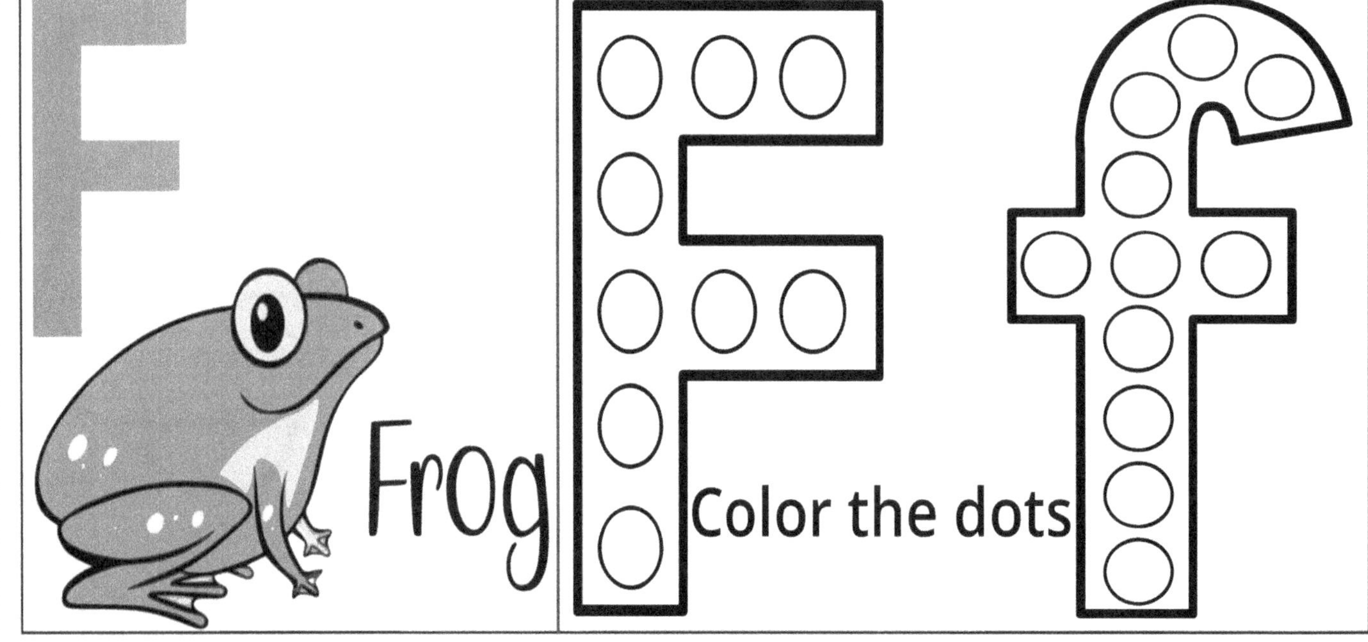

# Trace the letter

G G G G

g g g g

# Color the letters

G g

# Write the letter

G
g

# Find them

| | | | | |
|---|---|---|---|---|
| G | L | E | g | G |
| C | v | y | A | R |
| a | g | T | t | A |

Goose

## Color the dots

G g

## Trace the letter

H H H H

h h h h

## Color the letters

H h

## Write the letter

| | | | |
|---|---|---|---|
| H | | | |
| h | | | |

## Find them

d H E g A

C v h A R

a f T t H

H Hamster

## Color the dots

H h

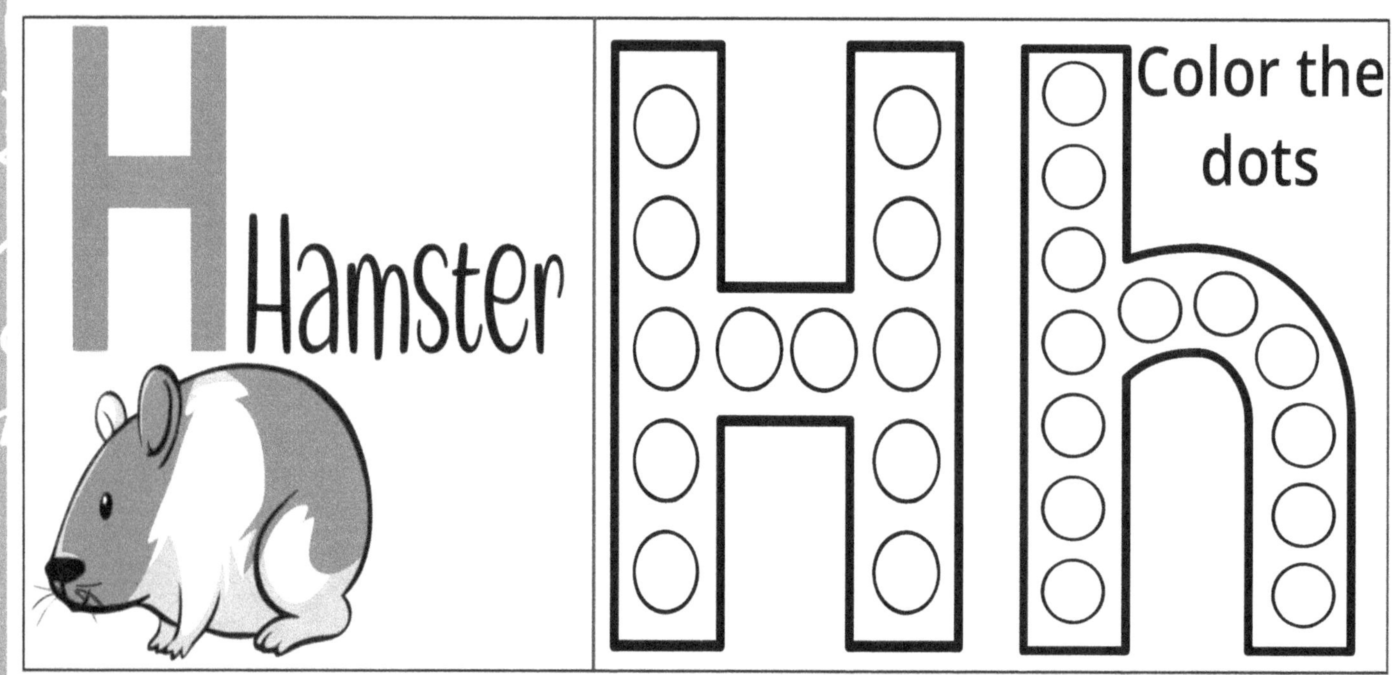

## Trace the letter

## Color the letters

I i

## Write the letter

I

i

## Find them

| | | | | |
|---|---|---|---|---|
| i | L | I | g | A |
| C | v | y | A | i |
| a | f | I | t | A |

I

Iguana

## Color the dots

I i

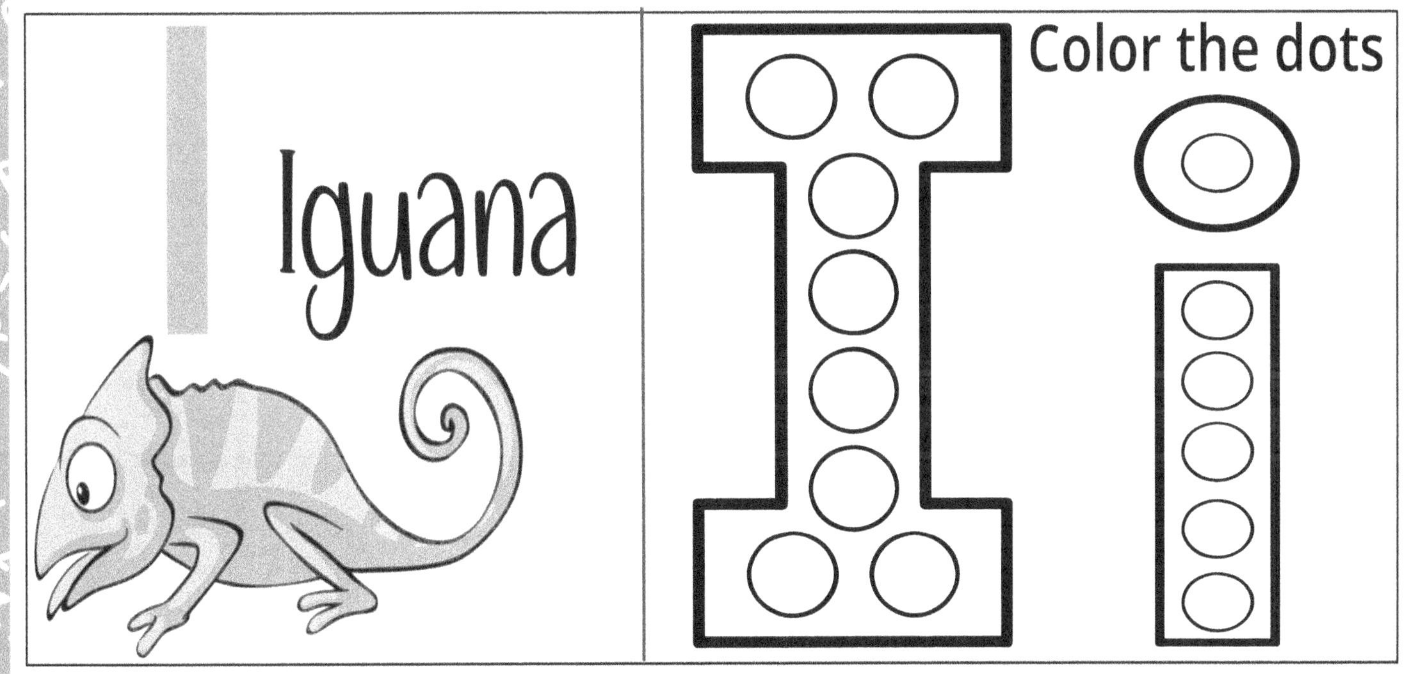

## Trace the letter

J J J J

j j j j

## Color the letters

J j

## Write the letter

| | | | |
|---|---|---|---|
| J | | | |
| j | | | |

## Find them

| | | | | |
|---|---|---|---|---|
| d | J | E | g | A |
| C | j | y | A | R |
| a | f | J | j | A |

J Jaguar

Color the dots

J j

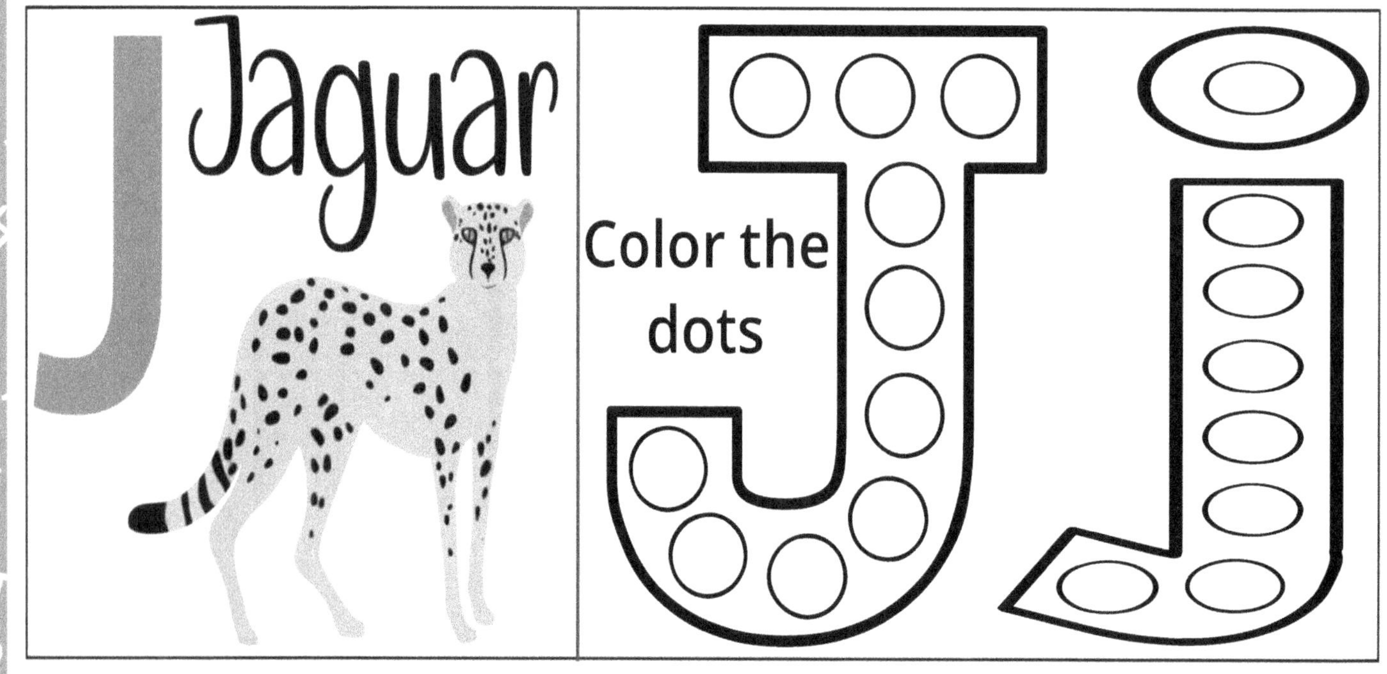

# Trace the letter

K  K  K  K

k  k  k  k

# Color the letters

K k

# Write the letter

K
k

# Find them

d L E g A

K v k A R

a f T k A

K  Kangaroo

Color the dots

## Trace the letter

L L L L

l l l l

## Color the letters

L l

## Write the letter

L

l

## Find them

d L E g A

C l y A I

I f T t A

L

Lemur

## Color the dots

L l

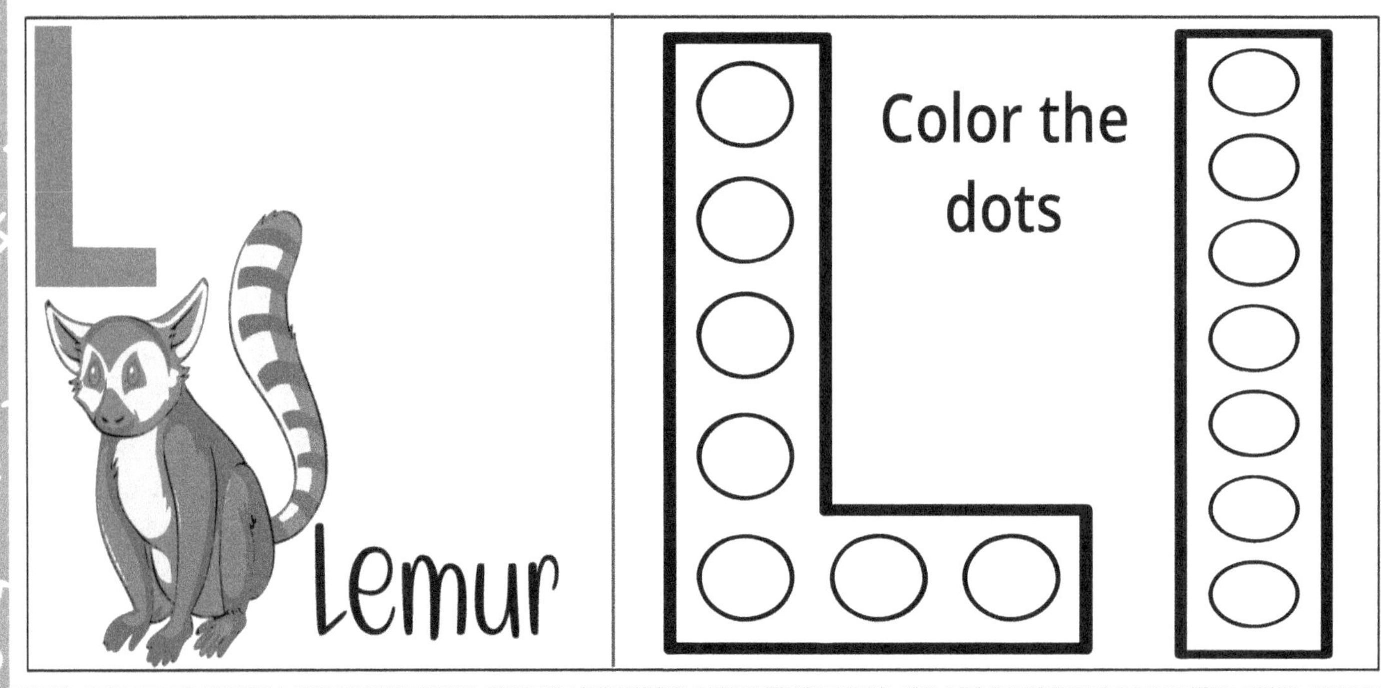

## Trace the letter

M M M M

m m m m

## Color the letters

M m

## Write the letter

M

m

## Find them

d M E g A

C v y A m

a m T M A

Mouse

M

Color the dots

M m

# Trace the letter

N N N N

n n n n

# Color the letters

N n

# Write the letter

N

n

# Find them

d L N g A

N v n A R

a f T n A

Nightingale

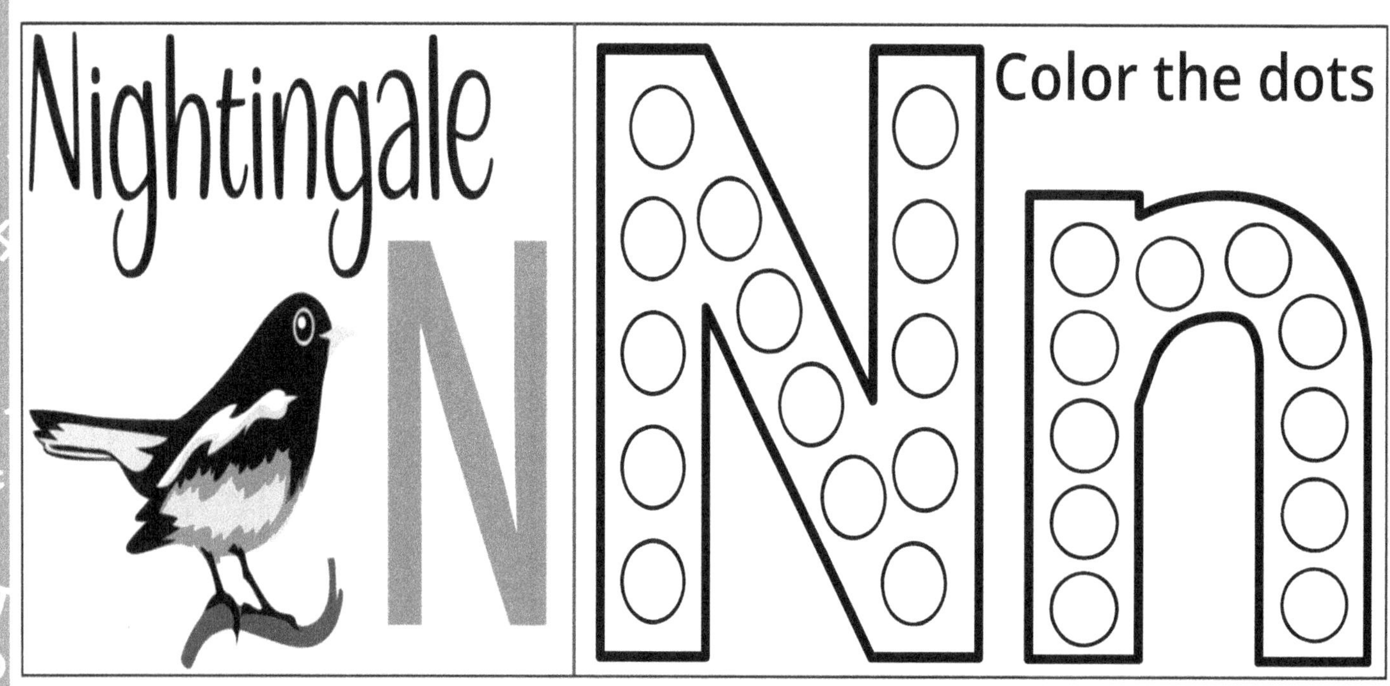

## Color the dots

N n

## Trace the letter

## Color the letters

O o

## Write the letter

O

o

## Find them

| | | | | |
|---|---|---|---|---|
| o | L | E | g | A |
| C | o | y | A | O |
| a | f | O | t | A |

O Otter

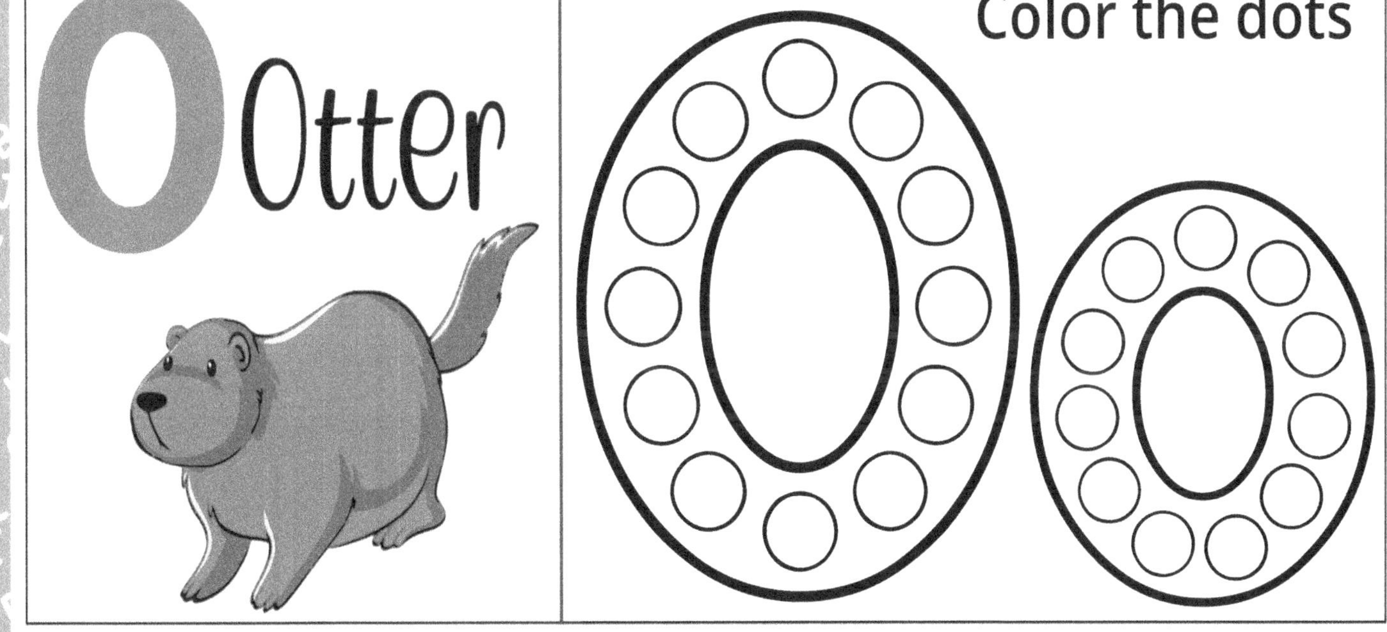

## Color the dots

# Trace the letter

P    P    P    P

p    p    p    p

# Color the letters

p   p

# Write the letter

P
p

# Find them

P   p   E   g   A
C   p   y   A   P
a   f   T   t   A

Penguin

# Color the dots

P   p

# Trace the letter

# Color the letters

Q q

# Write the letter

Q

q

# Find them

| q | Q | E | g | A |
| C | v | q | Q | R |
| a | f | T | q | A |

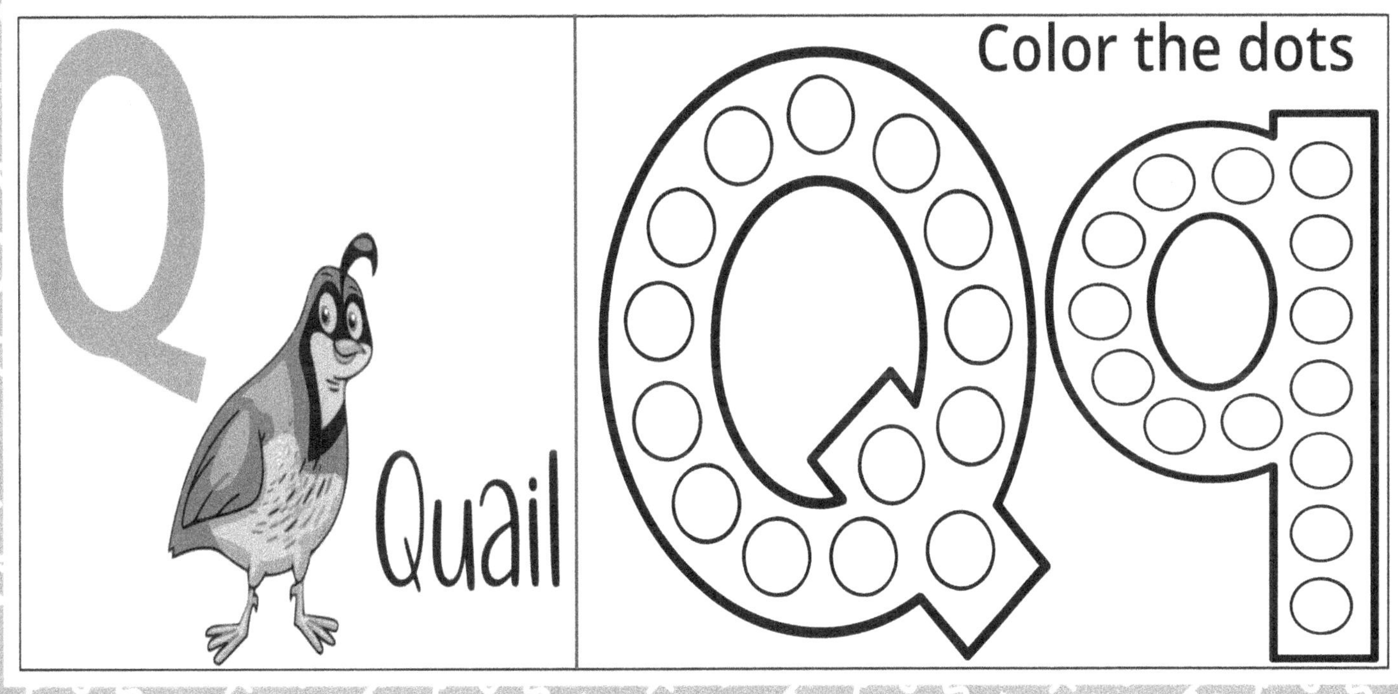

Quail

# Color the dots

Q q

# Trace the letter

R R R R

r r r r

# Color the letters

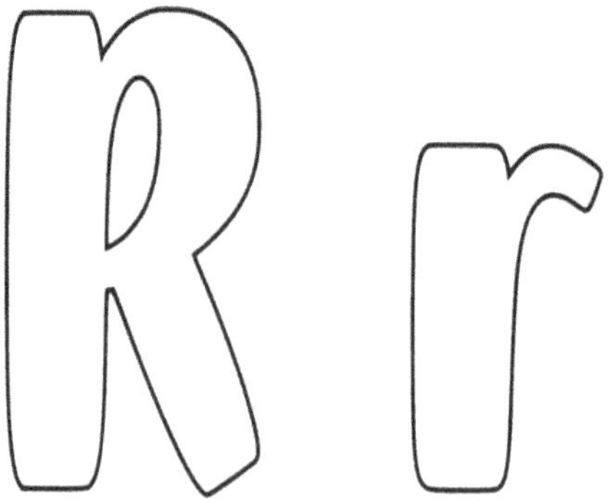

R r

# Write the letter

R

r

# Find them

d L R g A

C r y R R

a f T r A

Rabbit

## Color the dots

# Trace the letter

S   S   S   S

S   S   S   S

# Color the letters

S S

# Write the letter

S

S

# Find them

d   S   S   g   A

C   v   s   A   R

a   f   T   t   A

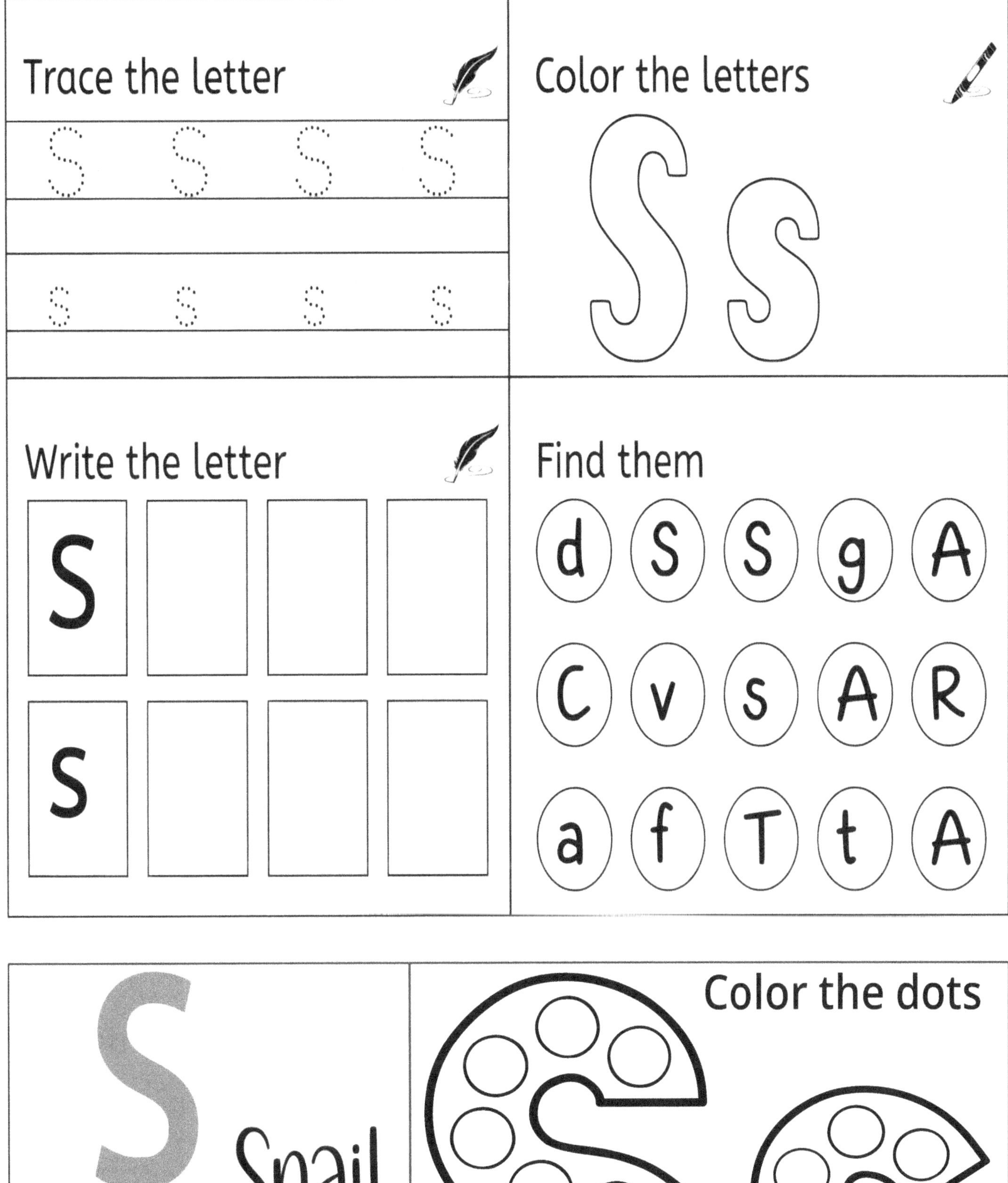

S

Snail

## Color the dots

S S

# Trace the letter

# Color the letters

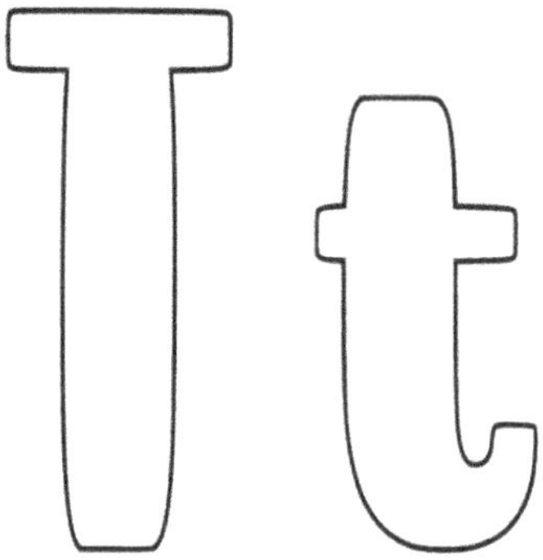

T t

# Write the letter

T
t

# Find them

d  T  E  g  A
C  t  y  T  R
a  f  T  t  A

T Tapir

Color the dots

# Trace the letter

# Color the letters

U u

# Write the letter

U
u

# Find them

d U E g A
C u y A R
a f U t A

Unicorn

# Color the dots

U u

## Trace the letter

V V V V

v v v v

## Color the letters

Vv

## Write the letter

V V V V
V V V V

## Find them

v L E g A
C v y A R
a f v t A

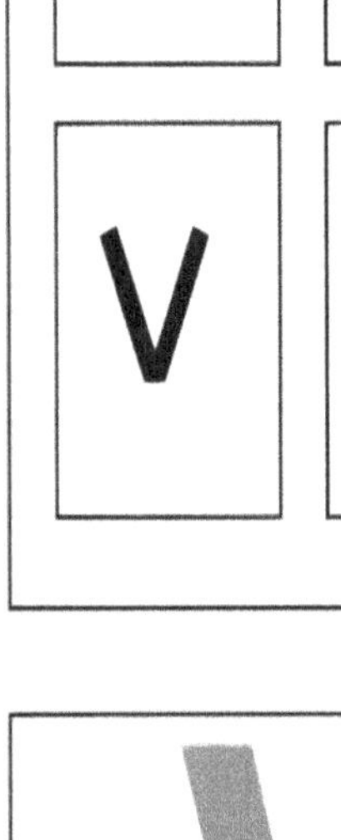

Vulture

## Color the dots

Vv

## Trace the letter

W W W W

w w w w

## Color the letters

W w

## Write the letter

W

w

## Find them

| | | | | |
|---|---|---|---|---|
| d | L | W | g | A |
| C | v | y | W | R |
| a | w | T | t | A |

W

Walrus

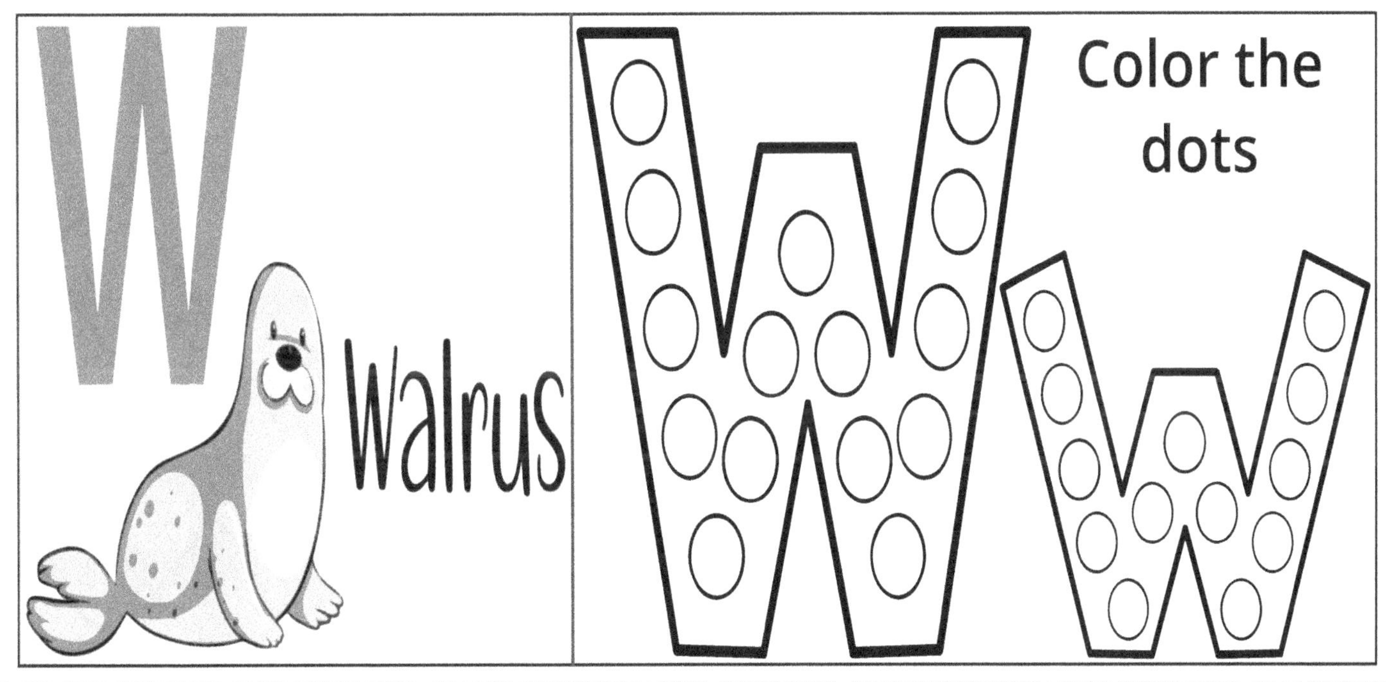

## Color the dots

W w

# Trace the letter

X X X X
X X X X

# Color the letters

Xx

# Write the letter

X
X

# Find them

x X E g A
C x y A R
a f T X A

X X-Ray Tetra

# Color the dots

Xx

# Trace the letter

# Color the letters

Y y

# Write the letter

Y

y

# Find them

Y  R  E  g  R

r  v  y  Y  R

a  f  T  t  A

Yak

## Color the dots

Y y

## Trace the letter

Z Z Z Z

Z Z Z Z

## Color the letters

Z z

## Write the letter

Z

Z

## Find them

z L E g z

C v Z A R

a f T t A

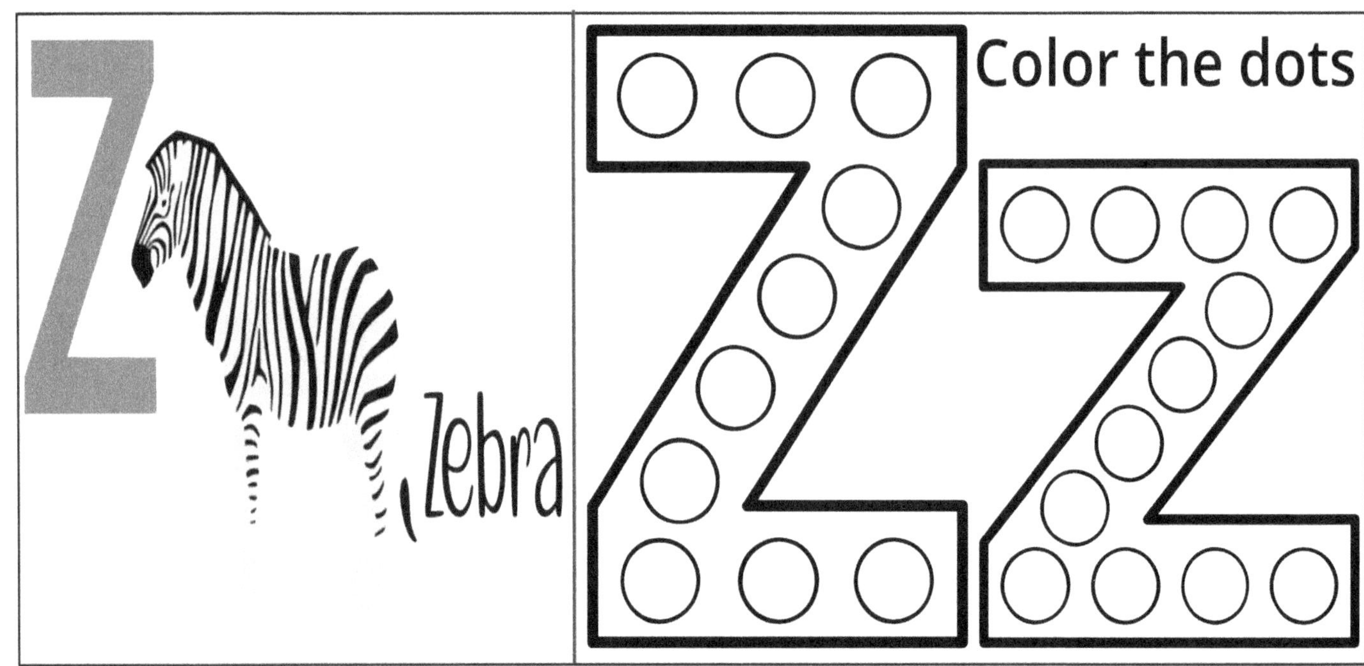


## Color the dots

Z Z

# Table of Contents – 405 Sight Words

Ⓐ – Ⓕ

| | | | | | | | |
|---|---|---|---|---|---|---|---|
| a | - page 33 | back | - page 84 | certain | - page 112 | earth | - page 94 |
| about | - page 78 | be | - page 75 | change | - page 91 | easy | - page 105 |
| above | - page 101 | because | - page 89 | children | - page 98 | eat | - page 100 |
| across | - page 106 | become | - page 105 | city | - page 94 | end | - page 88 |
| add | - page 93 | been | - page 81 | close | - page 96 | enough | - page 100 |
| after | - page 84 | before | - page 86 | cold | - page 111 | even | - page 88 |
| again | - page 90 | began | - page 99 | color | - page 104 | ever | - page 104 |
| against | - page 109 | begin | - page 96 | come | - page 44 | every | - page 93 |
| air | - page 91 | being | - page 102 | complete | - page 109 | example | - page 96 |
| all | - page 76 | below | - page 93 | could | - page 80 | eyes | - page 94 |
| almost | - page 101 | best | - page 106 | country | - page 93 | face | - page 100 |
| along | - page 96 | better | - page 106 | covered | - page 108 | fall | - page 111 |
| also | - page 87 | between | - page 93 | cried | - page 111 | family | - page 102 |
| always | - page 97 | big | - page 36 | cut | - page 102 | far | - page 101 |
| America | - page 92 | birds | - page 104 | day | - page 82 | farm | - page 110 |
| and | - page 34 | black | - page 107 | did | - page 82 | fast | - page 108 |
| and | - page 73 | blue | - page 37 | didn't | - page 105 | father | - page 94 |
| animal | - page 91 | body | - page 103 | different | - page 90 | feet | - page 98 |
| another | - page 88 | book | - page 99 | does | - page 88 | few | - page 95 |
| answer | - page 92 | both | - page 97 | dog | - page 103 | field | - page 112 |
| any | - page 86 | boy | - page 87 | don't | - page 95 | figure | - page 112 |
| are | - page 74 | but | - page 76 | door | - page 105 | find | - page 41 |
| area | - page 108 | by | - page 75 | down | - page 40 | fire | - page 112 |
| around | - page 92 | called | - page 81 | down | - page 82 | first | - page 81 |
| as | - page 79 | came | - page 87 | draw | - page 110 | fish | - page 103 |
| ask | - page 89 | can | - page 38 | during | - page 106 | five | - page 109 |
| at | - page 75 | car | - page 98 | each | - page 77 | follow | - page 87 |
| away | - page 35 | carry | - page 99 | early | - page 107 | food | - page 93 |

# Ⓕ – Ⓝ    Table of Contents – 405 Sight Words

| | | | | | | | |
|---|---|---|---|---|---|---|---|
| for | - page 42 | here | - page 46 | kind | - page 90 | map | - page 110 |
| form | - page 87 | here | - page 89 | king | - page 111 | mark | - page 103 |
| found | - page 92 | high | - page 93 | knew | - page 104 | may | - page 82 |
| four | - page 99 | him | - page 79 | know | - page 83 | me | - page 55 |
| friends | - page 105 | himself | - page 108 | land | - page 90 | means | - page 86 |
| from | - page 75 | his | - page 74 | large | - page 88 | measure | - page 107 |
| funny | - page 43 | hold | - page 108 | last | - page 94 | men | - page 89 |
| get | - page 82 | home | - page 90 | late | - page 100 | might | - page 96 |
| girl | - page 101 | horse | - page 104 | learn | - page 92 | mile | - page 98 |
| give | - page 84 | hours | - page 107 | leave | - page 102 | miss | - page 100 |
| go | - page 44 | house | - page 91 | left | - page 95 | money | - page 110 |
| good | - page 85 | how | - page 77 | let | - page 101 | more | - page 80 |
| got | - page 97 | however | - page 106 | letter | - page 92 | morning | - page 109 |
| great | - page 85 | hundred | - page 109 | life | - page 97 | most | - page 84 |
| ground | - page 111 | I | - page 47 | light | - page 95 | mother | - page 92 |
| group | - page 97 | idea | - page 100 | like | - page 79 | mountains | - page 101 |
| grow | - page 99 | if | - page 77 | line | - page 86 | move | - page 90 |
| had | - page 75 | I'll | - page 112 | list | - page 102 | much | - page 86 |
| hand | - page 90 | important | - page 98 | listen | - page 108 | music | - page 103 |
| happened | - page 107 | in | - page 48 | little | - page 52 | must | - page 88 |
| hard | - page 96 | Indian | - page 101 | live | - page 84 | my | - page 56 |
| has | - page 79 | into | - page 79 | long | - page 82 | name | - page 85 |
| have | - page 75 | is | - page 49 | look | - page 53 | near | - page 93 |
| he | - page 74 | it | - page 50 | low | - page 106 | need | - page 89 |
| head | - page 95 | it's | - page 102 | made | - page 82 | never | - page 94 |
| hear | - page 100 | jump | - page 51 | make | - page 54 | new | - page 83 |
| heard | - page 105 | just | - page 84 | many | - page 78 | next | - page 96 |
| help | - page 45 | keep | - page 94 | many | - page 78 | night | - page 98 |

# Table of Contents – 405 Sight Words  [N] – [T]


| | | | |
|---|---|---|---|
| north – page 110 | pattern – page 109 | say – page 85 | south – page 111 |
| not – page 57 | people – page 80 | school – page 94 | space – page 108 |
| not – page 76 | picture – page 90 | sea – page 99 | spell – page 91 |
| notice – page 111 | piece – page 104 | second – page 100 | stand – page 103 |
| now – page 81 | place – page 83 | see – page 63 | start – page 94 |
| number – page 80 | plan – page 111 | seem – page 96 | state – page 99 |
| numeral – page 109 | plant – page 93 | seen – page 110 | step – page 109 |
| of – page 73 | play – page 59 | sentence – page 85 | still – page 92 |
| off – page 91 | point – page 91 | set – page 88 | stop – page 100 |
| often – page 97 | problem – page 104 | several – page 108 | story – page 95 |
| oil – page 81 | products – page 107 | she – page 77 | study – page 92 |
| old – page 86 | pulled – page 110 | ship – page 106 | such – page 89 |
| once – page 99 | put – page 88 | short – page 106 | sun – page 103 |
| one – page 58 | questions – page 104 | should – page 92 | sure – page 105 |
| one – page 75 | reached – page 107 | show – page 87 | table – page 110 |
| only – page 83 | read – page 89 | side – page 98 | take – page 83 |
| open – page 96 | real – page 101 | since – page 104 | talk – page 102 |
| or – page 75 | red – page 60 | sing – page 111 | tell – page 86 |
| order – page 105 | red – page 105 | sit – page 81 | than – page 81 |
| other – page 78 | remember – page 107 | slowly – page 110 | that – page 73 |
| our – page 84 | right – page 86 | small – page 87 | the – page 64 |
| out – page 78 | river – page 99 | so – page 78 | their – page 77 |
| over – page 83 | rock – page 108 | some – page 79 | them – page 78 |
| own – page 93 | room – page 104 | something – page 96 | then – page 78 |
| page – page 91 | run – page 61 | sometimes – page 101 | there – page 77 |
| paper – page 97 | said – page 62 | song – page 102 | these – page 78 |
| part – page 82 | same – page 86 | soon – page 102 | they – page 74 |
| passed – page 109 | saw – page 95 | sound – page 83 | things – page 84 |

# Table of Contents – 405 Sight Words


|  |  | |  |  | |  |  |
|---|---|---|---|---|---|---|---|
| think | - page 85 | | use | - page 77 | | with | - page 74 |
| this | - page 75 | | usually | - page 105 | | without | - page 100 |
| those | - page 97 | | very | - page 84 | | wood | - page 112 |
| thought | - page 95 | | voice | - page 110 | | words | - page 75 |
| three | - page 65 | | vowel | - page 109 | | work | - page 83 |
| through | - page 85 | | walk | - page 98 | | world | - page 92 |
| time | - page 79 | | want | - page 87 | | would | - page 79 |
| to | - page 66 | | war | - page 111 | | write | - page 80 |
| today | - page 106 | | was | - page 74 | | years | - page 83 |
| together | - page 97 | | watch | - page 101 | | yellow | - page 71 |
| told | - page 104 | | water | - page 81 | | you | - page 72 |
| too | - page 86 | | waves | - page 107 | | young | - page 102 |
| took | - page 99 | | way | - page 80 | | | |
| top | - page 106 | | we | - page 69 | | | |
| toward | - page 108 | | well | - page 88 | | | |
| town | - page 112 | | went | - page 89 | | | |
| travel | - page 112 | | were | - page 76 | | | |
| tree | - page 94 | | what | - page 76 | | | |
| true | - page 109 | | when | - page 76 | | | |
| try | - page 90 | | where | - page 70 | | | |
| turn | - page 89 | | which | - page 77 | | | |
| two | - page 67 | | while | - page 95 | | | |
| under | - page 95 | | white | - page 98 | | | |
| unit | - page 112 | | who | - page 81 | | | |
| until | - page 98 | | whole | - page 107 | | | |
| up | - page 68 | | why | - page 89 | | | |
| upon | - page 112 | | will | - page 78 | | | |
| us | - page 90 | | wind | - page 108 | | | |


## ~ PART 2 ~

~ Sight Words Activities, Games & Word Search Puzzle Worksheets

### Benefits of Kids Learning Sight Words:

1. Memorizing & knowing sight words through repetition means they can build speed and fluency in reading in turn increasing reading comprehension.

2. They can be more fluent in reading because they don't have to stop and think about as many words.

3. They can understand more sentences by being able to make connections between sight words.

LEARNING IS FUN!

**Read it.**

a

**Trace it.**

a

**Trace and write.**

a a a
a a a
a

**Color by sight word.**

ORANGE a | GREEN a

**Decorate it.**

a

**Complete the sentence.**

I have a cat.

**Find and circle.**

| in | a | o | a | an |
|----|----|----|----|----|
| a | at | a | a | do |
| or | a | I | go | a |
| a | so | a | e | a |

**Fill in the missing letter.**

Read it.
and

Trace it.
and

Trace and write.
and    and
and    and
and

Decorate it.
and

Color by sight word.
PINK    and    |    GREEN    and

run
ant    and    can
and    and
and
and    and
go    and    an
the    and    and
a
my
end

Complete the sentence.
I like milk and bread.

Find and circle.
ant    and    and    mat    and
and    than    and    and    for
an    and    has    find    and
and    one    not    and    did

Fill in the missing letters.
a    d
n

**Read it.**

# away

**Trace it.**

**Trace and write.**

away   away

away   away

away

**Decorate it.**

away

**Color by sight word.**

ORANGE → away

YELLOW → *away*

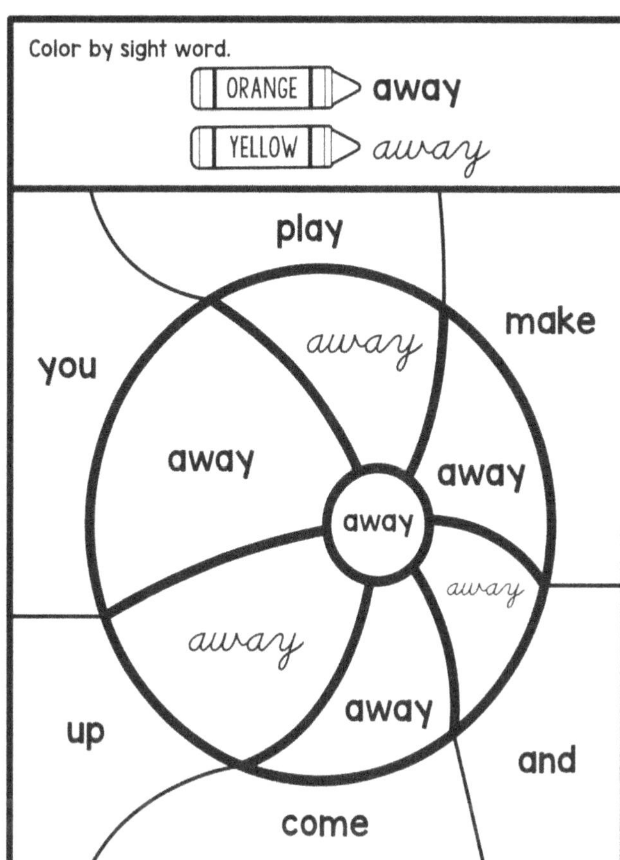


**Complete the sentence.**

The boy ran away.

**Find and circle.**

| away | day | am | away | way |
|---|---|---|---|---|
| can | away | and | may | away |
| away | say | away | yellow | out |
| what | away | they | away | pay |

**Fill in the missing letters.**

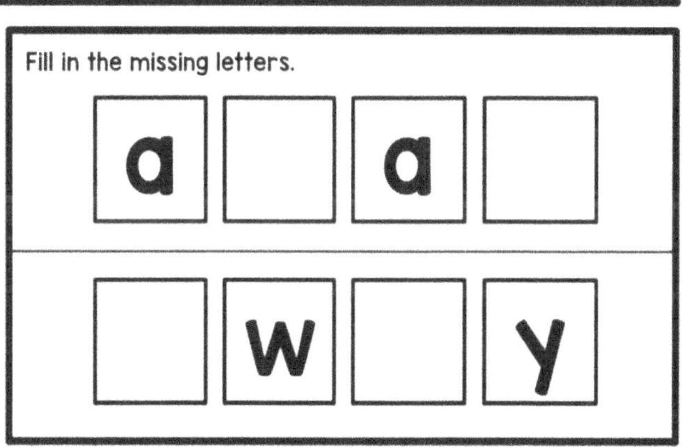

**Read it.**

big

**Trace it.**

big

**Trace and write.**

big big
big big
big

**Color by sight word.**

PINK **big** | BLUE *big*

**Decorate it.**

big

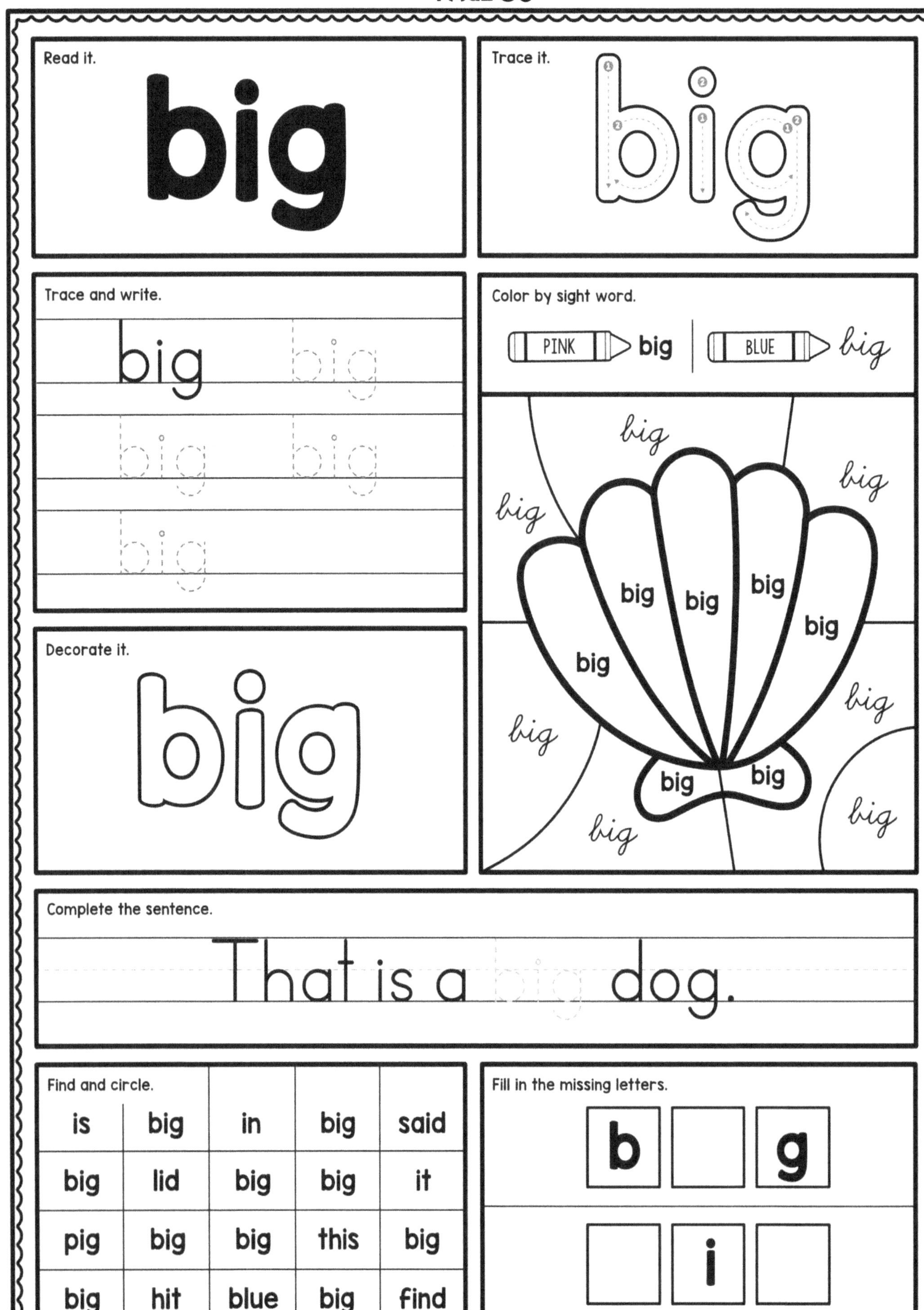

**Complete the sentence.**

That is a big dog.

**Find and circle.**

| is | big | in | big | said |
|---|---|---|---|---|
| big | lid | big | big | it |
| pig | big | big | this | big |
| big | hit | blue | big | find |

**Fill in the missing letters.**

| b |   | g |
|---|---|---|
|   | i |   |

Read it.

blue

Trace it.

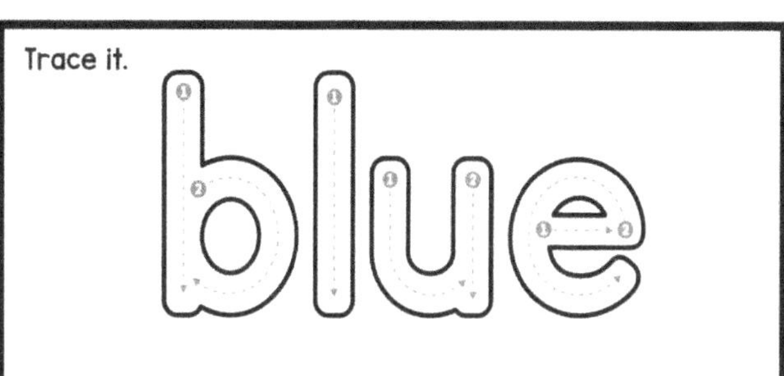

Trace and write.

blue   blue
blue   blue
blue

Decorate it.

blue

Color by sight word.

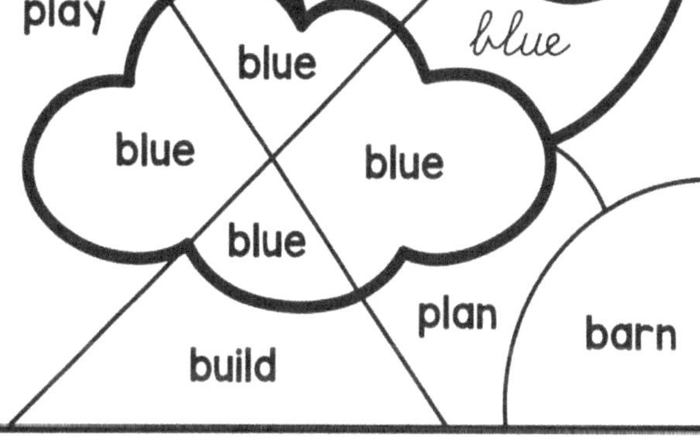


Complete the sentence.

She has a blue pen.

Find and circle.

| blue | be | blue | blue | born |
|------|------|------|------|------|
| glue | blue | been | bear | blue |
| blue | blue | dose | blue | big |
| plan | blue | blue | but | blue |

Fill in the missing letters.

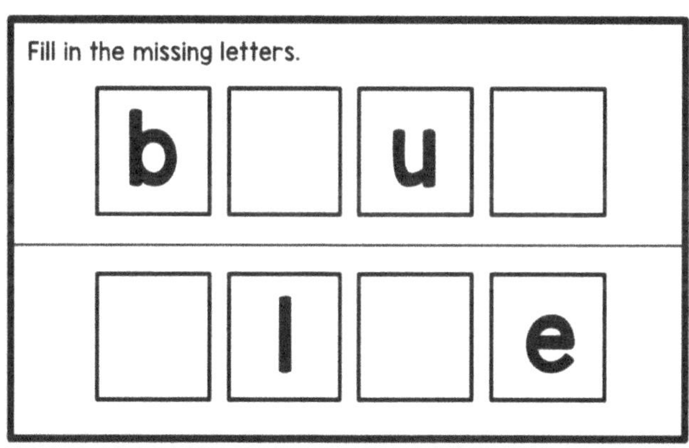

**Read it.**

# can

**Trace it.**

**Trace and write.**

can    can
can    can
can

**Color by sight word.**

BLACK ▷ **can**  |  PURPLE ▷ *can*

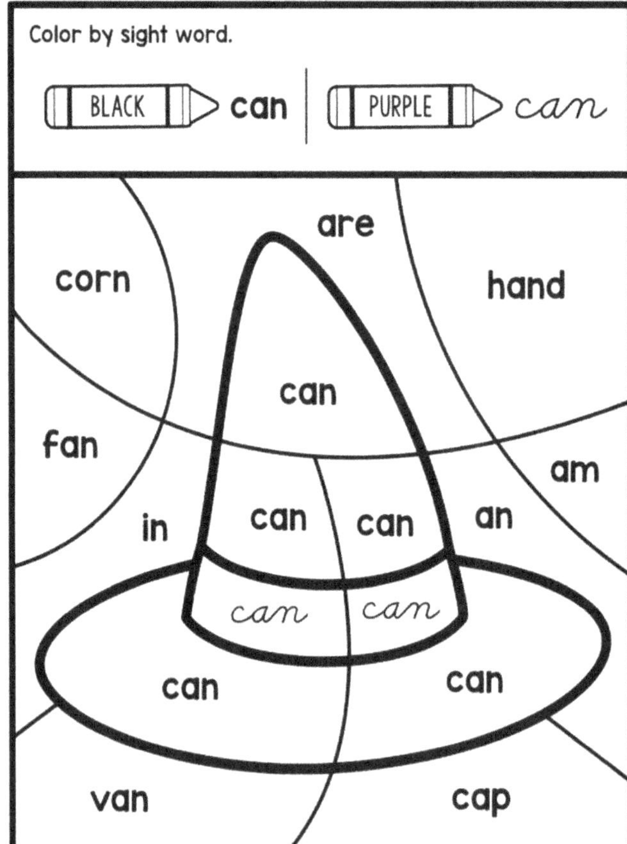


**Decorate it.**

can

**Complete the sentence.**

I can play the piano.

**Find and circle.**

| can | fan | can | an | can |
|---|---|---|---|---|
| can | but | can | can | ran |
| was | can | man | hand | can |
| sand | can | come | can | pan |

**Fill in the missing letters.**

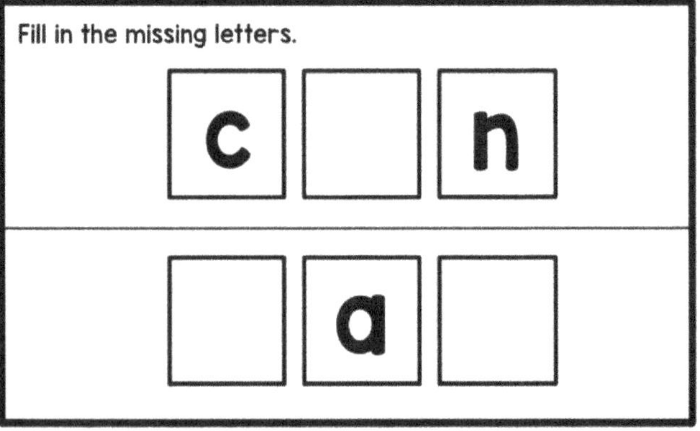

**Read it.**

# come

**Trace it.**

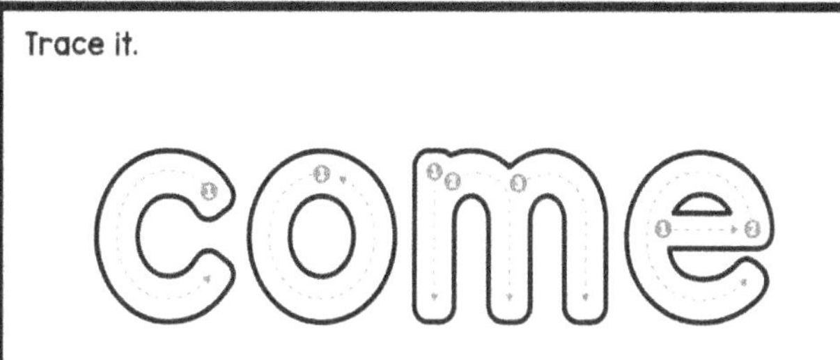

come

**Trace and write.**

come  come

come  come

come

**Color by sight word.**

YELLOW **come**

ORANGE *come*

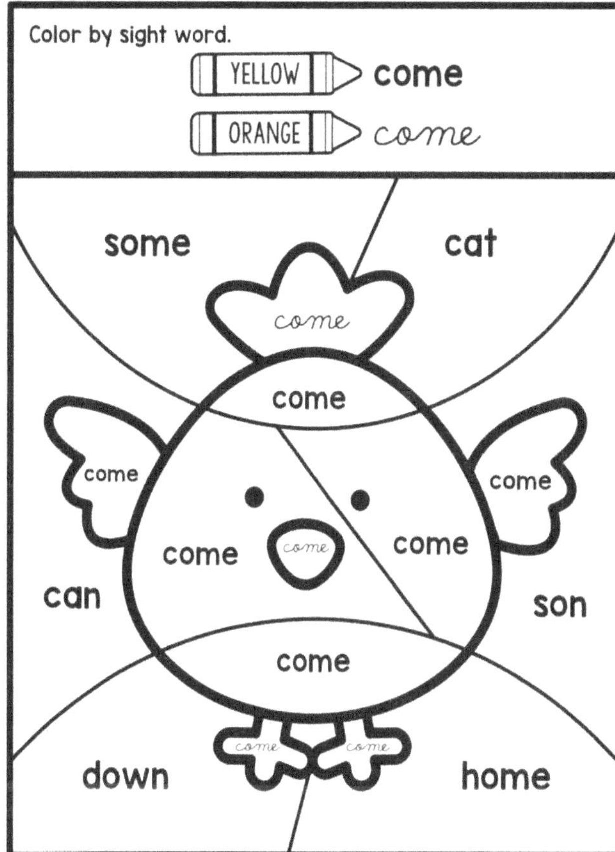


**Decorate it.**

come

**Complete the sentence.**

They come to study.

**Find and circle.**

| me | come | come | corn | time |
|---|---|---|---|---|
| come | coin | gone | come | come |
| them | come | mom | come | now |
| do | made | come | can | come |

**Fill in the missing letters.**

Read it.

# down

Trace it.

Trace and write.

down    down
down    down
down

Decorate it.

down

Color by sight word.

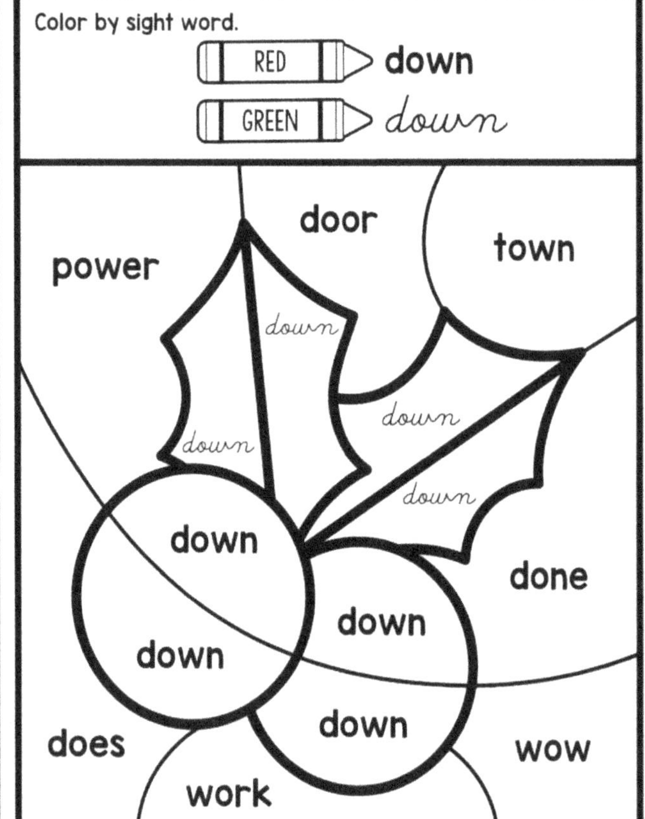


Complete the sentence.

The snow falls down.

Find and circle.

| down | own | born | down | owl |
|------|-----|------|------|-----|
| now | down | some | were | down |
| down | done | down | you | cow |
| come | down | can | down | down |

Fill in the missing letters.

| d |  | w |  |
|---|---|---|---|

| o |  | n |

Read it.

# find

Trace it.

Trace and write.

find  find
find  find
find

Color by sight word.

PINK → **find**
PURPLE → *find*

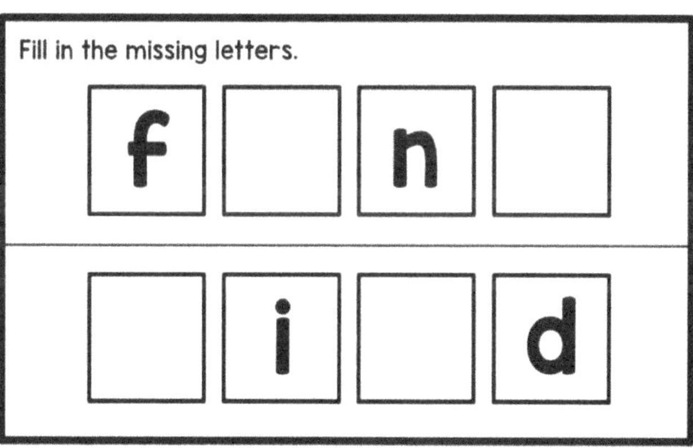


Decorate it.

Complete the sentence.

I want to find a bug.

Find and circle.

| mind | find | hi | find | land |
|------|------|------|------|------|
| very | for | fine | said | find |
| fall | find | find | kind | find |
| find | hand | find | down | old |

Fill in the missing letters.

| f | | n | |
|---|---|---|---|

| | i | | d |
|---|---|---|---|

**Read it.**

**Trace it.**

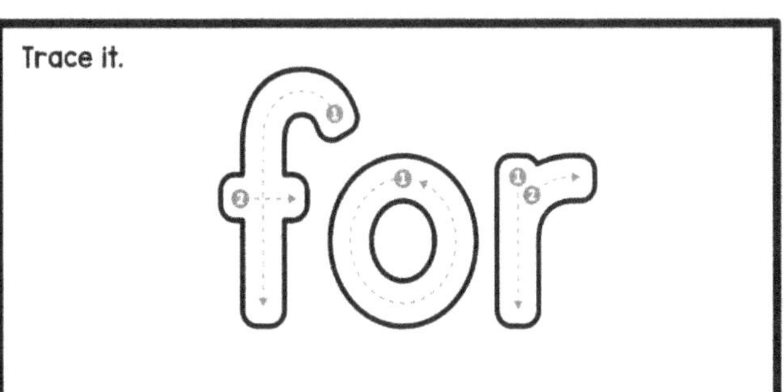

**Trace and write.**

for        for
for        for
for

**Color by sight word.**

RED ▶ for | BLACK ▶ for

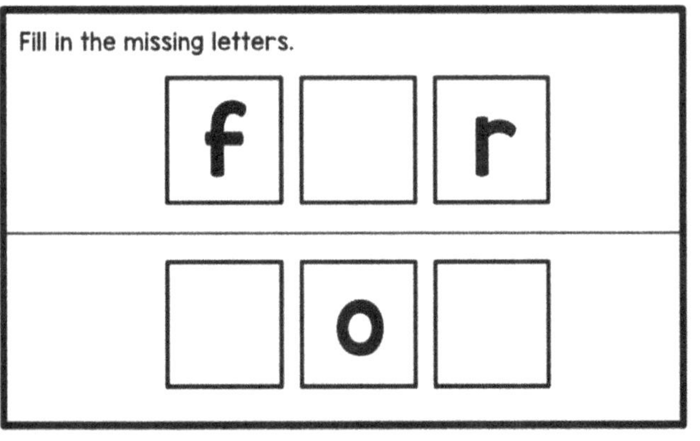


**Decorate it.**

**Complete the sentence.**

The gift is for you.

**Find and circle.**

| for | of | for | from | far |
|-----|-----|------|------|-----|
| do | for | more | for | off |
| for | farm | for | on | for |
| for | for | find | so | for |

**Fill in the missing letters.**

| f |  | r |
|---|---|---|
|  | o |  |

**Read it.**

# funny

**Trace it.**

**Trace and write.**

funny funny
funny funny
funny

**Color by sight word.**

ORANGE → **funny**
GRAY → *funny*

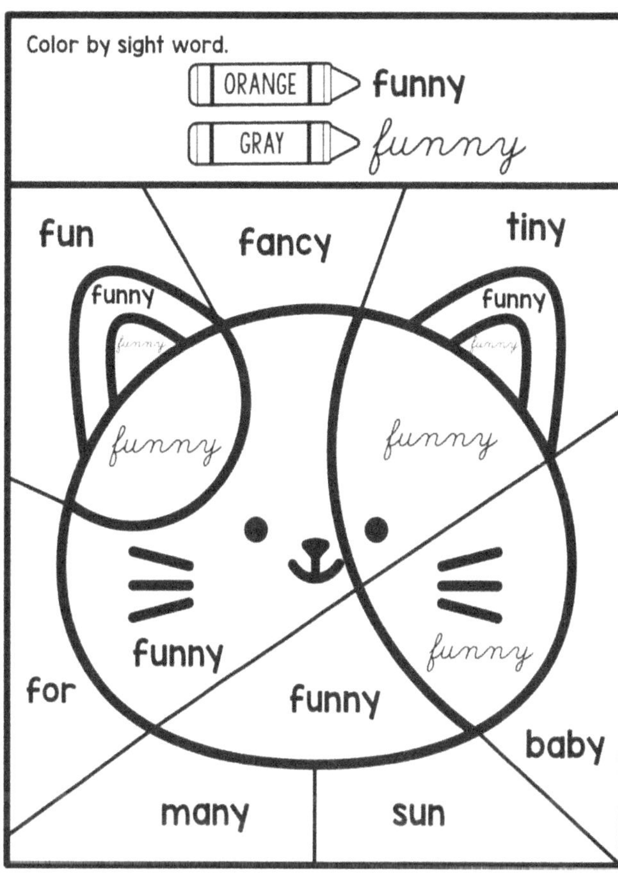


**Decorate it.**

funny

**Complete the sentence.**

This is a funny story.

**Find and circle.**

| run | funny | find | funny | this |
|-----|-------|------|-------|------|
| funny | day | than | have | funny |
| ready | may | funny | some | funny |
| your | funny | sunny | funny | many |

**Fill in the missing letters.**

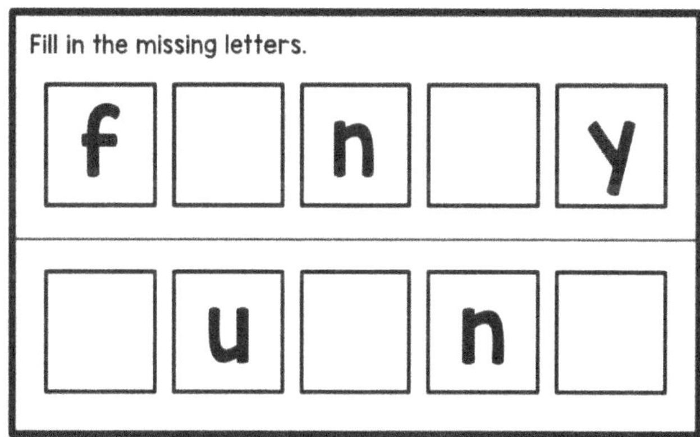

**Read it.**

# go

**Trace it.**

go

**Trace and write.**

go go go
go go go
go

**Color by sight word.**

YELLOW ▷ go | BROWN ▷ go

**Decorate it.**

go

**Complete the sentence.**

I go to the zoo.

**Find and circle.**

| no | go | gone | go | on |
|---|---|---|---|---|
| go | who | go | to | go |
| go | go | do | go | go |
| or | go | go | get | of |

**Fill in the missing letters.**

g ☐

☐ o

**Read it.**

# help

**Trace it.**

**Trace and write.**

help    help
help    help
help

**Color by sight word.**

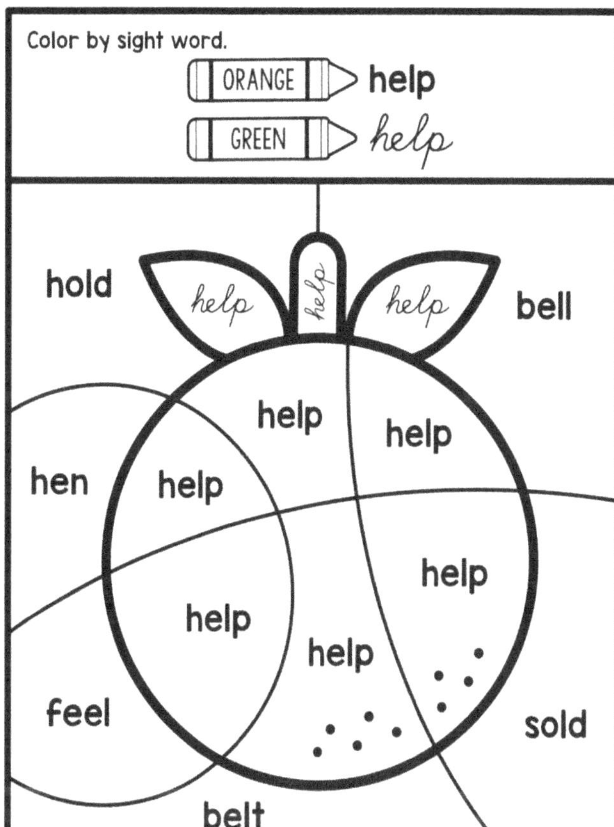


**Decorate it.**

**Complete the sentence.**

Can you help me?

**Find and circle.**

| help | him | help | he | with |
|------|------|------|-------|------|
| they | help | hope | help | five |
| help | help | here | three | help |
| help | long | each | help | then |

**Fill in the missing letters.**

**Read it.**

# here

**Trace it.**

**Trace and write.**

here    here

here    here

here

**Color by sight word.**

GRAY ▷ **here**

BLUE ▷ here

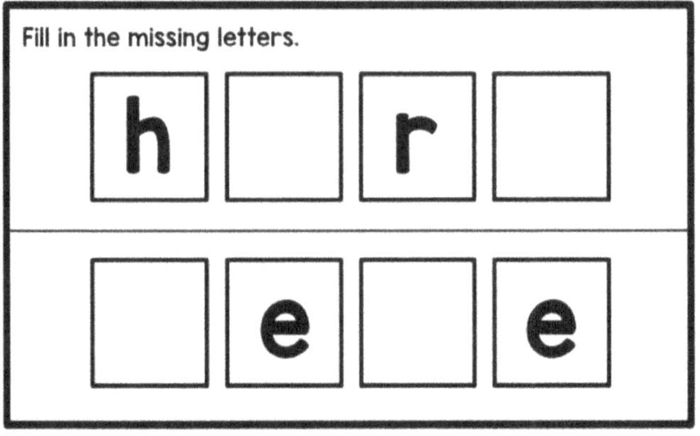


**Decorate it.**

here

**Complete the sentence.**

The pencil is here.

**Find and circle.**

| | | | | |
|---|---|---|---|---|
| here | have | there | here | help |
| ear | here | her | more | here |
| here | she | here | want | here |
| here | where | hear | here | were |

**Fill in the missing letters.**

| h | | r | |
|---|---|---|---|

| | e | | e |
|---|---|---|---|

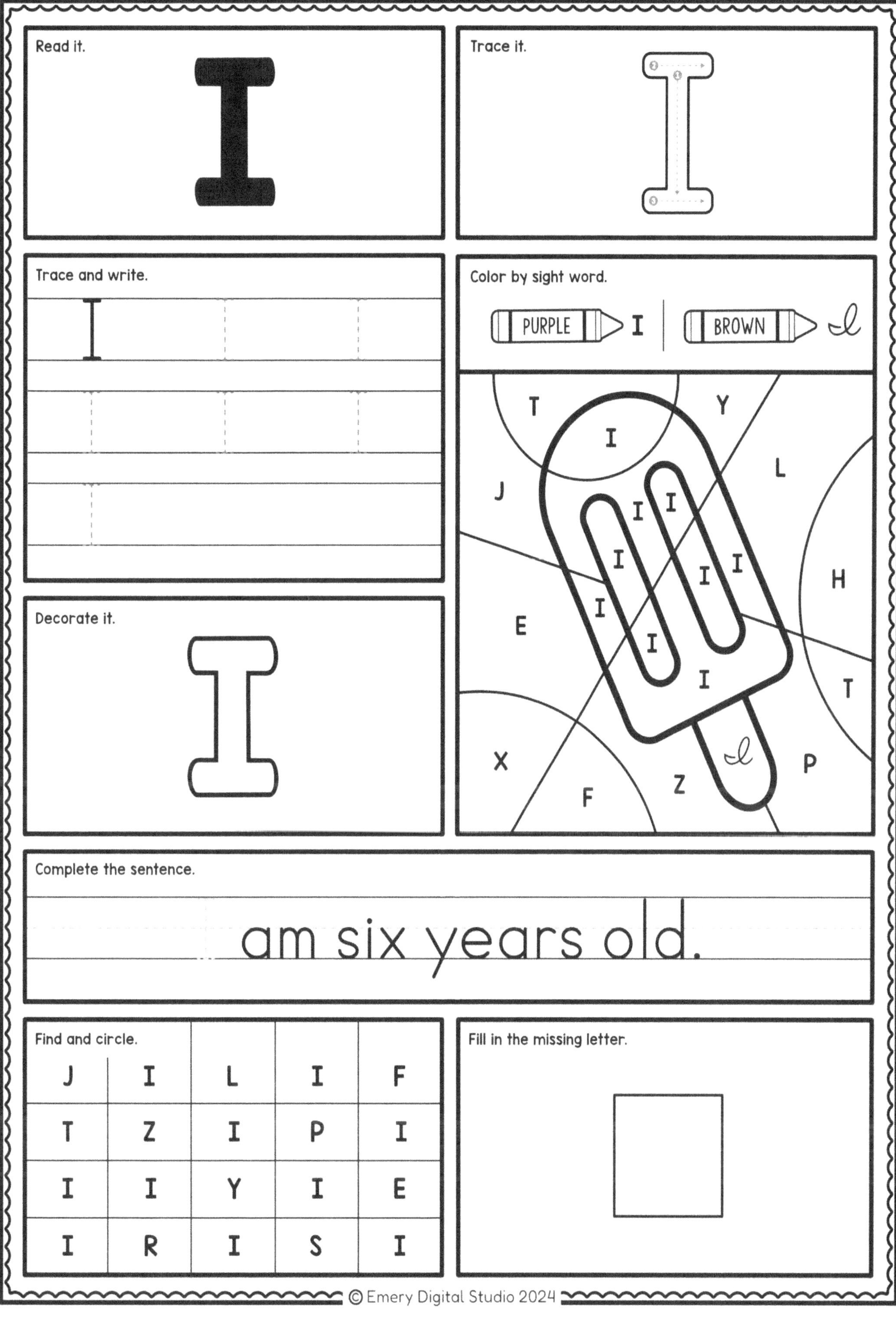

Read it.
I
Trace it.
Trace and write.
I
Decorate it.
Color by sight word.
PURPLE → I
BROWN → I
T
Y
I
J
L
I
I
I
I
I
I
H
E
I
I
T
X
I
P
F
Z
Complete the sentence.
am six years old.
Find and circle.
J   I   L   I   F
T   Z   I   P   I
I   I   Y   I   E
I   R   I   S   I
Fill in the missing letter.

Read it.
in
Trace it.
Trace and write.
in in in
in in in
in
Color by sight word.
PINK in
YELLOW in
in in in in in in in in in in in in in in in in in in in
Decorate it.
in
Complete the sentence.
The mail is in the box.
Find and circle.
in pin in in an
on in hi in in
it in in is fin
in if his in no
Fill in the missing letters.
i
n

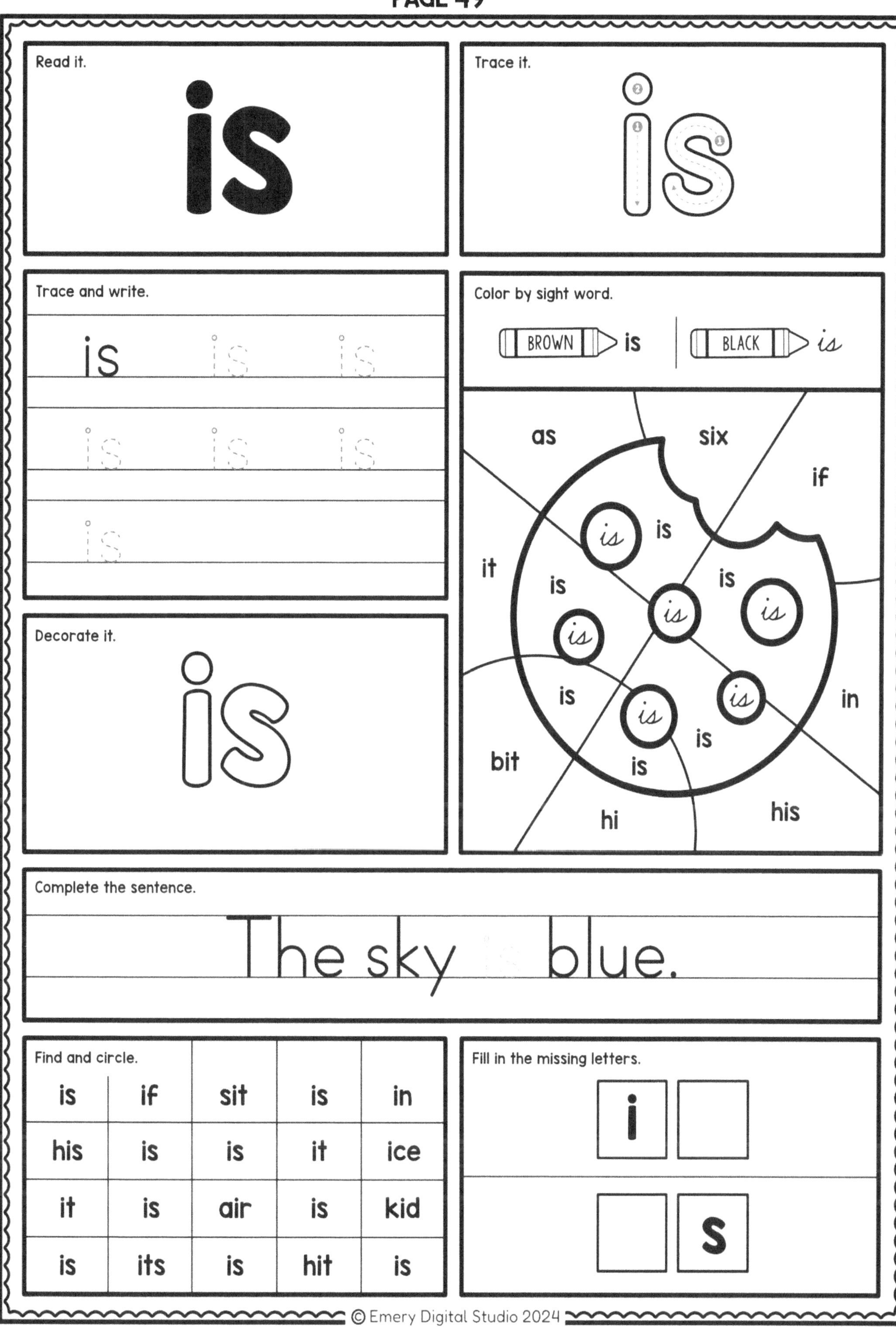
Read it.
is

Trace it.
is

Trace and write.
is    is    is
is    is    is
is

Color by sight word.
BROWN    is
BLACK    is

as
six
if
it
is
is
is
is
is
is
is
is
in
bit
is
his
hi

Decorate it.
is

Complete the sentence.
The sky      blue.

Find and circle.
is    if    sit    is    in
his    is    is    it    ice
it    is    air    is    kid
is    its    is    hit    is

Fill in the missing letters.
i
s

**Read it.**

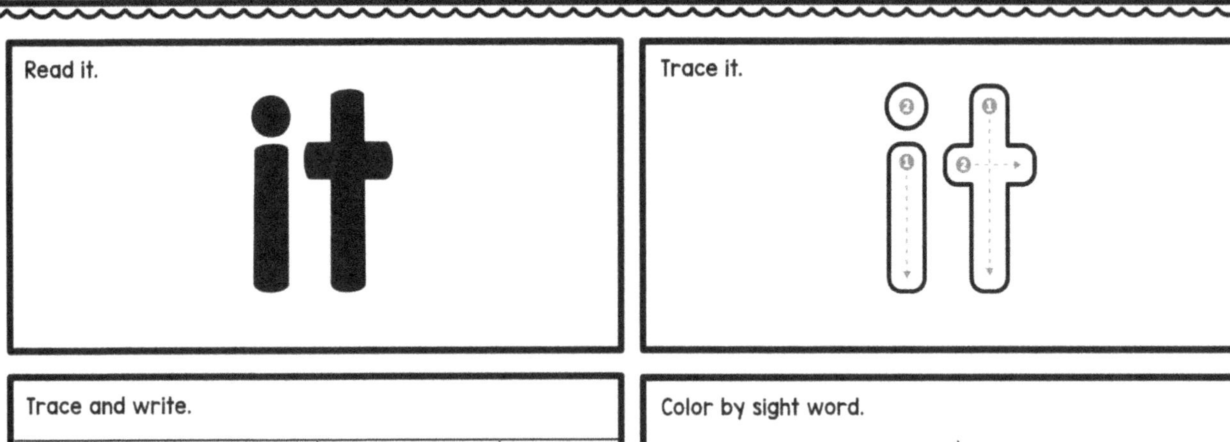

**Trace it.**

**Trace and write.**

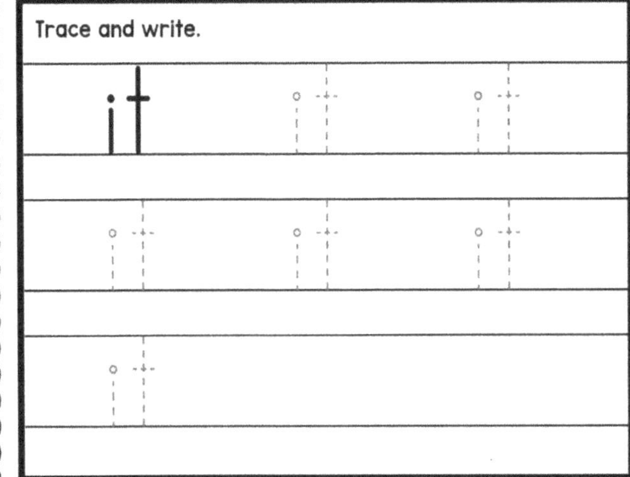

**Color by sight word.**

GREEN → it    GRAY → *it*

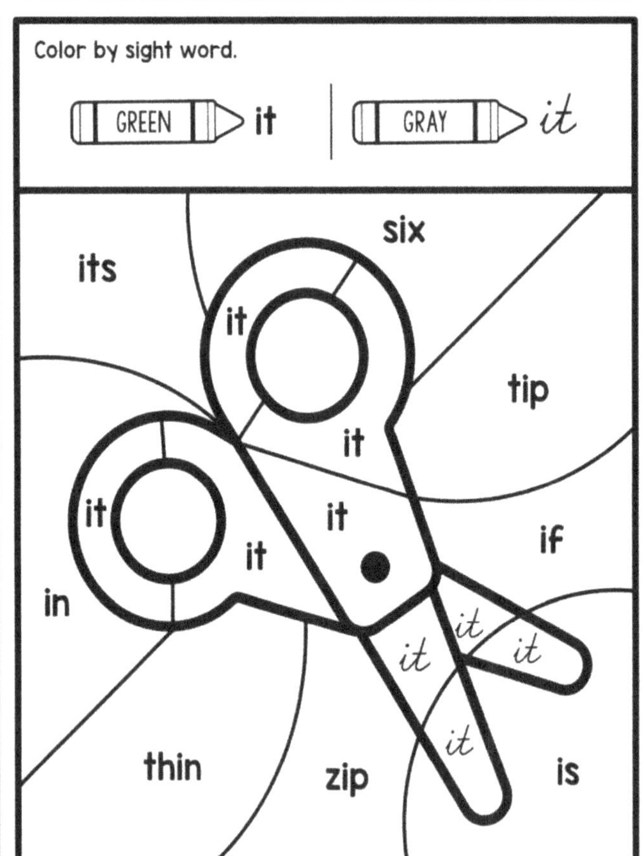


**Decorate it.**

**Complete the sentence.**

I like it very much.

**Find and circle.**

| it | is | in | us | it |
|----|----|----|----|----|
| let | it | or | it | if |
| it | be | it | lie | it |
| ate | it | list | it | as |

**Fill in the missing letters.**

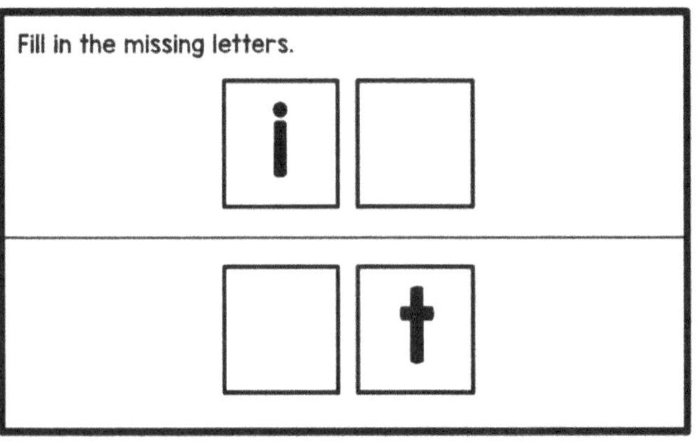

**Read it.**

# jump

**Trace it.**

**Trace and write.**

jump    jump
jump    jump
jump

**Color by sight word.**

YELLOW → **jump**
ORANGE → *jump*

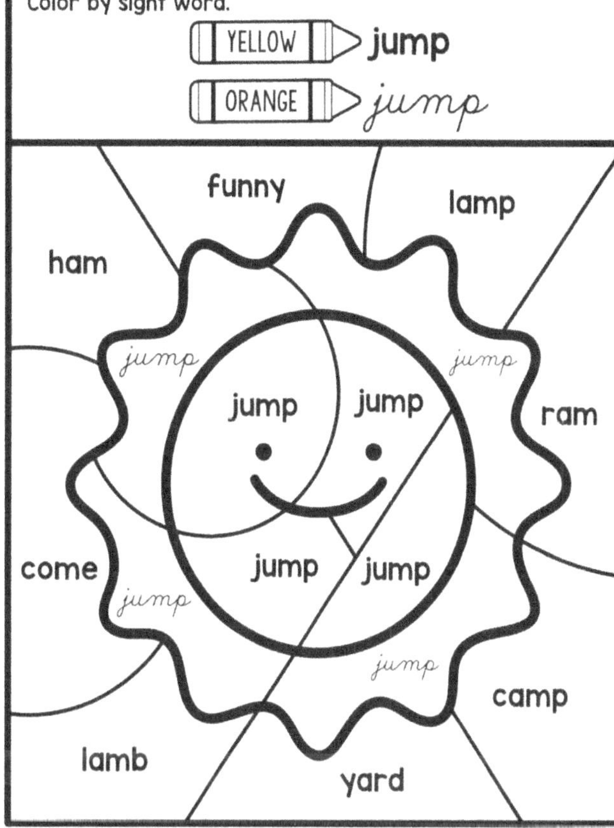


**Decorate it.**

jump

**Complete the sentence.**

A dog can jump.

**Find and circle.**

| jump | home | jump | must | jump |
|------|------|------|------|------|
| jar | jam | jump | jump | think |
| jeans | jump | came | jug | jump |
| just | jump | jump | farm | play |

**Fill in the missing letters.**

**Read it.**

little

**Trace it.**

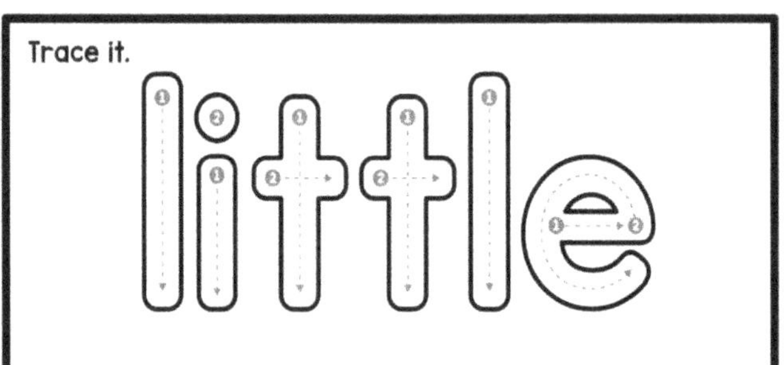

**Trace and write.**

little

**Color by sight word.**

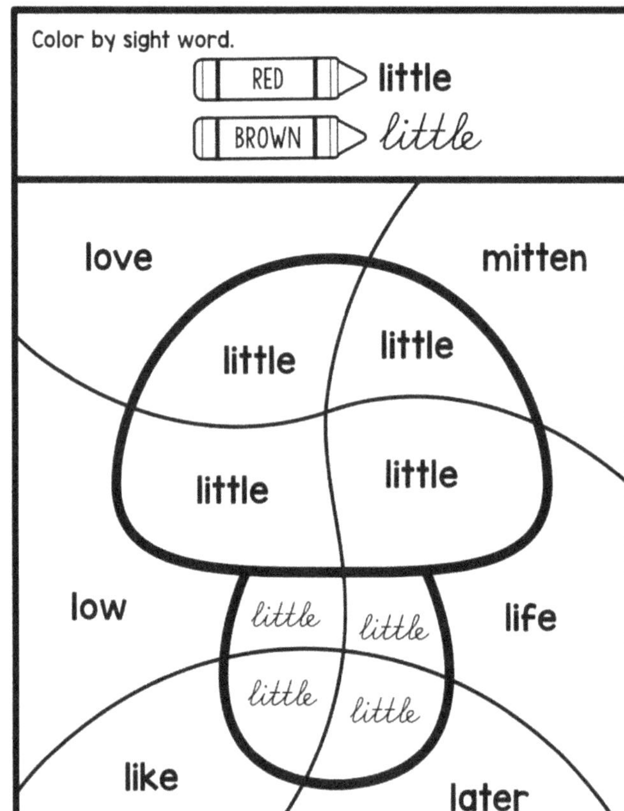


**Decorate it.**

little

**Complete the sentence.**

There is a little bird.

**Find and circle.**

| land | little | letter | kind | little |
|------|--------|--------|------|--------|
| little | long | little | little | live |
| tell | little | still | kitten | little |
| little | small | little | line | little |

**Fill in the missing letters.**

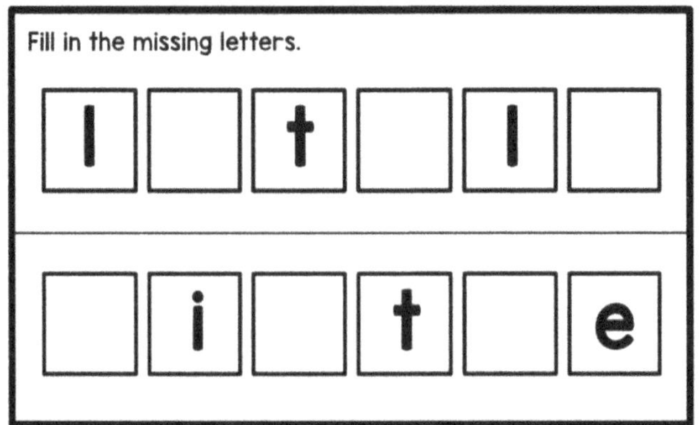

Read it.

**look**

Trace it.

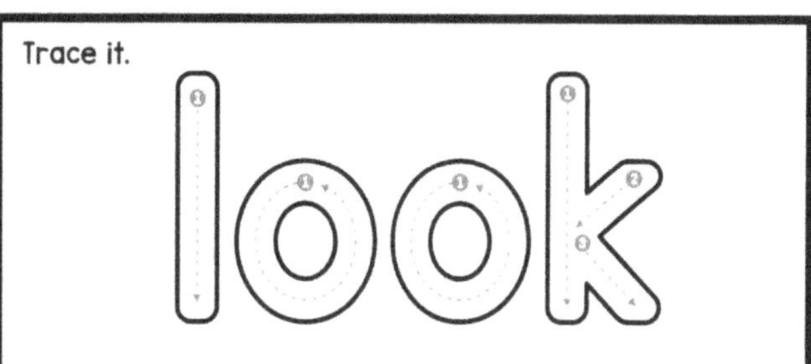

Trace and write.

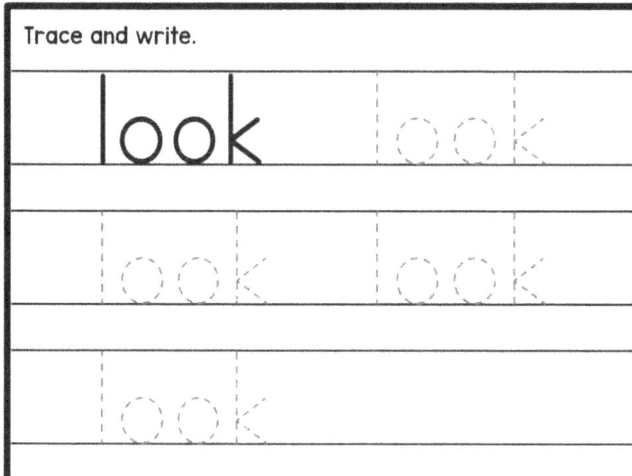

Color by sight word.

GREEN ▷ **look**
BLUE ▷ *look*

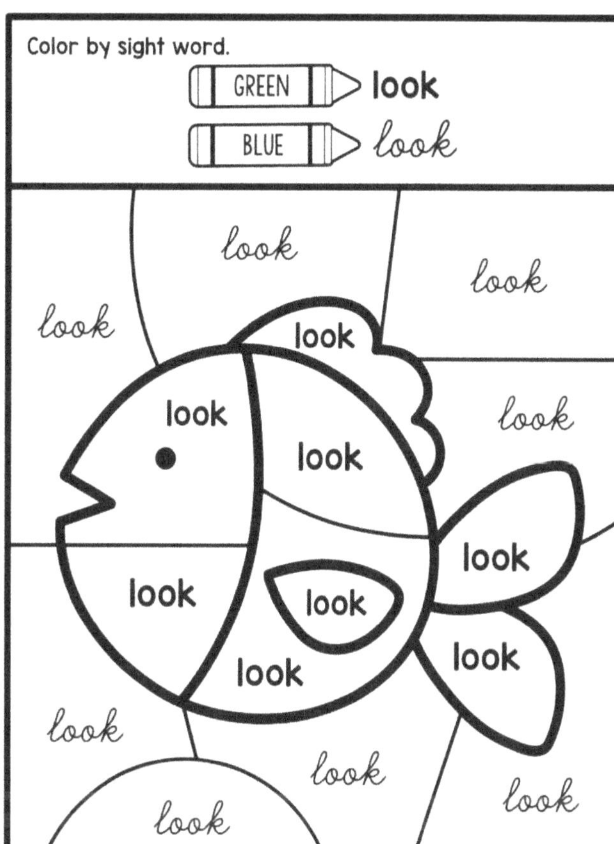

Decorate it.

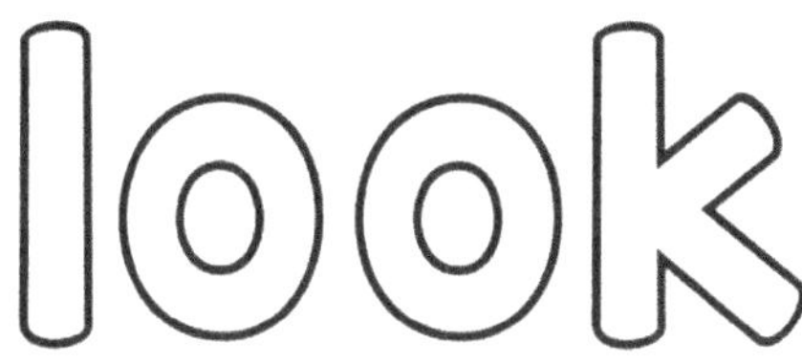

Complete the sentence.

I will ______ for my bag.

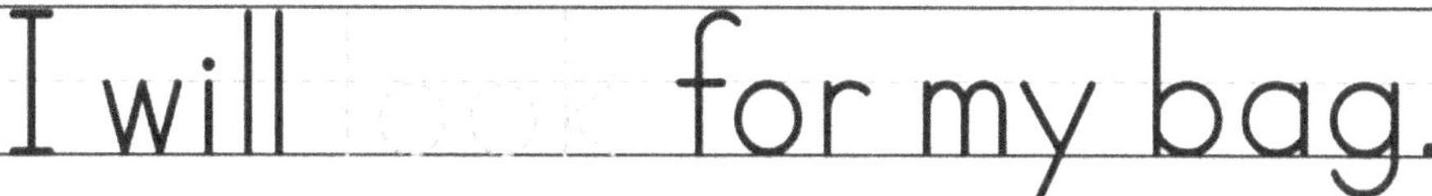

Find and circle.

| look | took | walk | look | luck |
| cook | look | look | too | look |
| look | door | look | look | look |
| for | look | book | look | done |

Fill in the missing letters.

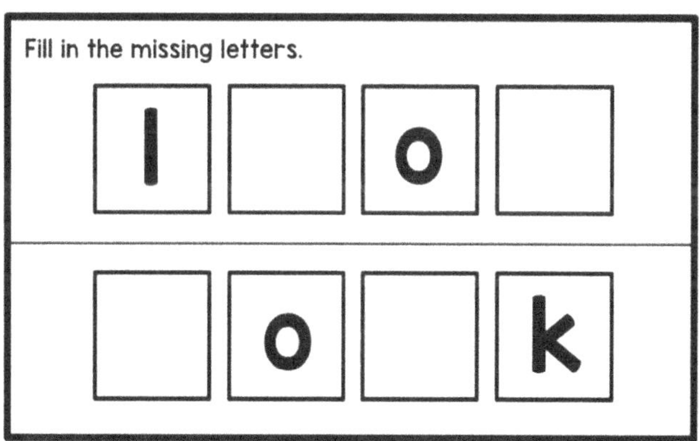

## Read it.

# make

## Trace it.

## Trace and write.

make  make

make  make

make

## Color by sight word.

ORANGE → **make**

PURPLE → *make*

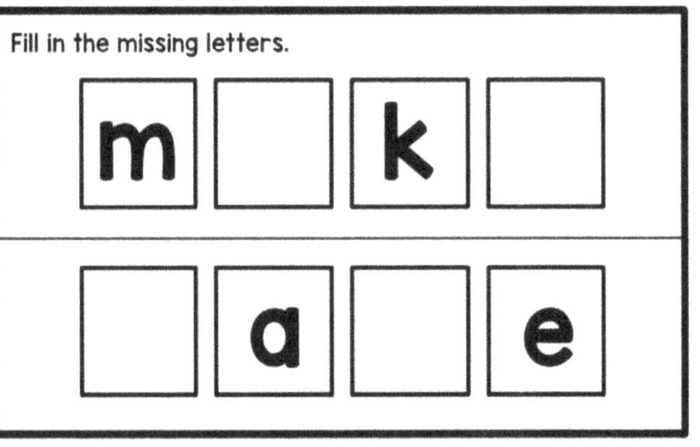


## Decorate it.

## Complete the sentence.

She will make a cake.

## Find and circle.

| milk | make | moo | make | make |
|------|------|-----|------|------|
| make | more | mom | make | leg |
| man | make | lake | me | make |
| make | jet | make | make | men |

## Fill in the missing letters.

| m |  | k |  |
|---|---|---|---|

| | a | | e |
|---|---|---|---|

## Read it.

# me

## Trace it.

# me

## Trace and write.

me  me  me

me  me  me

me

## Decorate it.

# me

## Color by sight word.

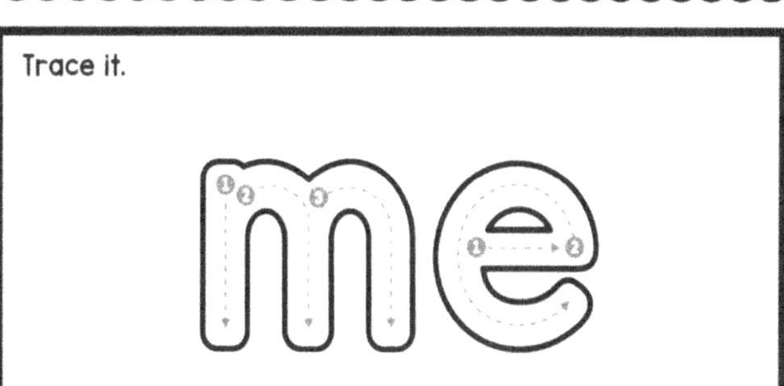


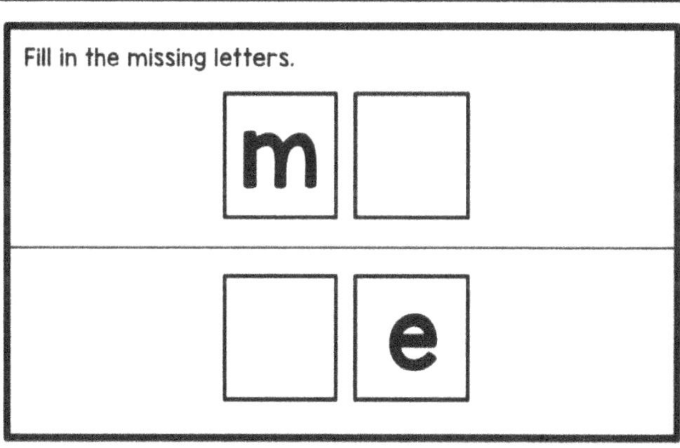


## Complete the sentence.

You make me happy.

## Find and circle.

| me | my | me | no | me |
|----|----|----|----|----|
| bee | me | me | me | she |
| me | to | we | me | me |
| see | me | me | do | me |

## Fill in the missing letters.

m ☐

☐ e

**Read it.**

my

**Trace it.**

my

**Trace and write.**

my my my
my my my
my

**Color by sight word.**

BLUE → my | YELLOW → my

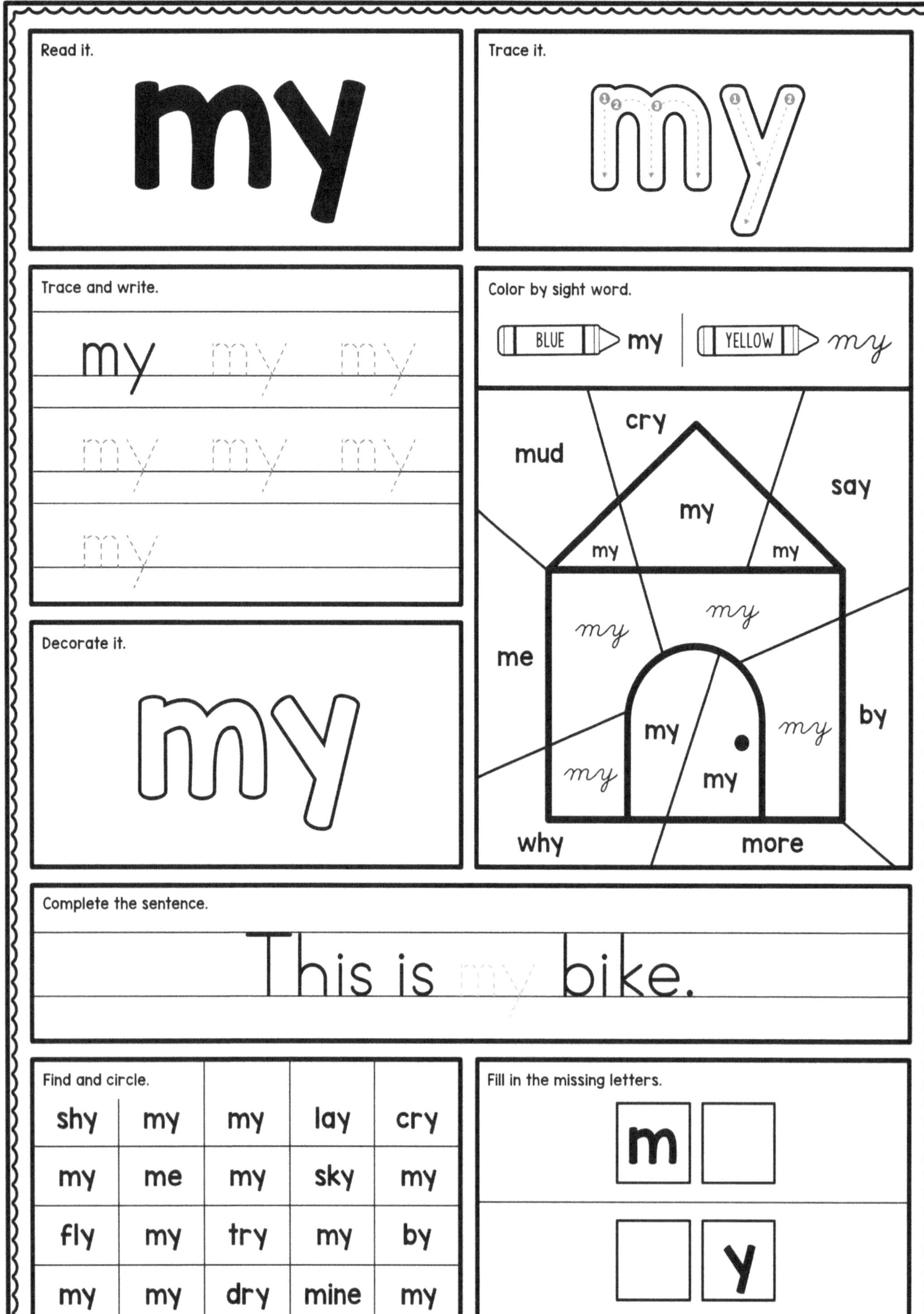


**Decorate it.**

my

**Complete the sentence.**

This is my bike.

**Find and circle.**

| shy | my | my | lay | cry |
|-----|-----|-----|-----|-----|
| my | me | my | sky | my |
| fly | my | try | my | by |
| my | my | dry | mine | my |

**Fill in the missing letters.**

m

y

**Read it.**

# not

**Trace it.**

**Trace and write.**

not    not
not    not
not

**Color by sight word.**

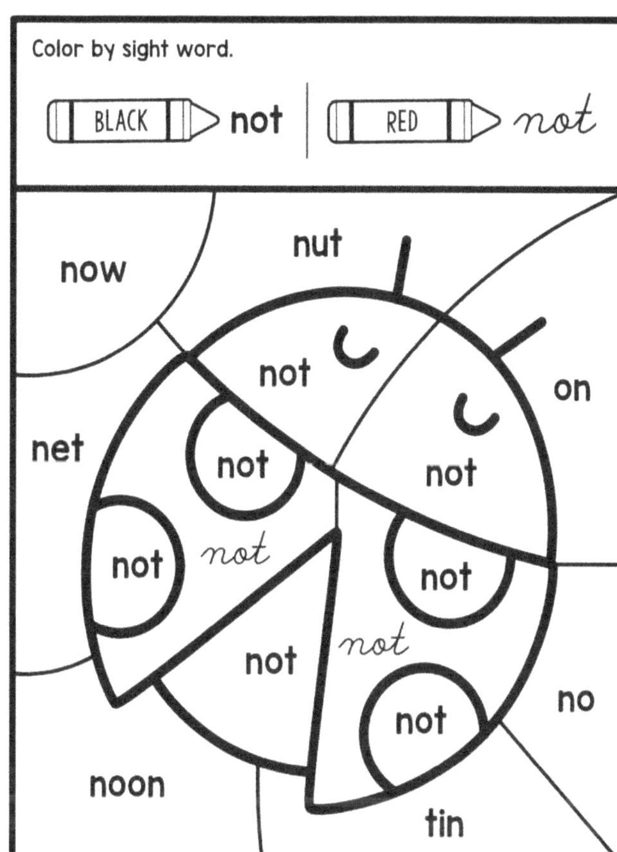


**Decorate it.**

**Complete the sentence.**

It is ____ my ring.

**Find and circle.**

| not | note | got | not | not |
|-----|------|-----|-----|-----|
| you | not | not | to | fox |
| not | lot | not | no | not |
| go | not | none | not | mop |

**Fill in the missing letters.**

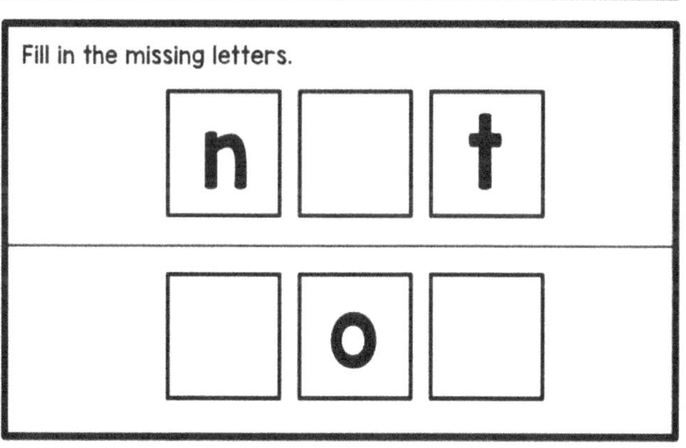

**Read it.**

# one

**Trace it.**

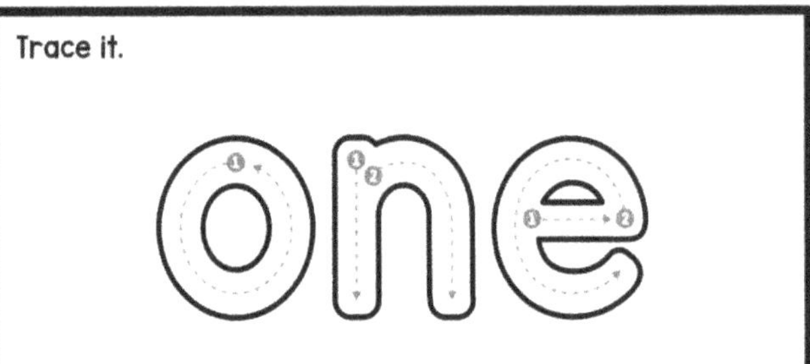

**Trace and write.**

one one

one one

one

**Color by sight word.**

ORANGE ▷ **one** | GREEN ▷ *one*

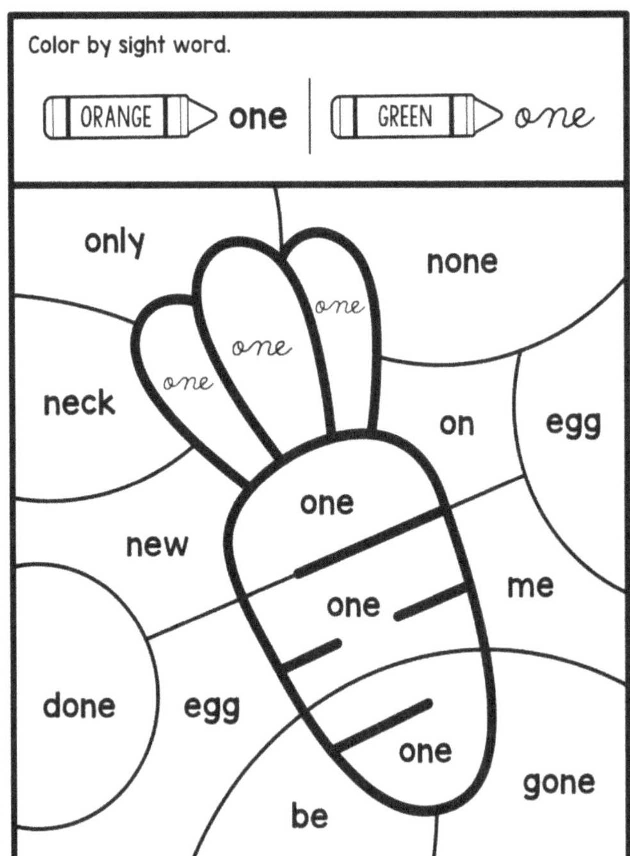


**Decorate it.**

one

**Complete the sentence.**

He has one ball.

**Find and circle.**

| on | one | one | one | he |
|------|-------|------|------|------|
| one | moon | no | one | one |
| own | one | one | noon | he |
| one | owl | one | open | one |

**Fill in the missing letters.**

| o | | e |
|---|---|---|
| | n | |

Read it.

Trace it.

Trace and write.

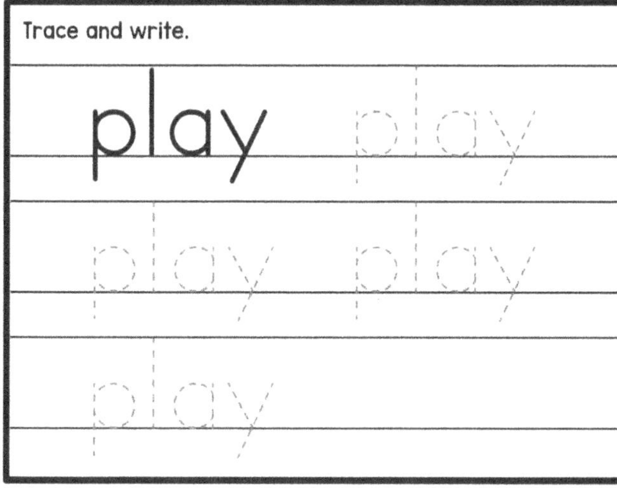

Color by sight word.

PURPLE ➤ **play**
YELLOW ➤ *play*

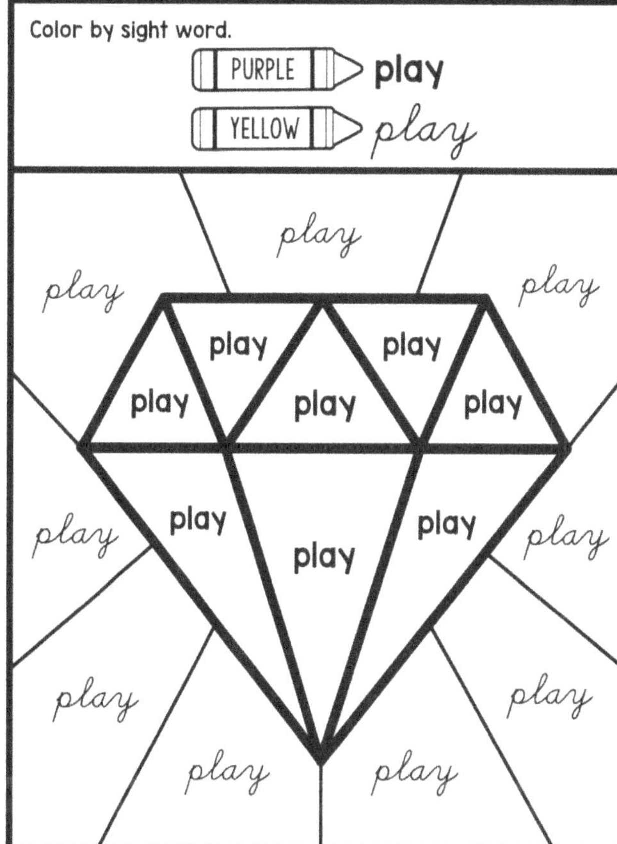

Decorate it.

Complete the sentence.

We play with toys.

Find and circle.

| play | pie | say | play | lay |
|------|------|------|------|------|
| play | reply | play | play | play |
| buy | play | you | sky | play |
| they | play | play | play | blue |

Fill in the missing letters.

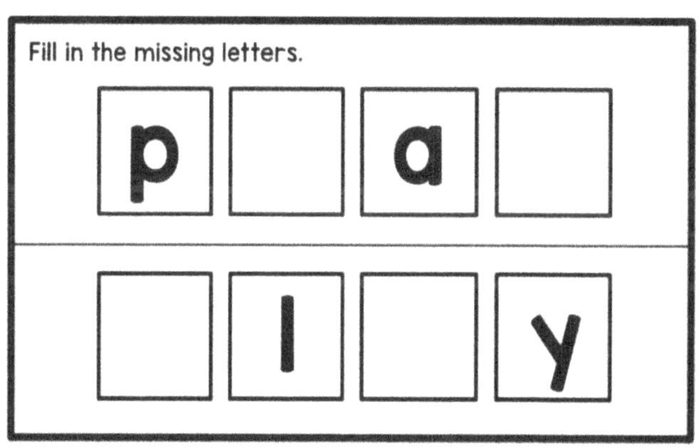

**Read it.**

# red

**Trace it.**

**Trace and write.**

red red
red red
red

**Color by sight word.**

RED ▷ **red**  |  BLUE ▷ *red*

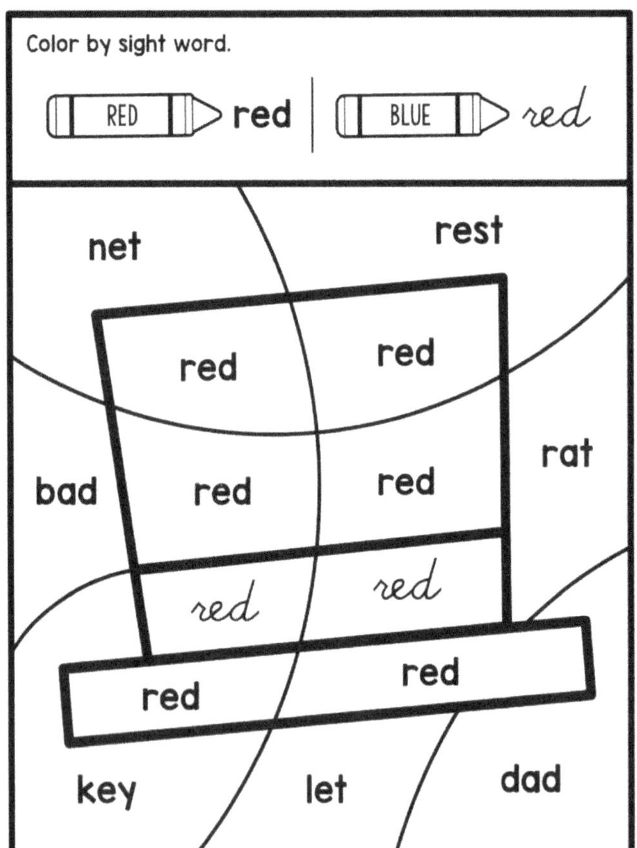


**Decorate it.**

**Complete the sentence.**

It is a red hat.

**Find and circle.**

| get | red | red | set | rod |
|-----|-----|-----|------|-----|
| red | red | may | road | red |
| ray | red | red | red | vet |
| red | read | net | road | red |

**Fill in the missing letters.**

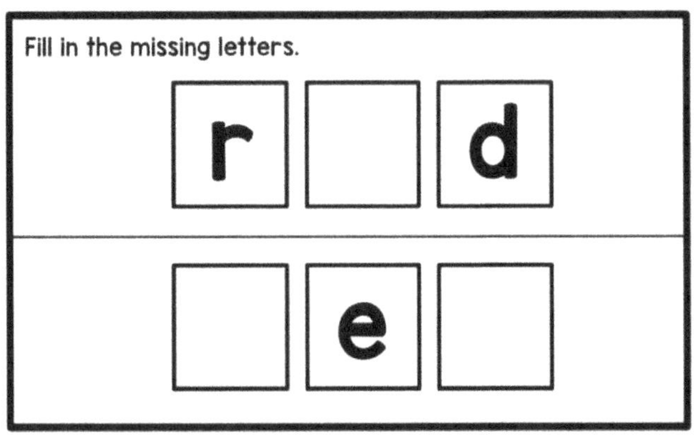

**Read it.**

# run

**Trace it.**

**Trace and write.**

run   run

run   run

run

**Color by sight word.**



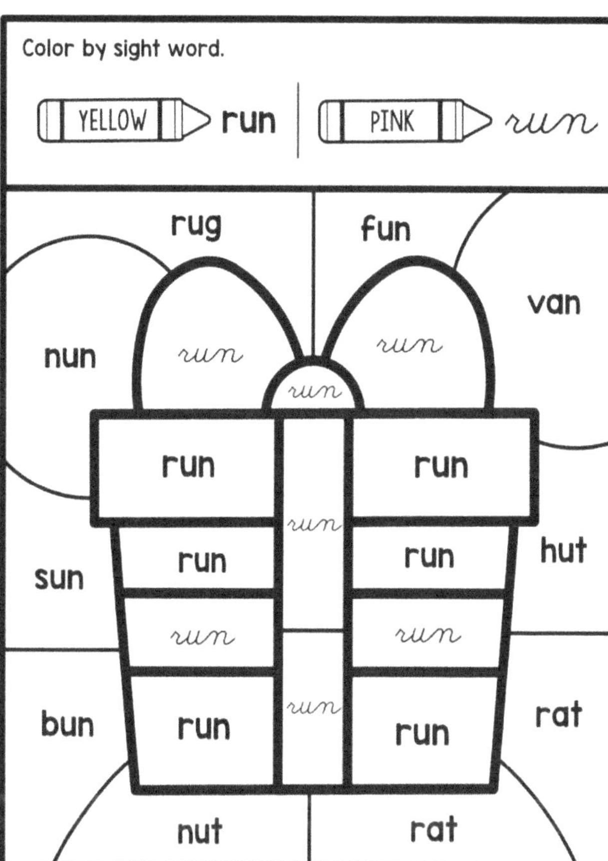


**Decorate it.**

# run

**Complete the sentence.**

I run in the garden.

**Find and circle.**

| run | ride | fun | run | rat |
| --- | --- | --- | --- | --- |
| hen | nut | run | run | run |
| run | sun | run | kite | run |
| run | run | bun | run | red |

**Fill in the missing letters.**

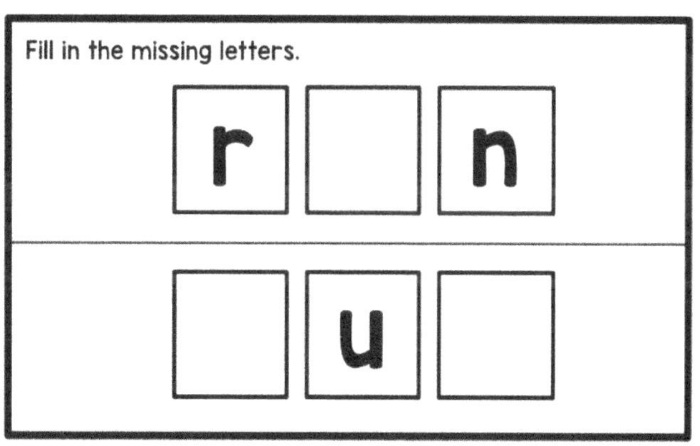

**Read it.**

# said

**Trace it.**

**Trace and write.**

said  said
said  said
said

**Color by sight word.**

GREEN ▷ **said**
RED ▷ *said*

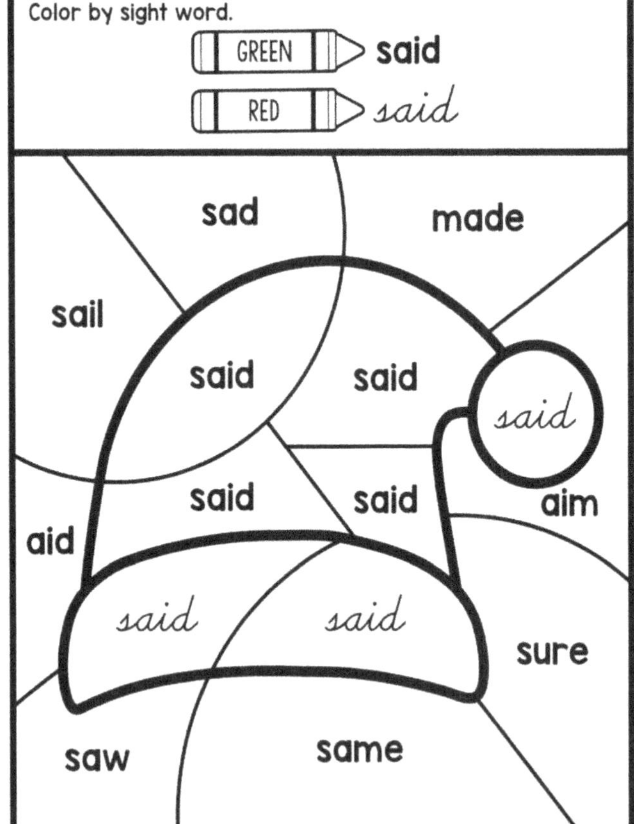


**Decorate it.**

said

**Complete the sentence.**

She said to him.

**Find and circle.**

| paid | said | said | and | soon |
| --- | --- | --- | --- | --- |
| said | join | said | make | said |
| find | said | done | said | say |
| said | lead | said | die | said |

**Fill in the missing letters.**

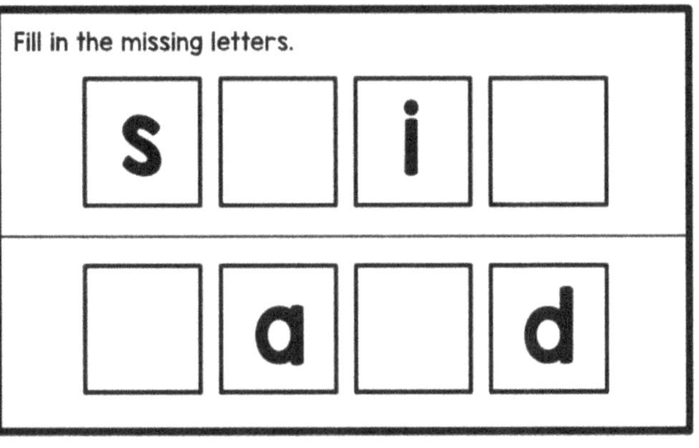

Read it.

Trace it.

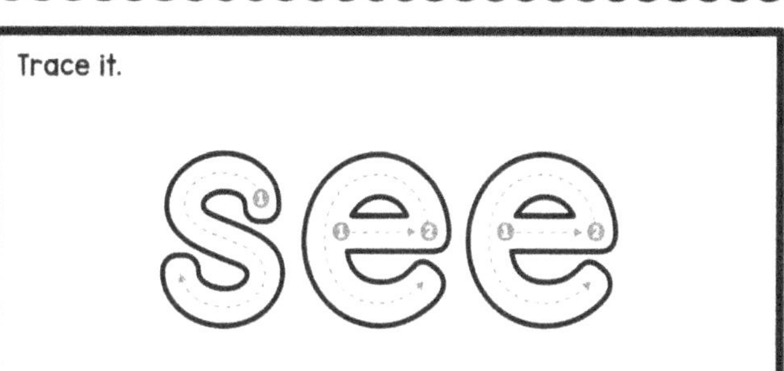

Trace and write.

see    see
see    see
see

Color by sight word.

ORANGE → **see** | BROWN → *see*

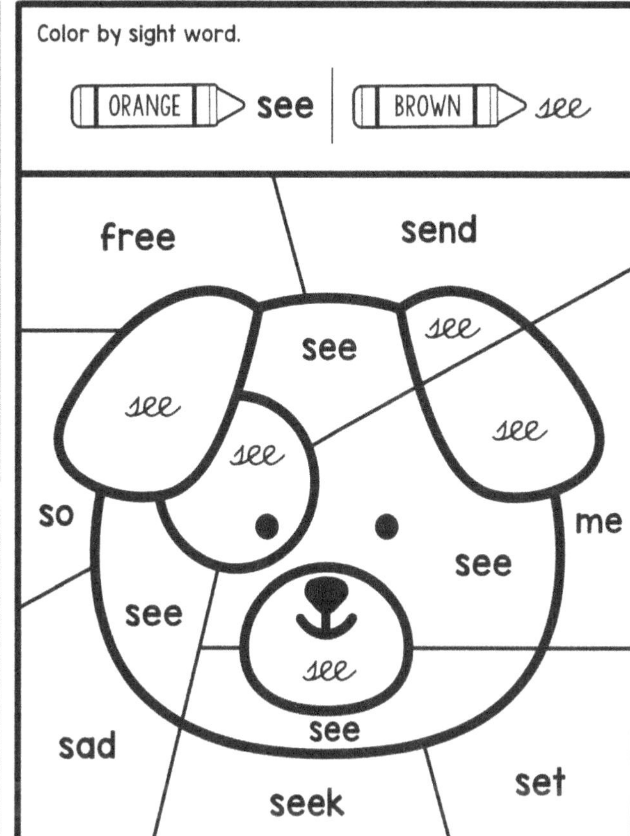


Decorate it.

Complete the sentence.

Do you see the bus?

Find and circle.

| see | sun | see | see | bee |
|-----|-----|-----|------|-----|
| for | see | see | cake | see |
| the | here | see | feed | say |
| see | see | three | see | see |

Fill in the missing letters.

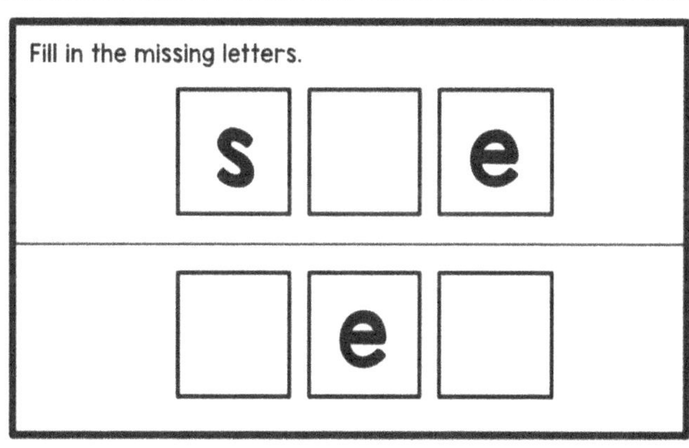

**Read it.**

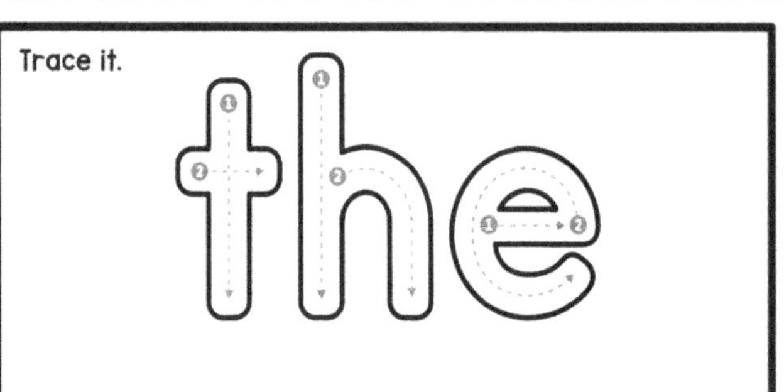

**the**

**Trace it.**

**Trace and write.**

**Color by sight word.**

YELLOW → **the** | BLUE → the

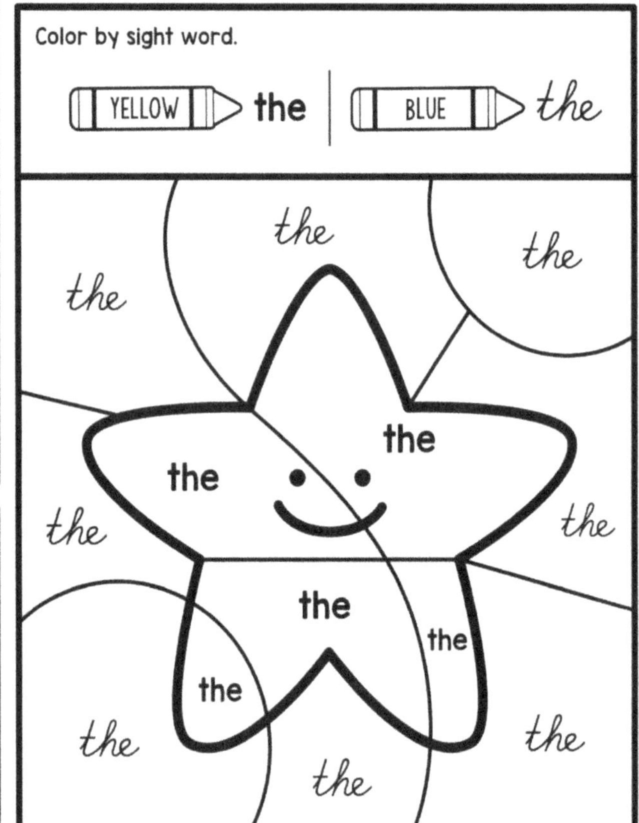


**Decorate it.**

**Complete the sentence.**

We play in the park.

**Find and circle.**

| the | he | the | the | three |
|---|---|---|---|---|
| the | we | the | she | the |
| the | the | toy | the | they |
| then | there | the | the | here |

**Fill in the missing letters.**

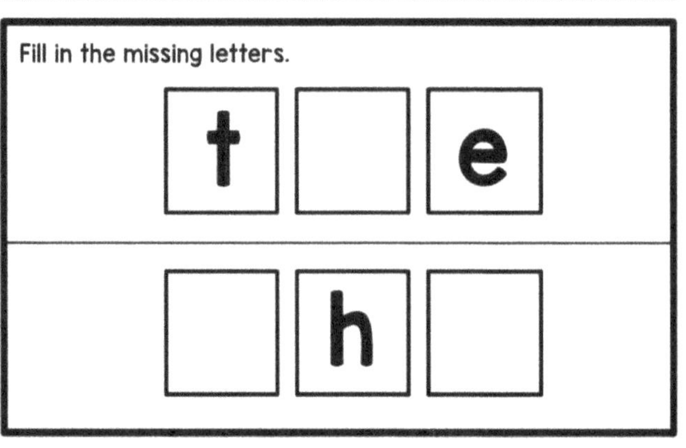

**Read it.**

# three

**Trace it.**

**Trace and write.**

three three
three three
three

**Color by sight word.**

PINK ➤ **three**
BROWN ➤ *three*

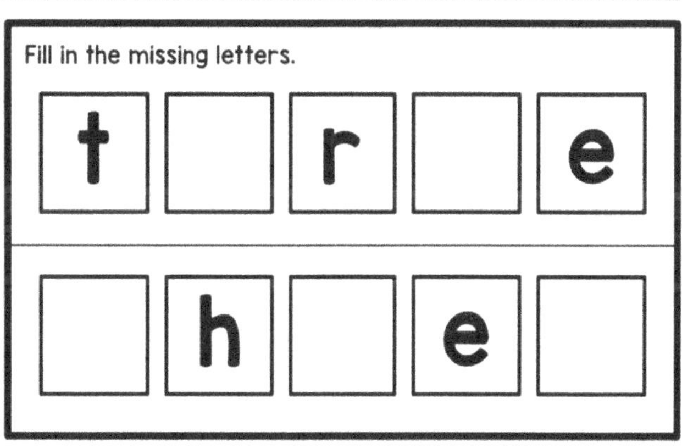


**Decorate it.**

**Complete the sentence.**

It was three o'clock.

**Find and circle.**

| tree | three | play | three | the |
|---|---|---|---|---|
| three | see | away | free | three |
| little | three | three | where | three |
| help | three | when | three | down |

**Fill in the missing letters.**

| t | | r | | e |
|---|---|---|---|---|

| | h | | e | |
|---|---|---|---|---|

**Read it.**

to

**Trace it.**

to

**Trace and write.**

to    to    to
to    to    to
to

**Color by sight word.**

PURPLE → to    GREEN → to

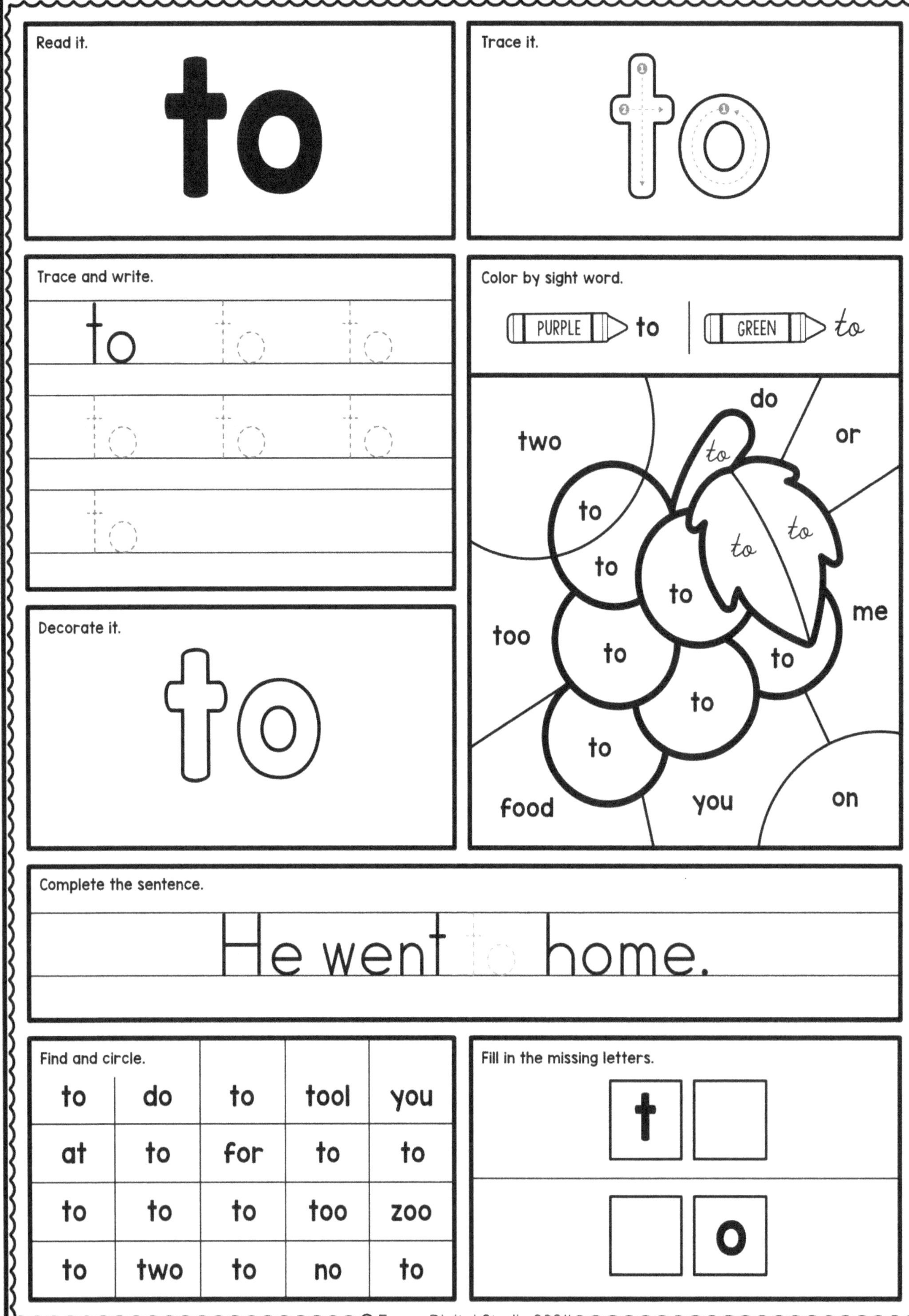


**Decorate it.**

to

**Complete the sentence.**

He went to home.

**Find and circle.**

| to | do | to | tool | you |
|----|----|----|------|-----|
| at | to | for | to | to |
| to | to | to | too | zoo |
| to | two | to | no | to |

**Fill in the missing letters.**

| t |  |
|---|---|

|  | o |
|---|---|

## Read it.

two

## Trace it.

## Trace and write.

two   two

two   two

two

## Color by sight word.

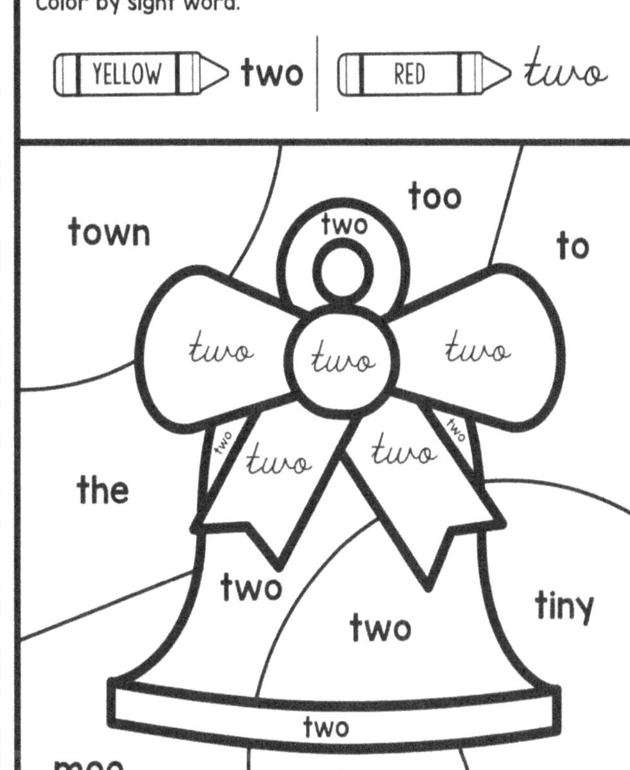


## Decorate it.

## Complete the sentence.

I ate two cookies.

## Find and circle.

| can | two | ten | two | wet |
| --- | --- | --- | --- | --- |
| two | find | two | this | two |
| cool | two | two | we | two |
| toe | two | fun | two | pool |

## Fill in the missing letters.

| t | | o |
| --- | --- | --- |
| | w | |

**Read it.**

**Trace it.**

**Trace and write.**

**Color by sight word.**



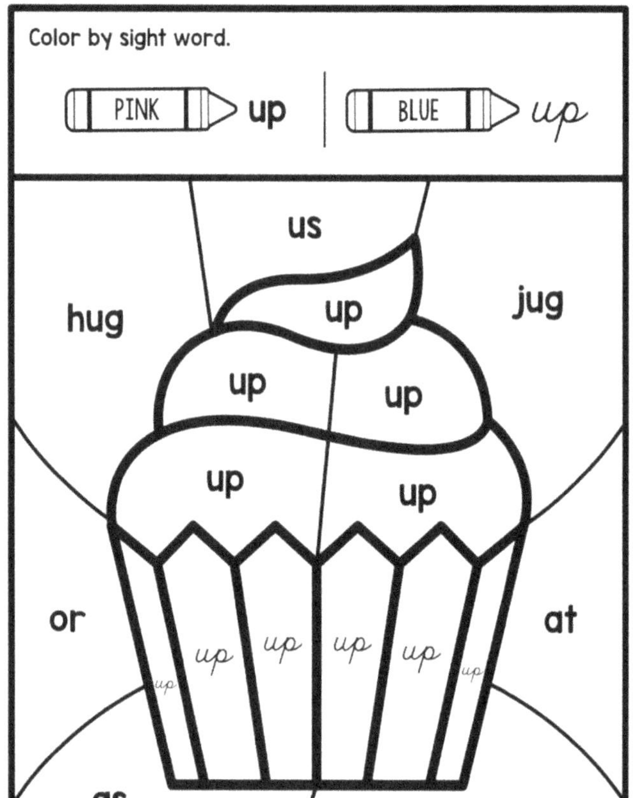

**Decorate it.**

**Complete the sentence.**

The plane goes up.

**Find and circle.**

| up | but | up | cut | put |
|----|-----|-----|------|-----|
| run | up | up | blue | up |
| up | up | at | up | one |
| up | in | up | an | up |

**Fill in the missing letters.**

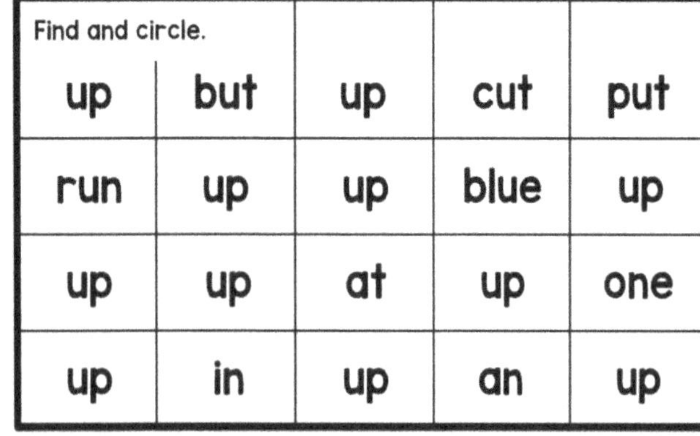

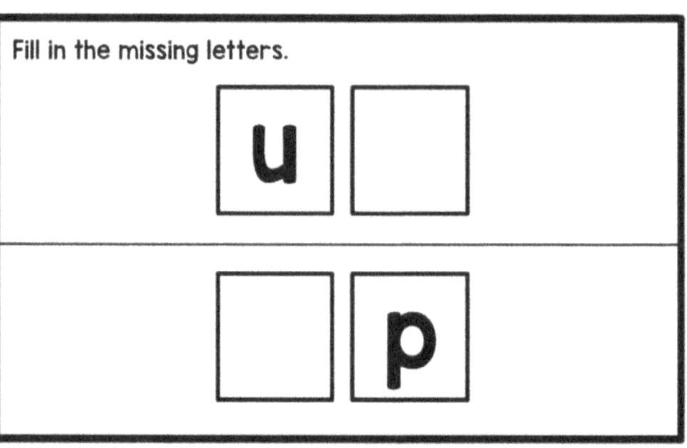

**Read it.**

# we

**Trace it.**

**Trace and write.**

we    we    we

we    we    we

we

**Color by sight word.**



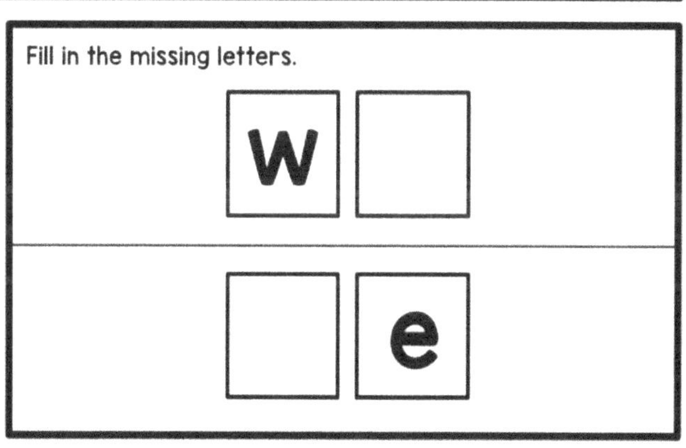


**Decorate it.**

**Complete the sentence.**

We can dance.

**Find and circle.**

| be | we | me | we | him |
| --- | --- | --- | --- | --- |
| are | we | we | time | we |
| my | we | will | we | now |
| we | am | we | we | want |

**Fill in the missing letters.**

| W |   |
| --- | --- |

|   | e |
| --- | --- |

**Read it.**

# where

**Trace it.**

**Trace and write.**

where  where

where  where

where

**Color by sight word.**

BLUE → **where**

PURPLE → *where*

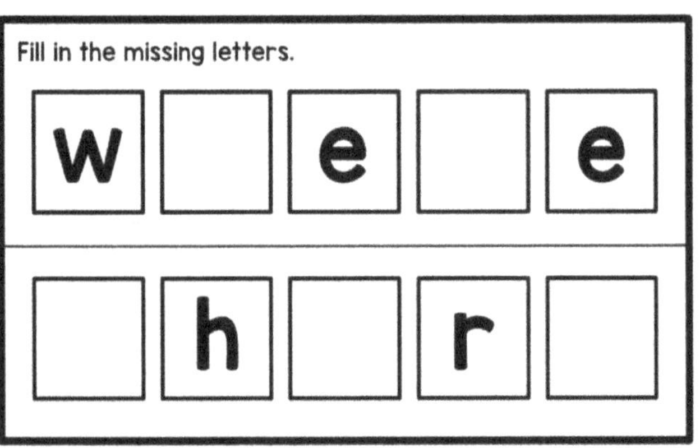


**Decorate it.**

where

**Complete the sentence.**

Where did you go?

**Find and circle.**

| where | care | bear | where | dear |
|---|---|---|---|---|
| with | where | where | here | where |
| where | when | who | where | now |
| was | where | what | where | win |

**Fill in the missing letters.**

| w |  | e |  | e |
|---|---|---|---|---|

| h |  | r |  |  |

**Read it.**

# yellow

**Trace it.**

**Trace and write.**

yellow yellow
yellow yellow
yellow

**Color by sight word.**



**Decorate it.**

# yellow

**Complete the sentence.**

He holds a yellow book.

**Find and circle.**

| many | tall | yellow | word | yellow |
|---|---|---|---|---|
| from | yellow | low | yellow | now |
| yellow | snow | yellow | hard | yellow |
| yarn | yellow | yellow | walk | below |

**Fill in the missing letters.**

| y |  | l |  | o |  |
|---|---|---|---|---|---|

|  | e |  | l |  | w |
|---|---|---|---|---|---|

**Read it.**

# you

**Trace it.**

**Trace and write.**

you     you

you     you

you

**Color by sight word.**



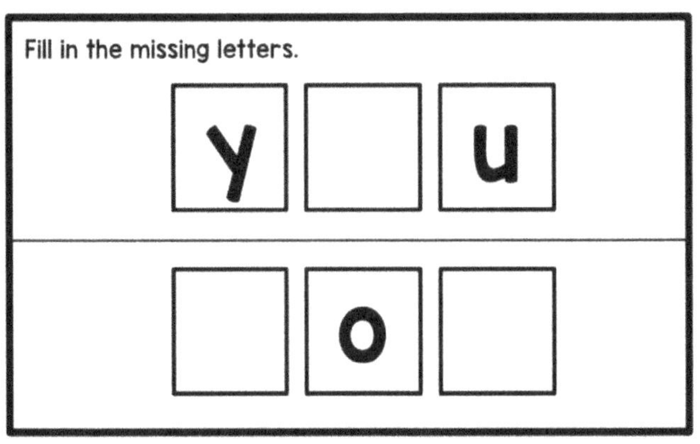


**Decorate it.**

you

**Complete the sentence.**

I love you so much.

**Find and circle.**

| you | you | are | you | who |
|-----|-----|-----|-----|-----|
| one | long | you | our | you |
| any | you | why | you | just |
| you | joy | you | you | old |

**Fill in the missing letters.**

| y |  | u |
|---|---|---|
| o |  |  |

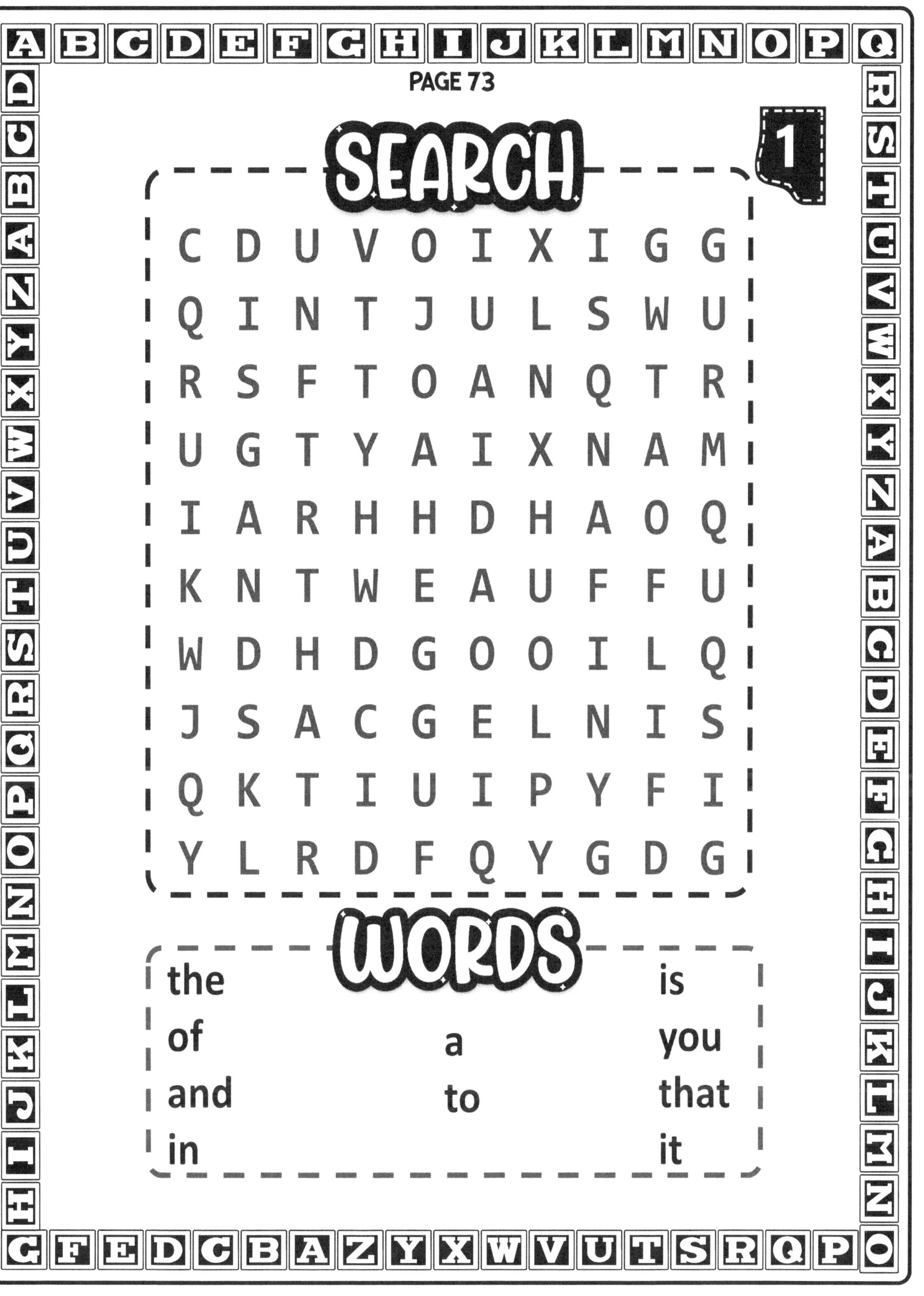
SEARCH

1

C D U V O I X I G G
Q I N T J U L S W U
R S F T O A N Q T R
U G T Y A I X N A M
I A R H H D H A O Q
K N T W E A U F F U
W D H D G O O I L Q
J S A C G E L N I S
Q K T I U I P Y F I
Y L R D F Q Y G D G

WORDS

the
of
and
in

a
to

is
you
that
it

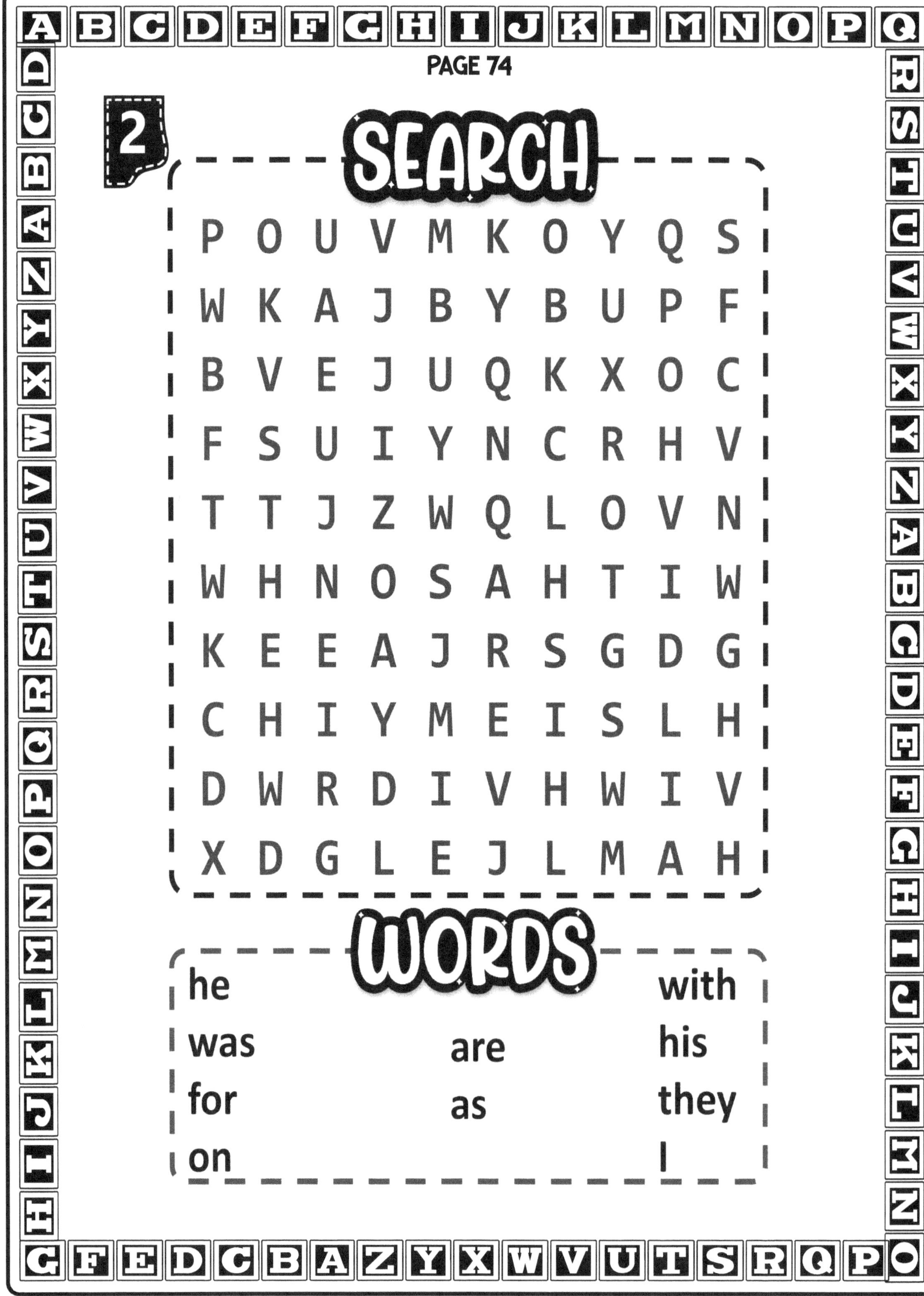

2

SEARCH

P O U V M K O Y Q S
W K A J B Y B U P F
B V E J U Q K X O C
F S U I Y N C R H V
T T J Z W Q L O V N
W H N O S A H T I W
K E E A J R S G D G
C H I Y M E I S L H
D W R D I V H W I V
X D G L E J L M A H

WORDS

he                            with
was            are            his
for            as             they
on

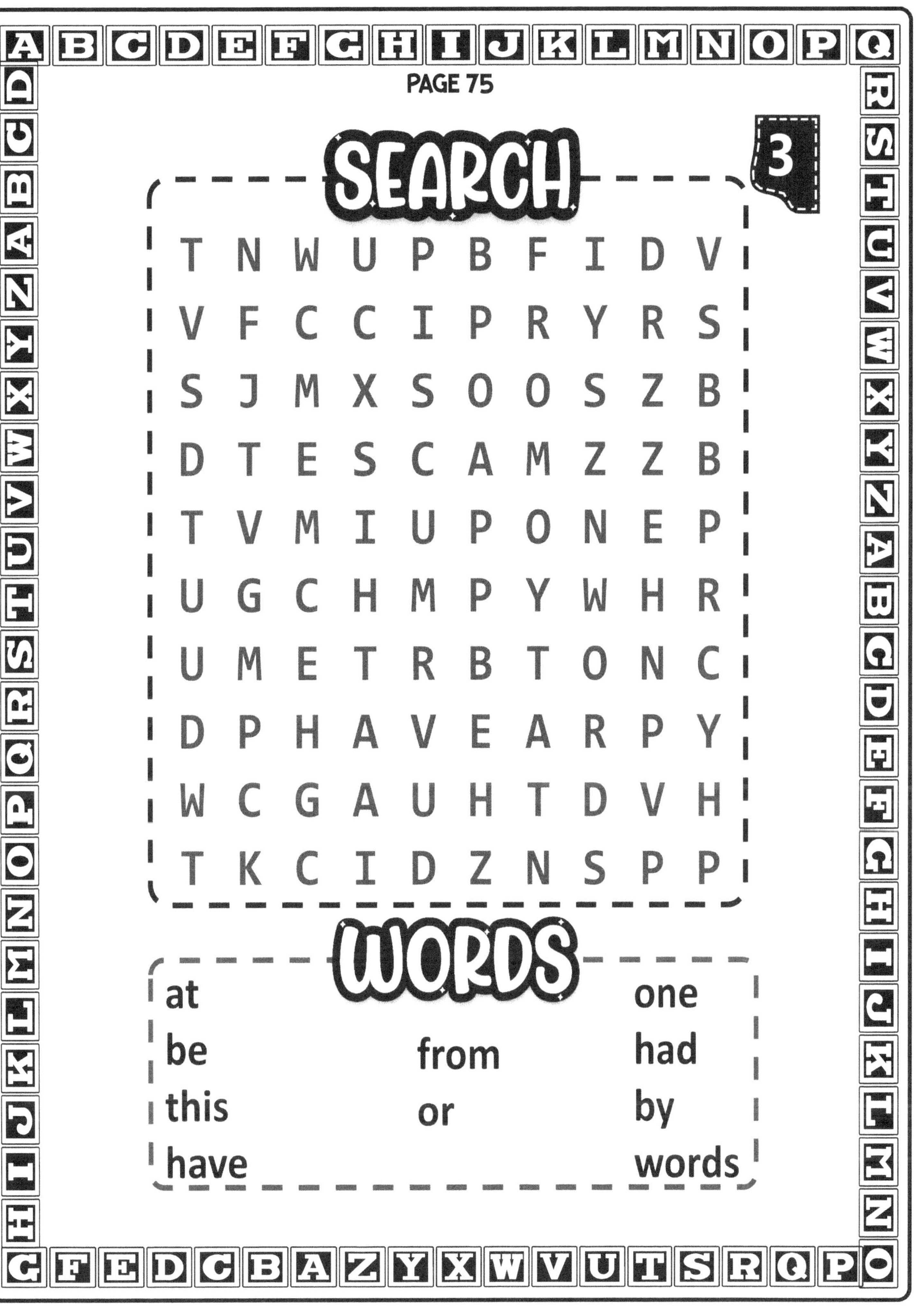

SEARCH
3

T N W U P B F I D V
V F C C I P R Y R S
S J M X S O O S Z B
D T E S C A M Z Z B
T V M I U P O N E P
U G C H M P Y W H R
U M E T R B T O N C
D P H A V E A R P Y
W C G A U H T D V H
T K C I D Z N S P P

WORDS

at
be
this
have

from
or

one
had
by
words

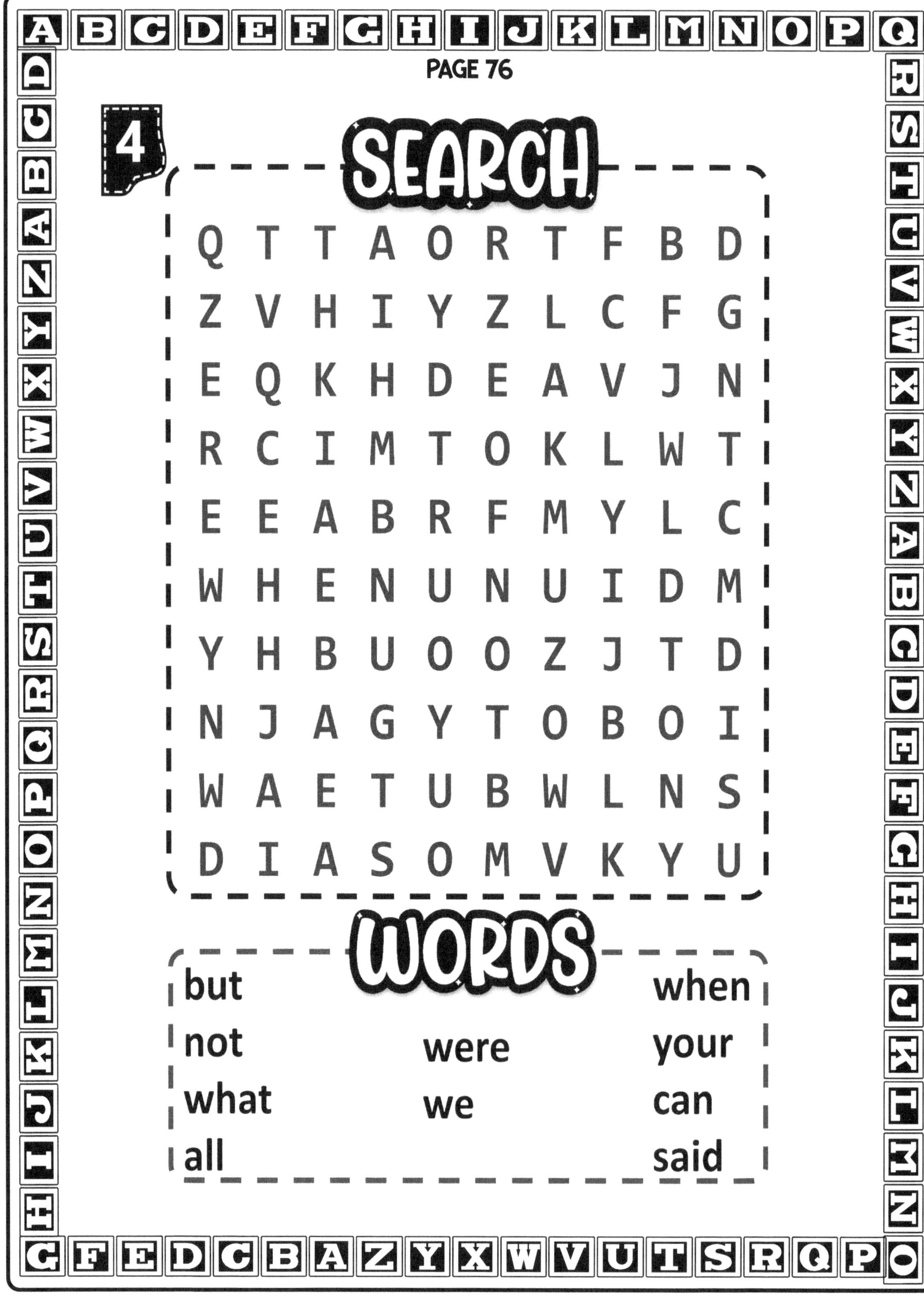

4

SEARCH

Q T T A O R T F B D
Z V H I Y Z L C F G
E Q K H D E A V J N
R C I M T O K L W T
E E A B R F M Y L C
W H E N U N U I D M
Y H B U O O Z J T D
N J A G Y T O B O I
W A E T U B W L N S
D I A S O M V K Y U

WORDS

but                          when
not          were            your
what         we              can
all                          said

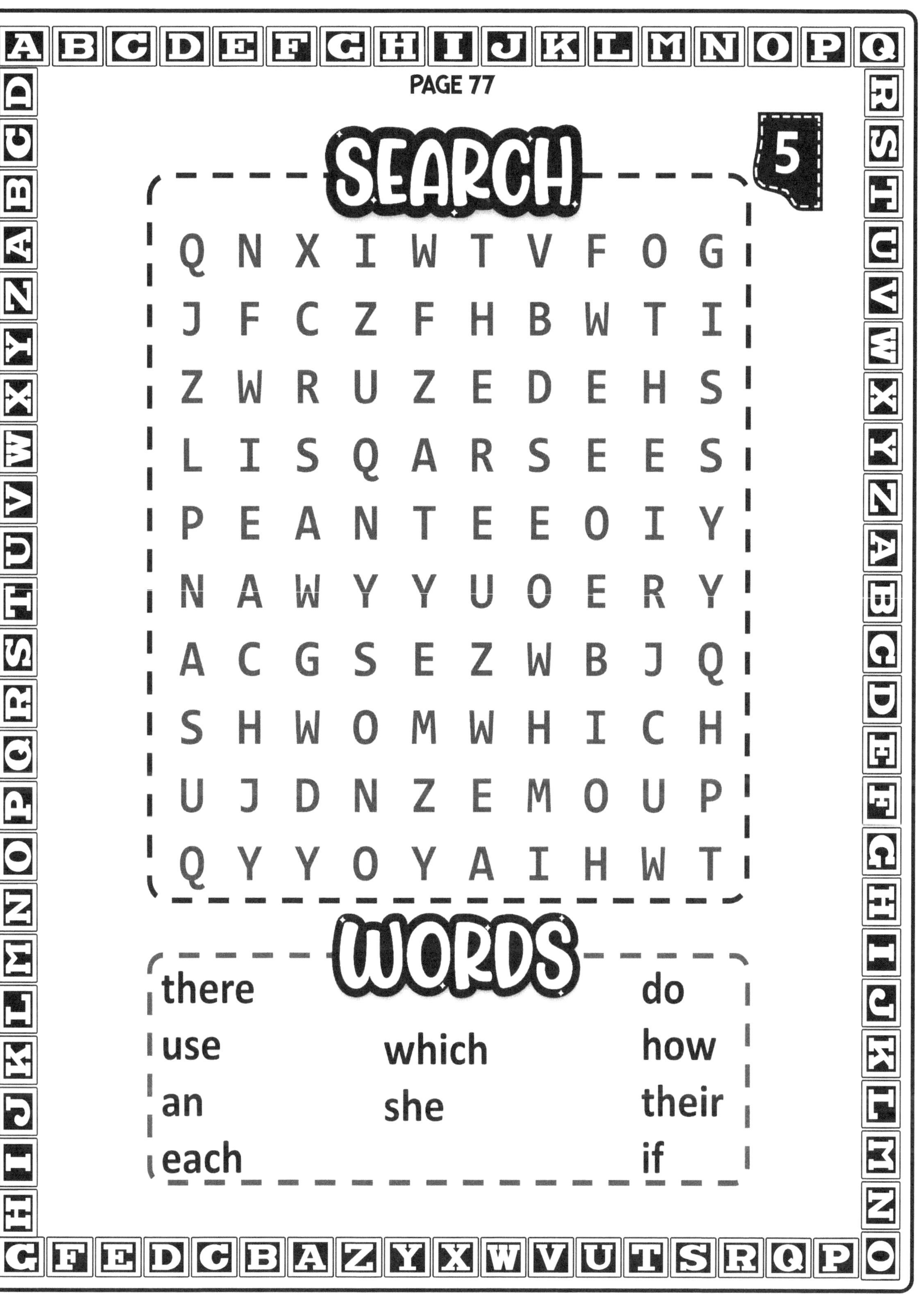


SEARCH
5

Q N X I W T V F O G
J F C Z F H B W T I
Z W R U Z E D E H S
L I S Q A R S E E S
P E A N T E E O I Y
N A W Y Y U O E R Y
A C G S E Z W B J Q
S H W O M W H I C H
U J D N Z E M O U P
Q Y Y O Y A I H W T

WORDS

there
use
an
each

which
she

do
how
their
if

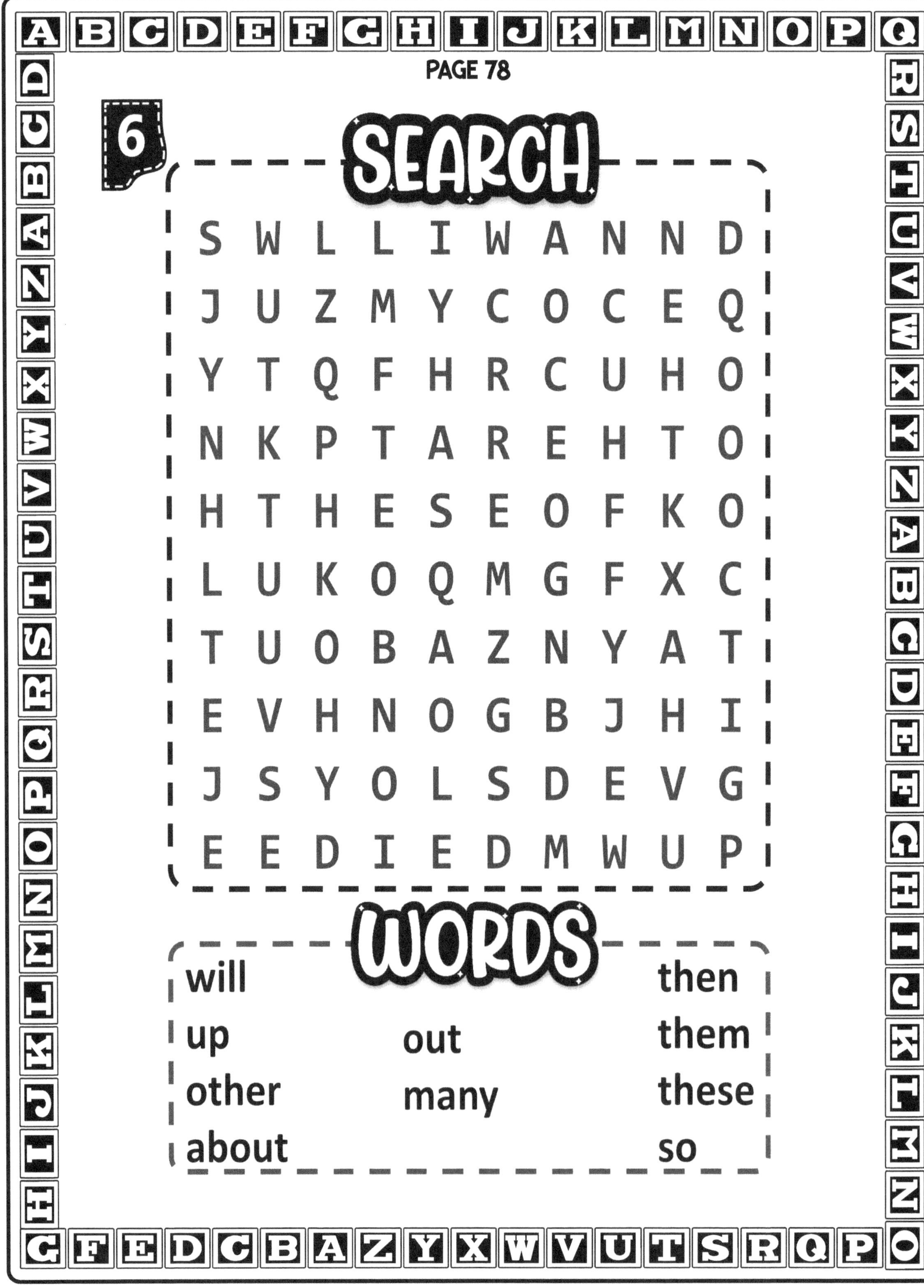
PAGE 78

6

SEARCH

S W L L I W A N N D
J U Z M Y C O C E Q
Y T Q F H R C U H O
N K P T A R E H T O
H T H E S E O F K O
L U K O Q M G F X C
T U O B A Z N Y A T
E V H N O G B J H I
J S Y O L S D E V G
E E D I E D M W U P

WORDS

will
up
other
about
out
many
then
them
these
so

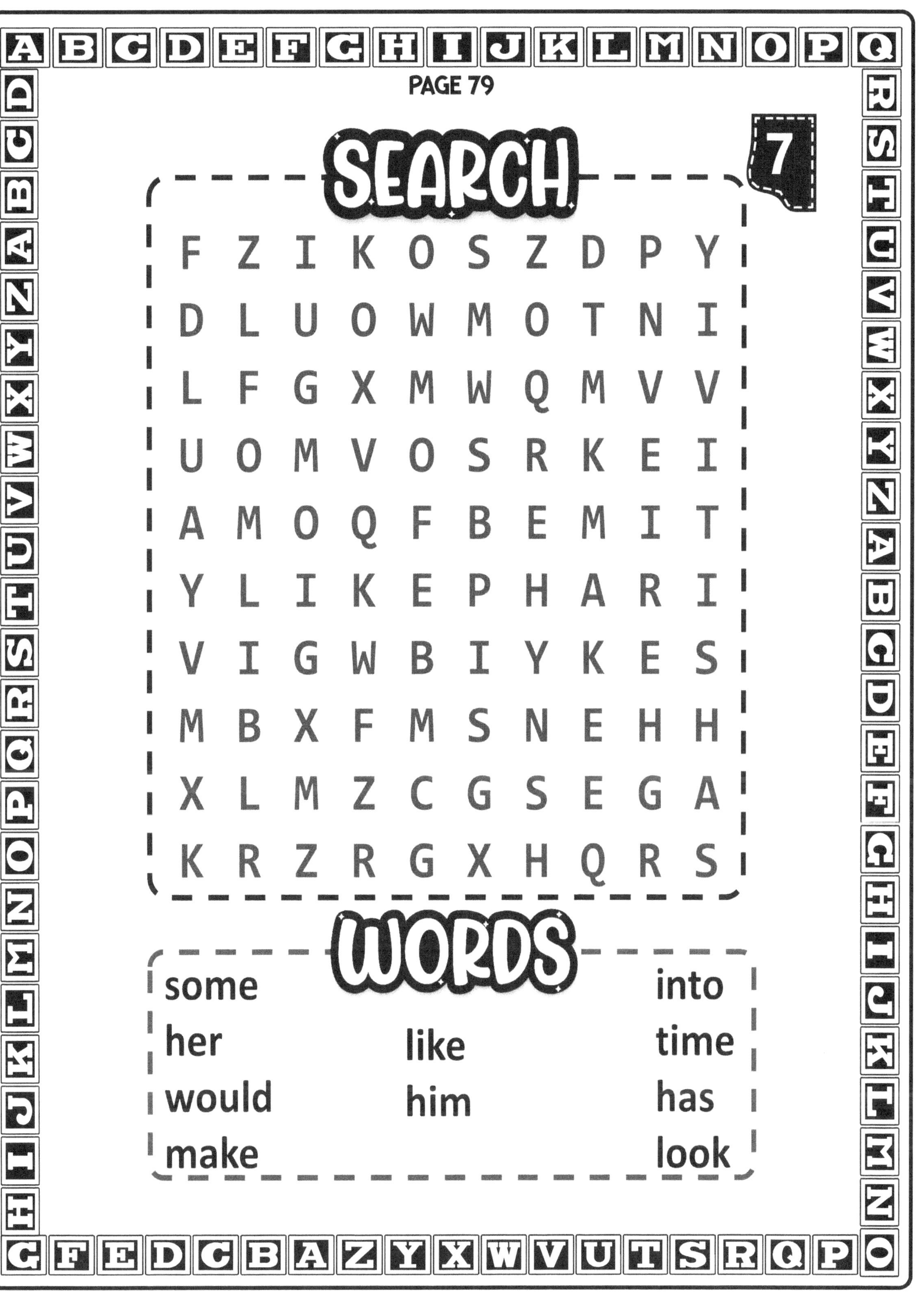
SEARCH
7
F Z I K O S Z D P Y
D L U O W M O T N I
L F G X M W Q M V V
U O M V O S R K E I
A M O Q F B E M I T
Y L I K E P H A R I
V I G W B I Y K E S
M B X F M S N E H H
X L M Z C G S E G A
K R Z R G X H Q R S
WORDS
some
her
would
make
like
him
into
time
has
look

8
SEARCH

X O D H R X Z Y A W
O W M Y E R O M B V
T T W D B R C H E H
H A I X M O I E L I
O Q W Z U S S T S Y
O G W L N D F I W J
O K D P M I E R P A
E D D H G S D W H I
X V E L P O E P J S
B V C B H N O G Y X

WORDS

two                         no
more        see             way
write       number          could
go                          people

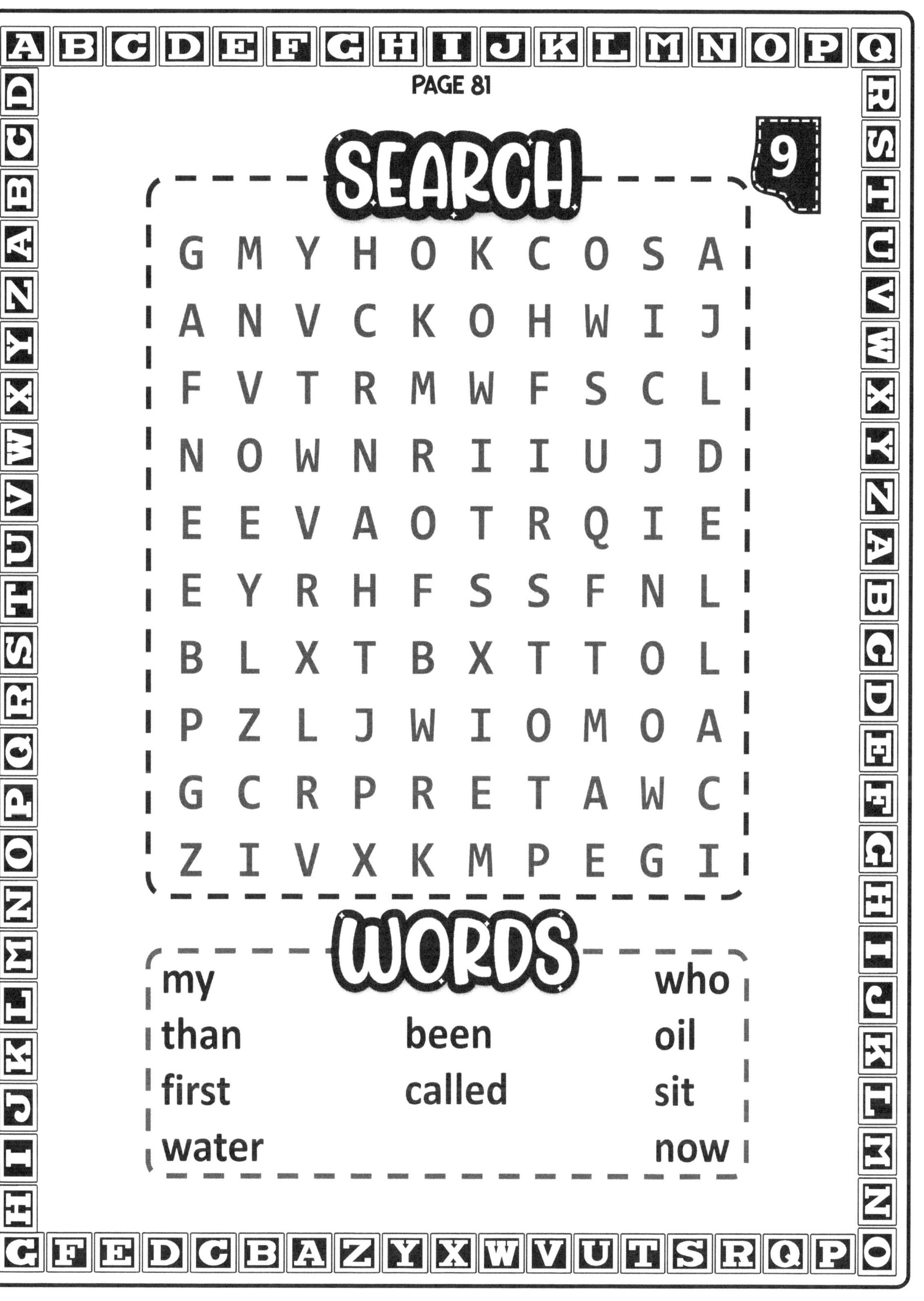


SEARCH
9
G M Y H O K C O S A
A N V C K O H W I J
F V T R M W F S C L
N O W N R I I U J D
E E V A O T R Q I E
E Y R H F S S F N L
B L X T B X T T O L
P Z L J W I O M O A
G C R P R E T A W C
Z I V X K M P E G I
WORDS
my
than
first
water
been
called
who
oil
sit
now

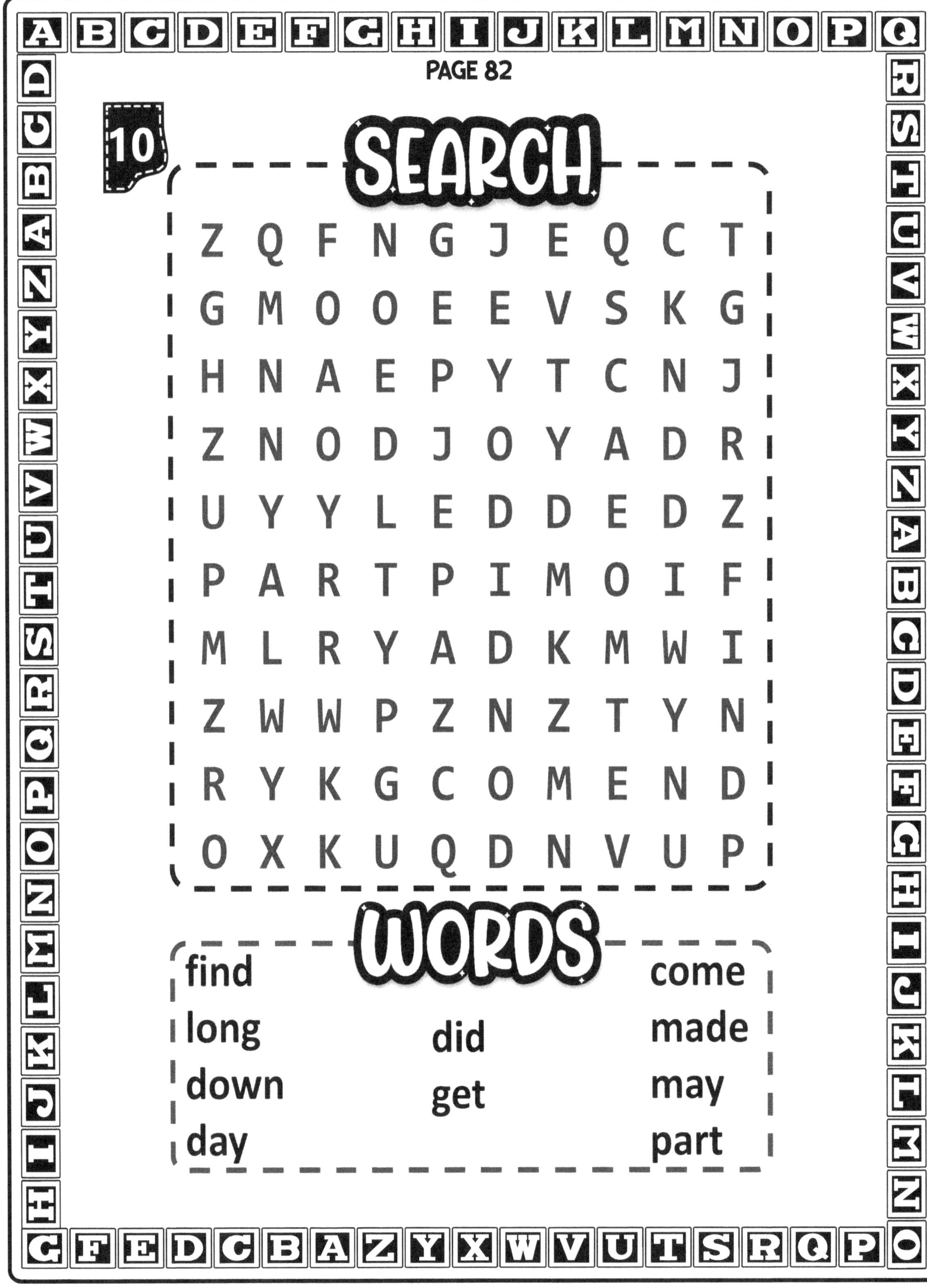
10
SEARCH

Z Q F N G J E Q C T
G M O O E E V S K G
H N A E P Y T C N J
Z N O D J O Y A D R
U Y Y L E D D E D Z
P A R T P I M O I F
M L R Y A D K M W I
Z W W P Z N Z T Y N
R Y K G C O M E N D
O X K U Q D N V U P

WORDS

find
long
down
day

did
get

come
made
may
part

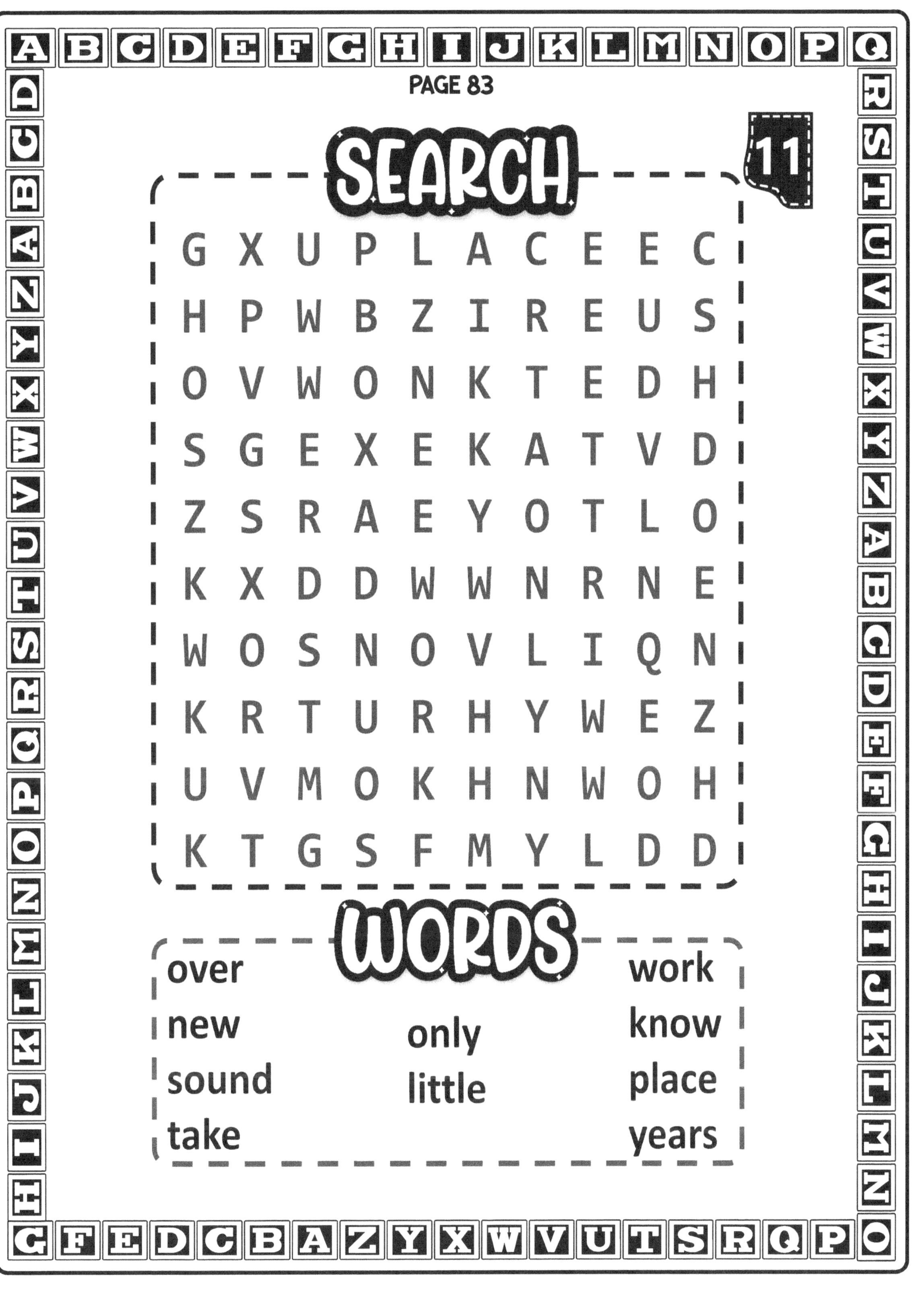


SEARCH
11
G X U P L A C E E C
H P W B Z I R E U S
O V W O N K T E D H
S G E X E K A T V D
Z S R A E Y O T L O
K X D D W W N R N E
W O S N O V L I Q N
K R T U R H Y W E Z
U V M O K H N W O H
K T G S F M Y L D D
WORDS
over
new
sound
take
only
little
work
know
place
years

12

SEARCH

B T G R X V G X W O
C D I Q R U B L W W
N T V Q E T O A E G
A W E O T D I U C M
X M E F F G N B R K
Q O L V A J V M M A
Z S G N I H T E R E
T T D I U L G F R L
F U N J U S T P M Y
U S S B C O M K V M

WORDS

live
me
back
give
most
very
after
things
our
just

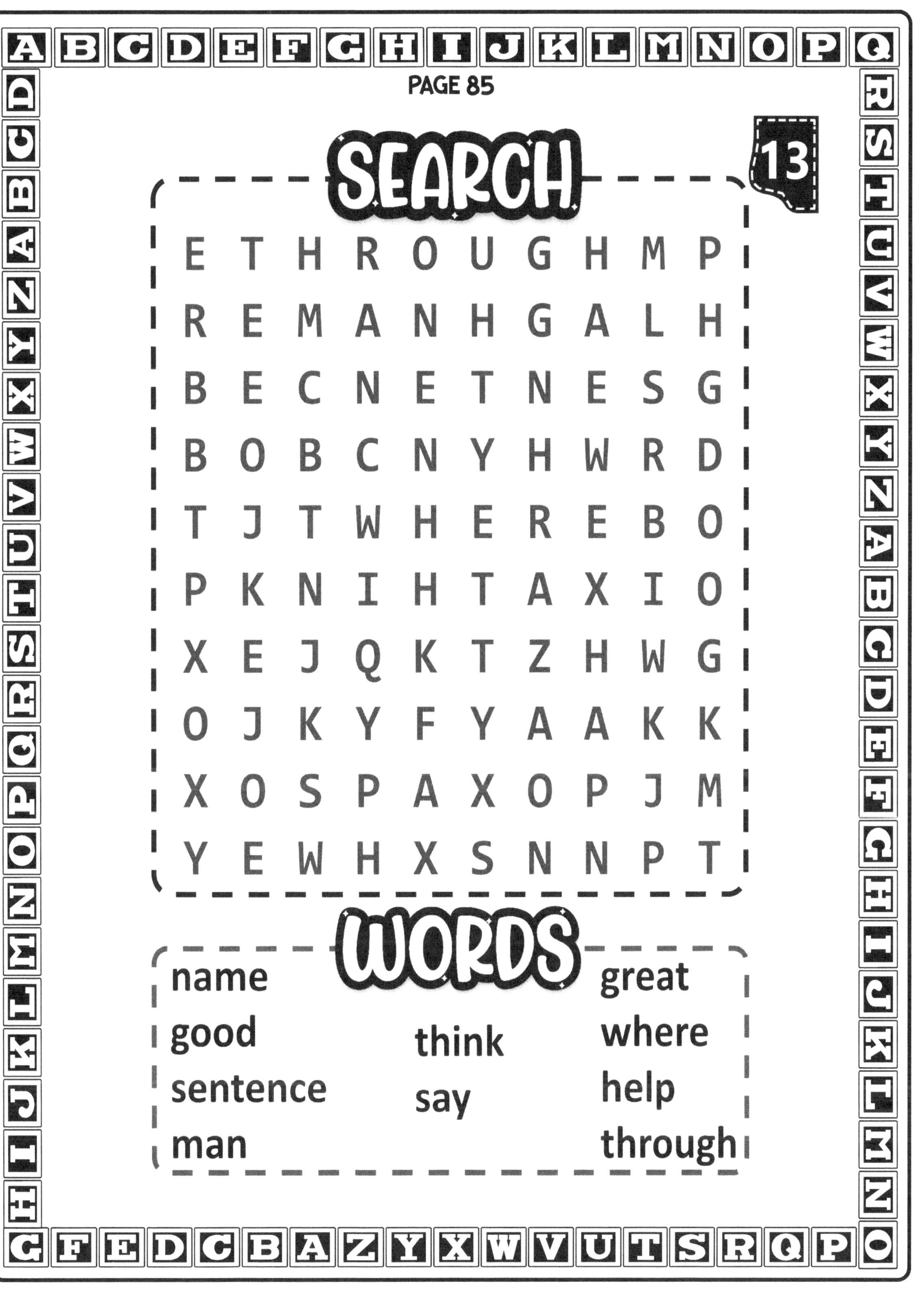
SEARCH
13

E T H R O U G H M P
R E M A N H G A L H
B E C N E T N E S G
B O B C N Y H W R D
T J T W H E R E B O
P K N I H T A X I O
X E J Q K T Z H W G
O J K Y F Y A A K K
X O S P A X O P J M
Y E W H X S N N P T

WORDS
name
good
sentence
man
think
say
great
where
help
through

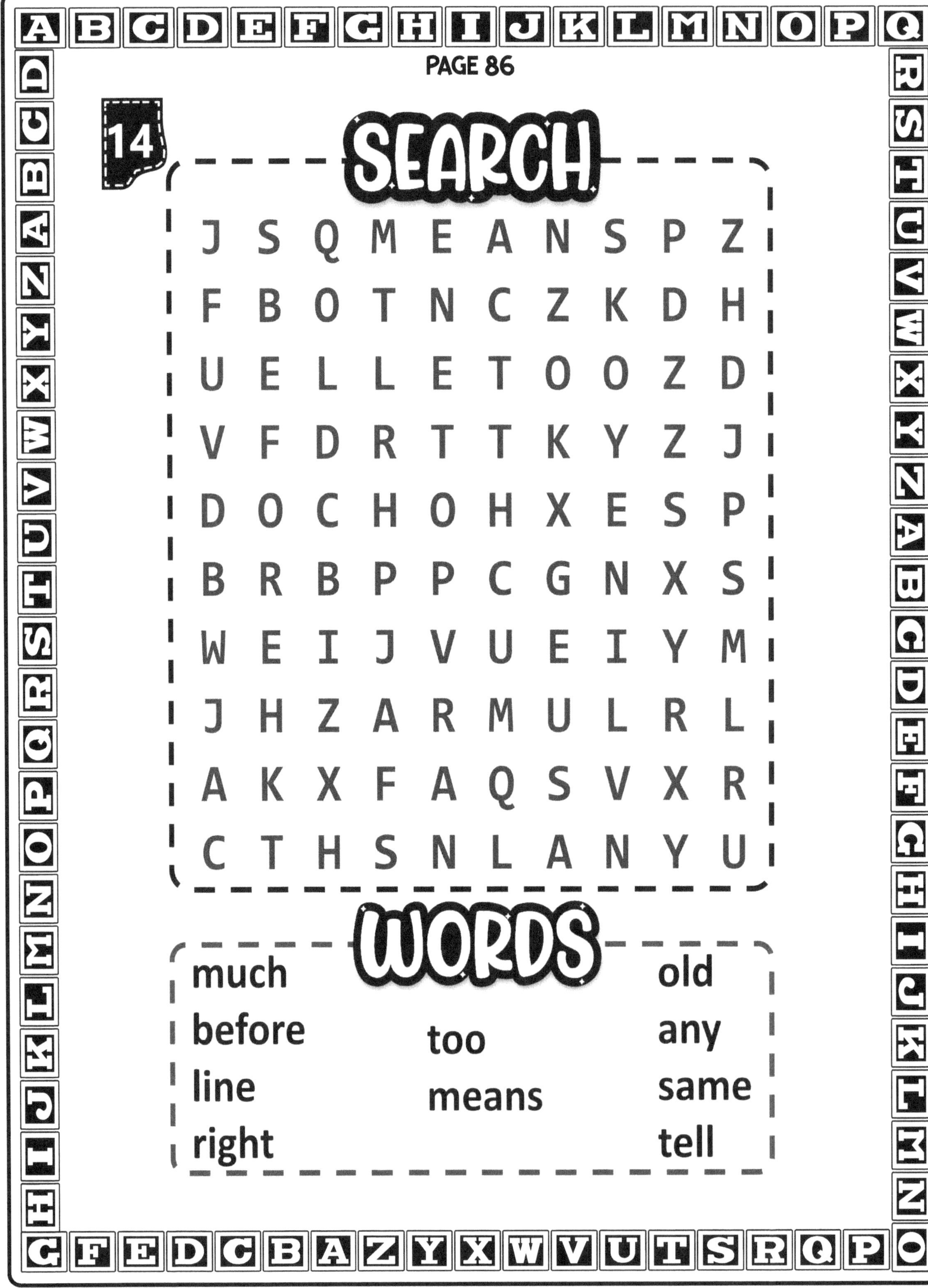


14

SEARCH

J S Q M E A N S P Z
F B O T N C Z K D H
U E L L E T O O Z D
V F D R T T K Y Z J
D O C H O H X E S P
B R B P P C G N X S
W E I J V U E I Y M
J H Z A R M U L R L
A K X F A Q S V X R
C T H S N L A N Y U

WORDS

much
before
line
right

too
means

old
any
same
tell

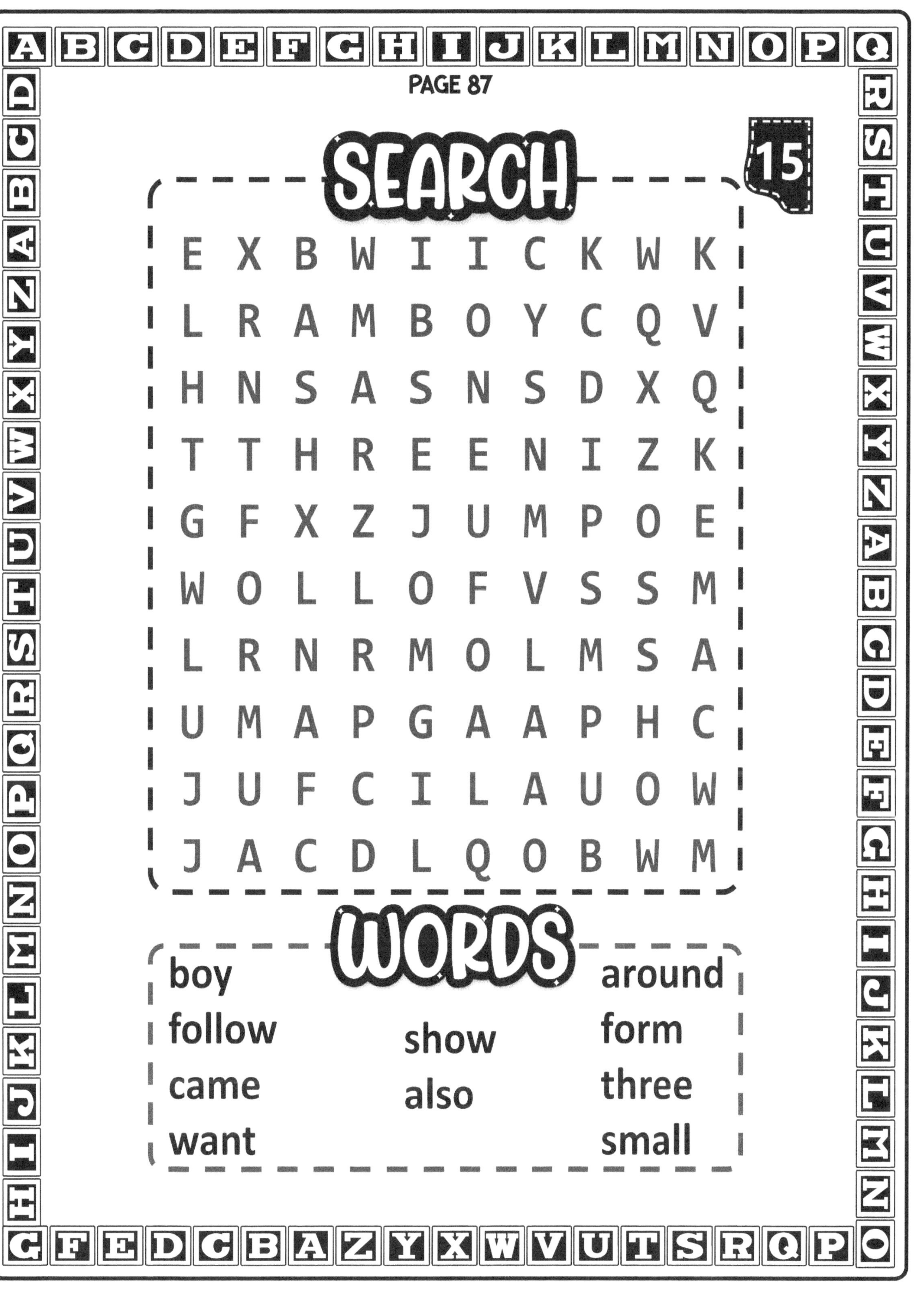


SEARCH
15

E X B W I I C K W K
L R A M B O Y C Q V
H N S A S N S D X Q
T T H R E E N I Z K
G F X Z J U M P O E
W O L L O F V S S M
L R N R M O L M S A
U M A P G A A P H C
J U F C I L A U O W
J A C D L Q O B W M

WORDS
boy
follow
came
want
show
also
around
form
three
small

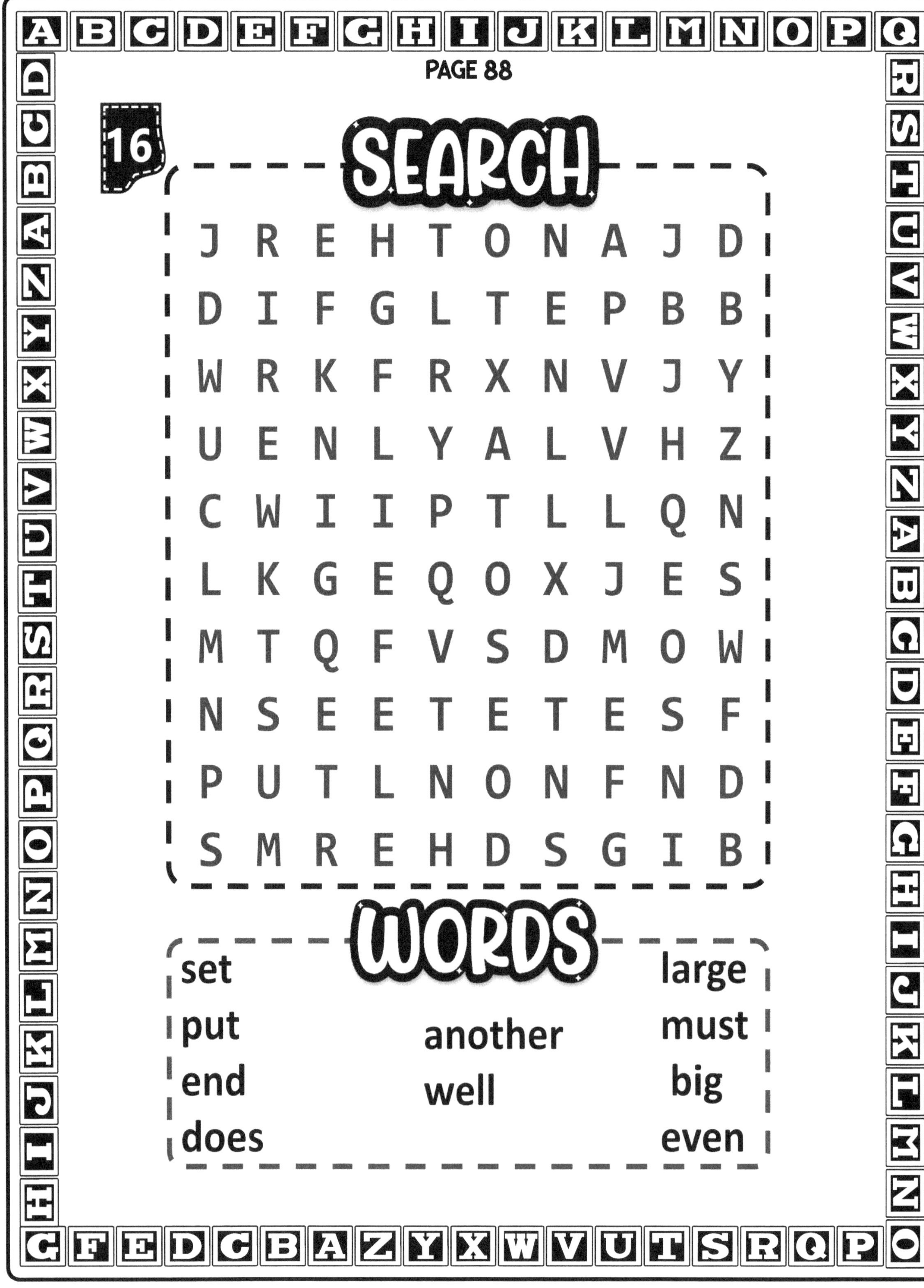

16
SEARCH

J R E H T O N A J D
D I F G L T E P B B
W R K F R X N V J Y
U E N L Y A L V H Z
C W I I P T L L Q N
L K G E Q O X J E S
M T Q F V S D M O W
N S E E T E T E S F
P U T L N O N F N D
S M R E H D S G I B

WORDS

set
put
end
does

another
well

large
must
big
even

# SEARCH

**17**

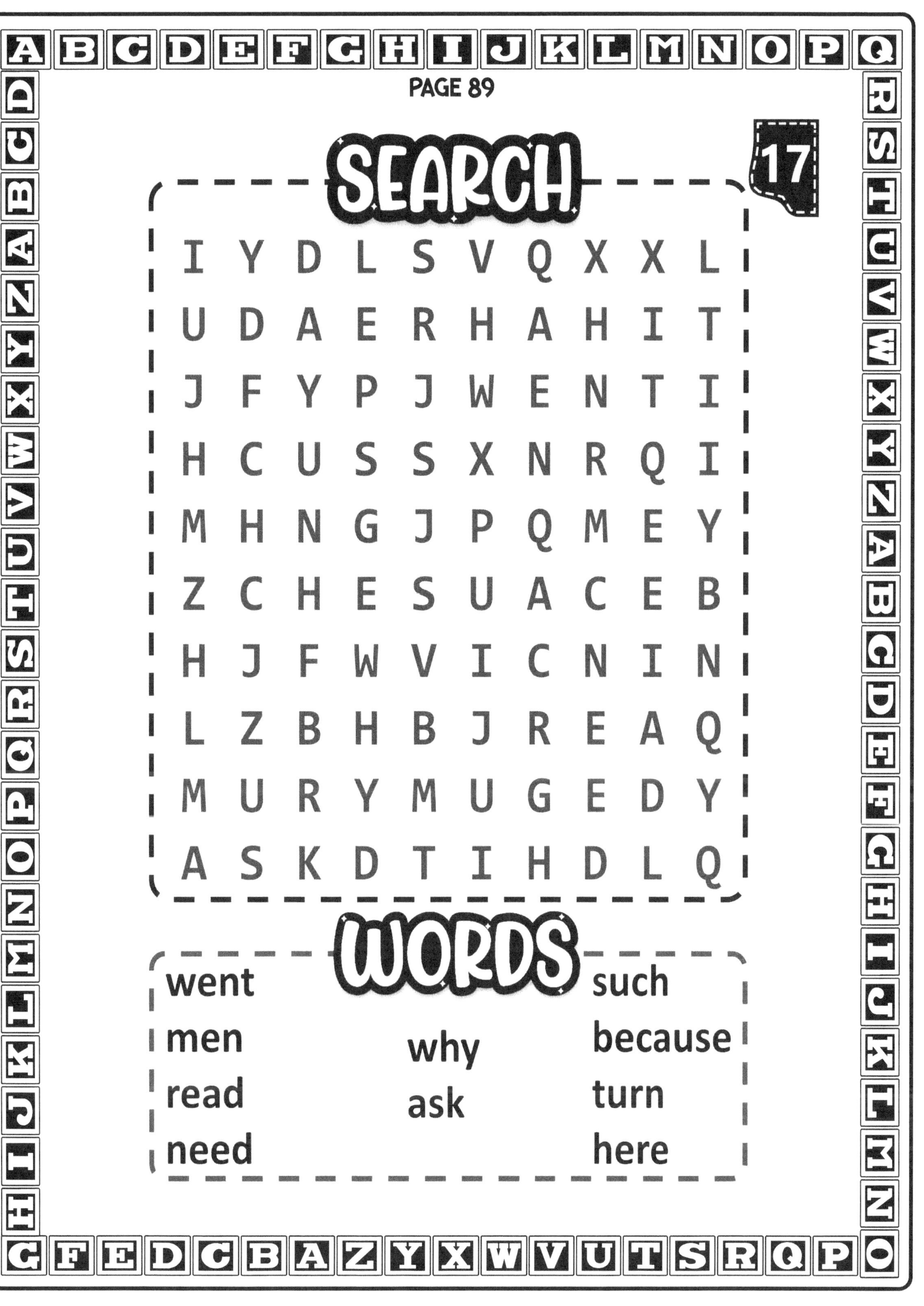



# WORDS

went

men

read

need

why

ask

such

because

turn

here

# SEARCH

**18**

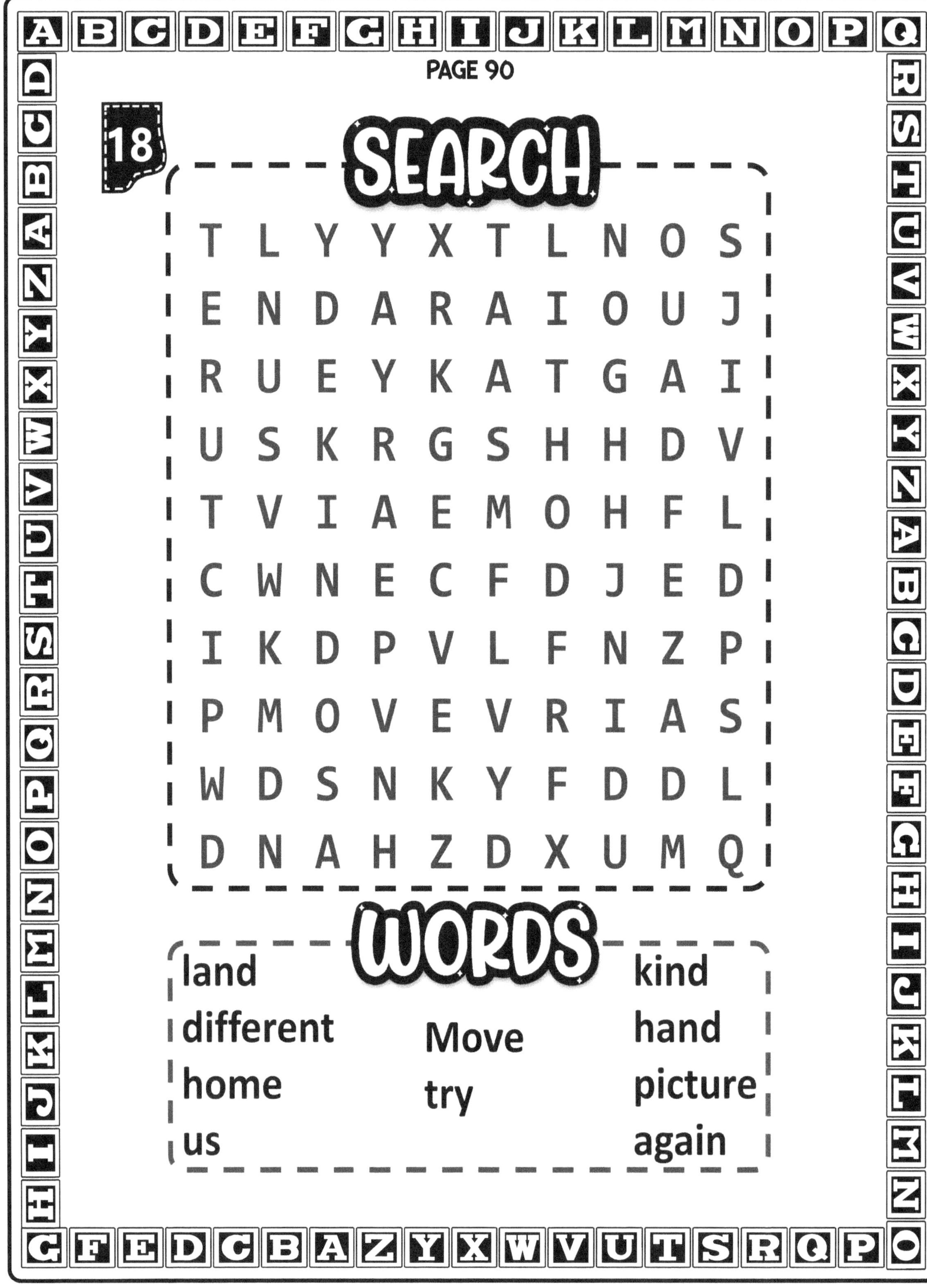



## WORDS

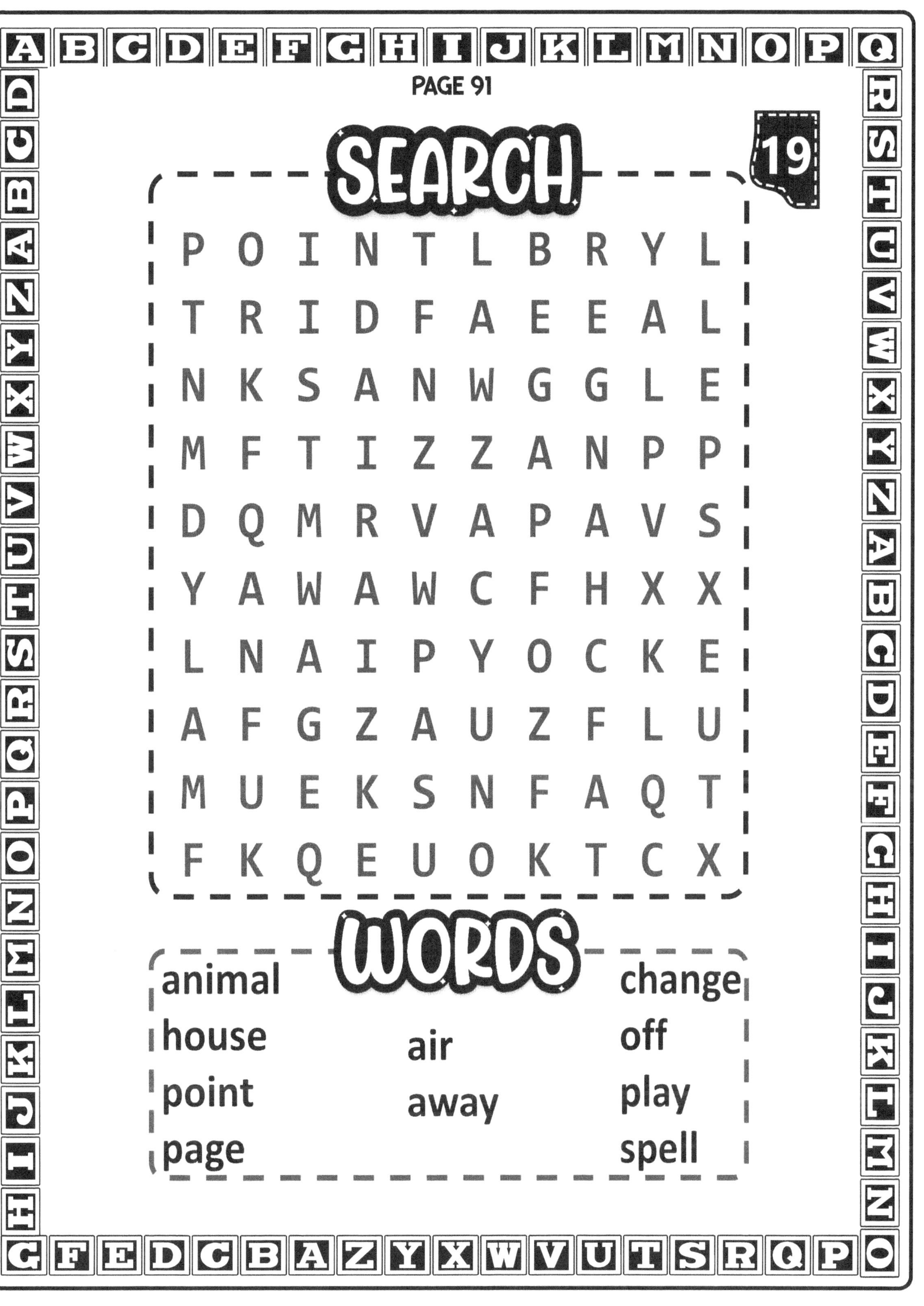
SEARCH
19
P O I N T L B R Y L
T R I D F A E E A L
N K S A N W G G L E
M F T I Z Z A N P P
D Q M R V A P A V S
Y Y A W A W C F H X X
L N A I P Y O C K E
A F G Z A U Z F L U
M U E K S N F A Q T
F K Q E U O K T C X
WORDS
animal
house
point
page
air
away
change
off
play
spell

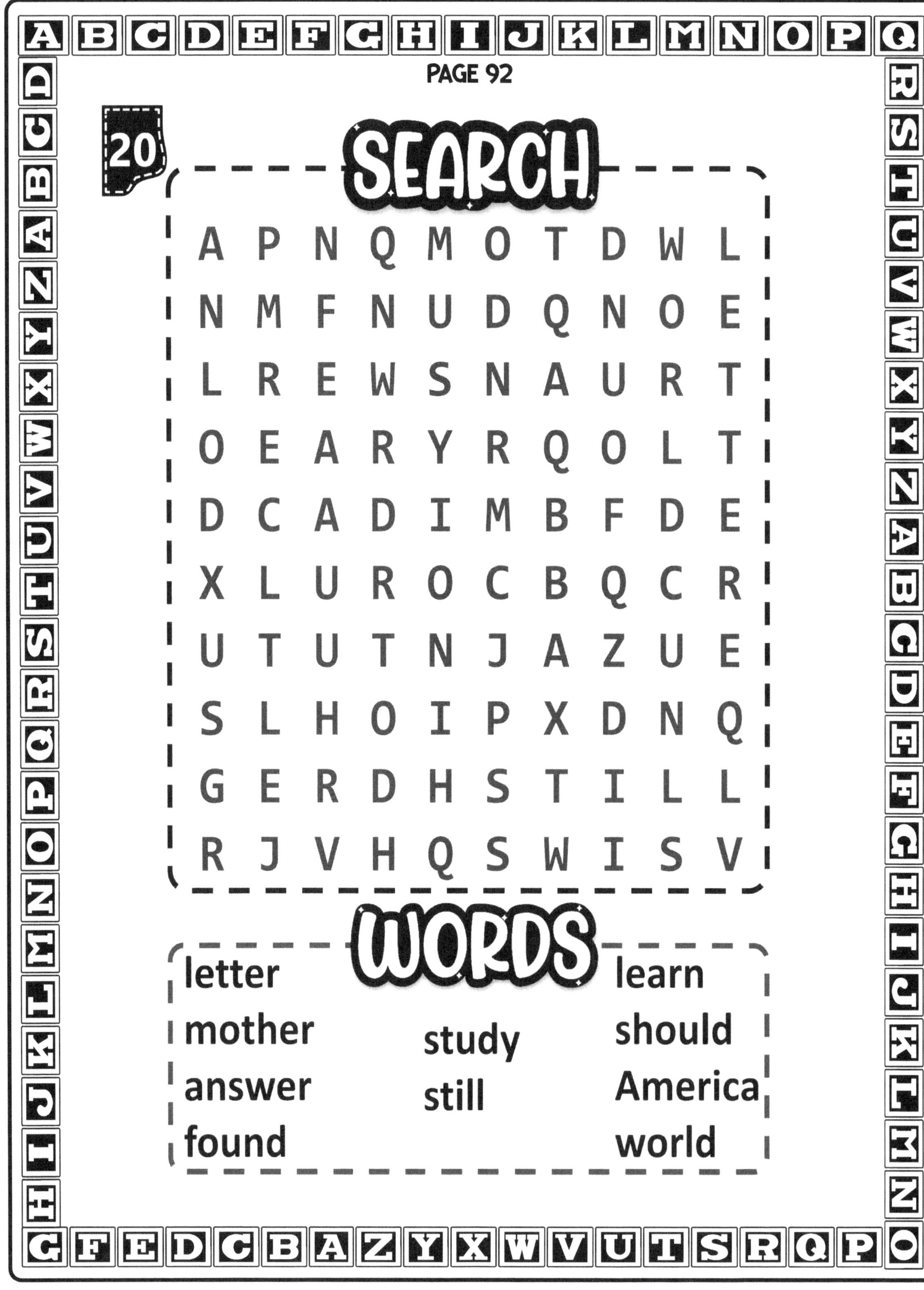

20
SEARCH

A P N Q M O T D W L
N M F N U D Q N O E
L R E W S N A U R T
O E A R Y R Q O L T
D C A D I M B F D E
X L U R O C B Q C R
U T U T N J A Z U E
S L H O I P X D N Q
G E R D H S T I L L
R J V H Q S W I S V

WORDS

letter
mother
answer
found

study
still

learn
should
America
world

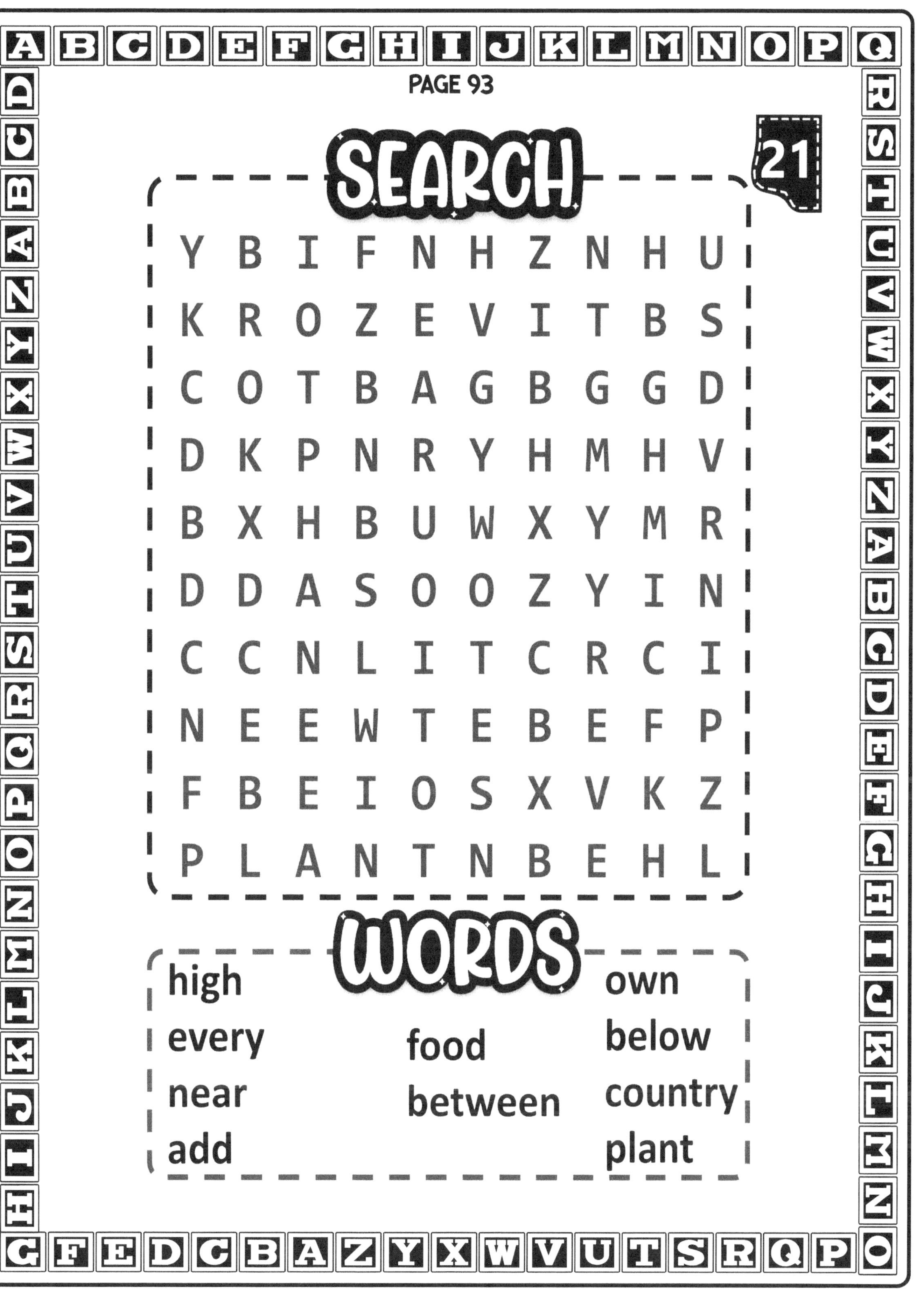
SEARCH
21

Y B I F N H Z N H U
K R O Z E V I T B S
C O T B A G B G G D
D K P N R Y H M H V
B X H B U W X Y M R
D D A S O O Z Y I N
C C N L I T C R C I
N E E W T E B E F P
F B E I O S X V K Z
P L A N T N B E H L

WORDS

high
every
near
add

food
between

own
below
country
plant

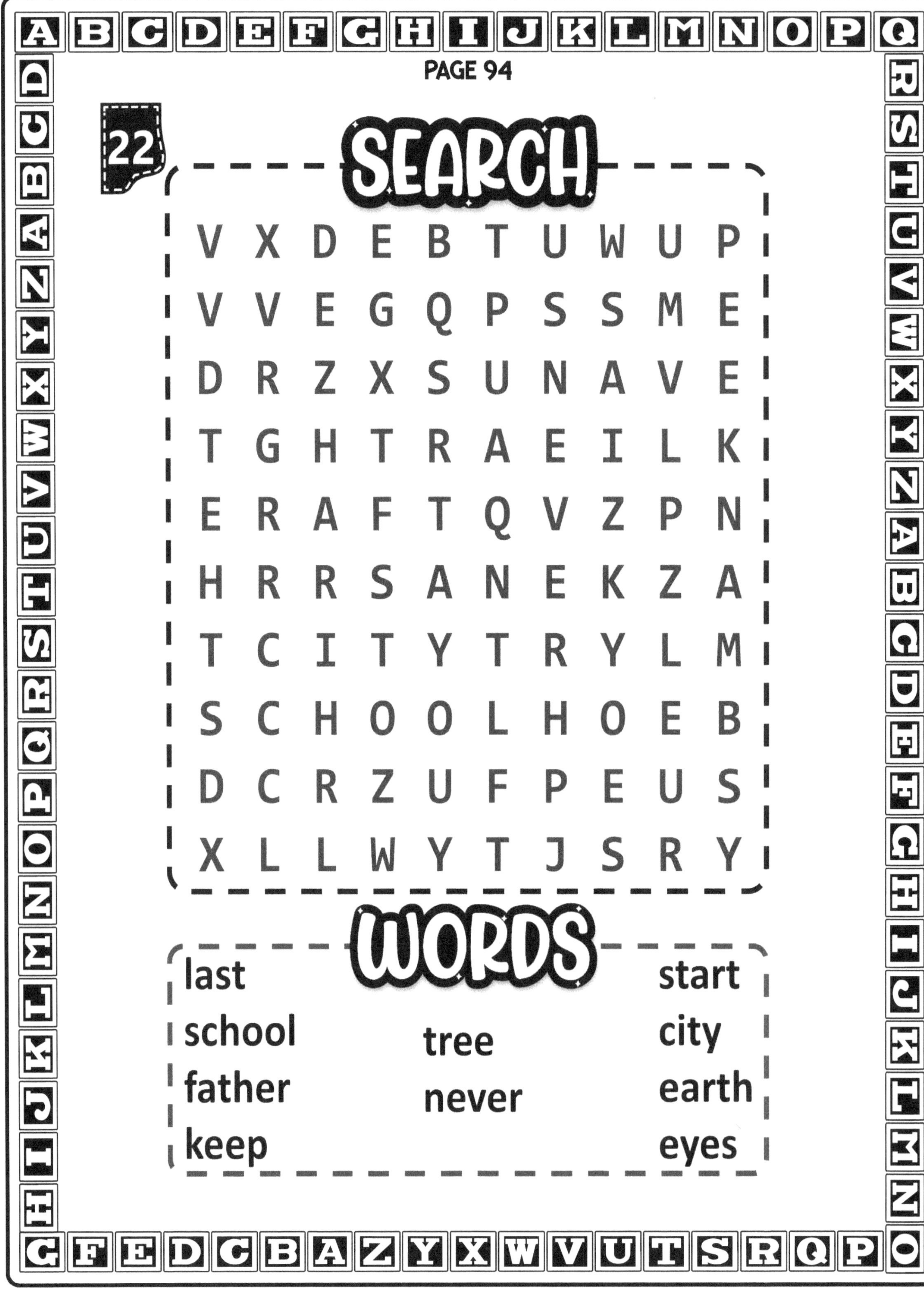
22
SEARCH

V X D E B T U W U P
V V E G Q P S S M E
D R Z X S U N A V E
T G H T R A E I L K
E R A F T Q V Z P N
H R R S A N E K Z A
T C I T Y T R Y L M
S C H O O L H O E B
D C R Z U F P E U S
X L L W Y T J S R Y

WORDS

last
school
father
keep

tree
never

start
city
earth
eyes

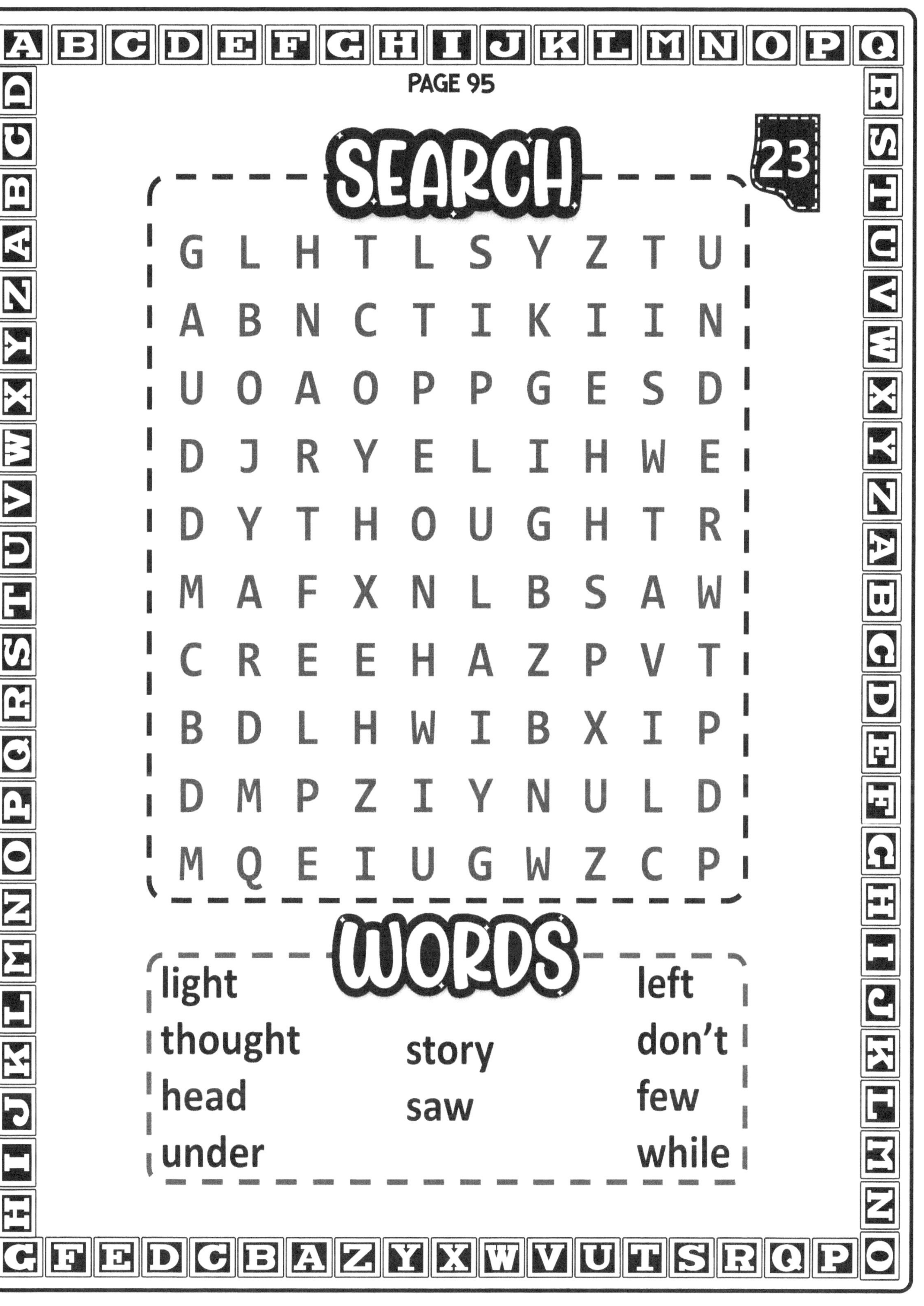

SEARCH
23

G L H T L S Y Z T U
A B N C T I K I I N
U O A O P P G E S D
D J R Y E L I H W E
D Y T H O U G H T R
M A F X N L B S A W
C R E E H A Z P V T
B D L H W I B X I P
D M P Z I Y N U L D
M Q E I U G W Z C P

WORDS

light
thought
head
under

story
saw

left
don't
few
while

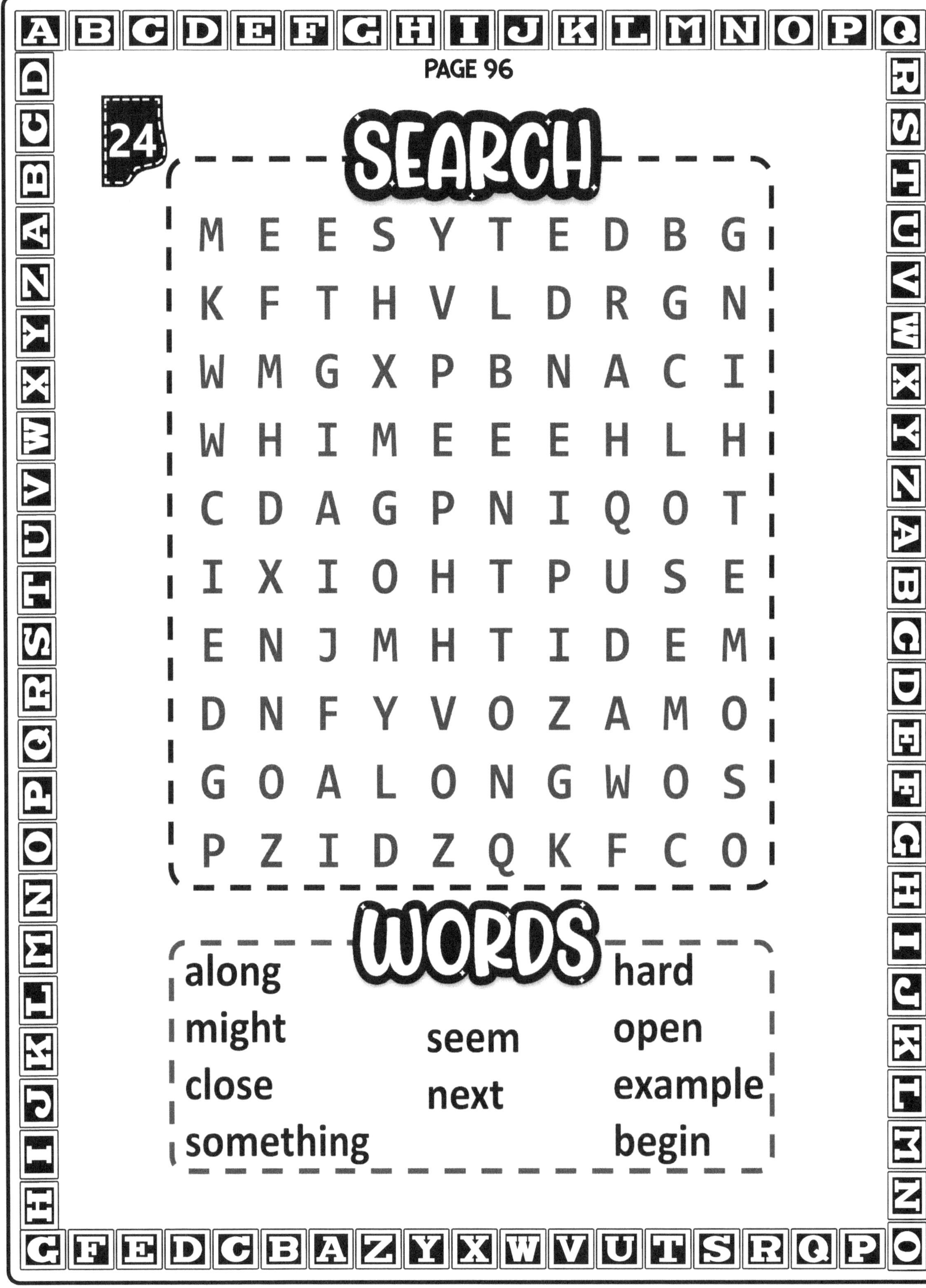

24

SEARCH

M E E S Y T E D B G
K F T H V L D R G N
W M G X P B N A C I
W H I M E E E H L H
C D A G P N I Q O T
I X I O H T P U S E
E N J M H T I D E M
D N F Y V O Z A M O
G O A L O N G W O S
P Z I D Z Q K F C O

WORDS

along
might
close
something

seem
next

hard
open
example
begin

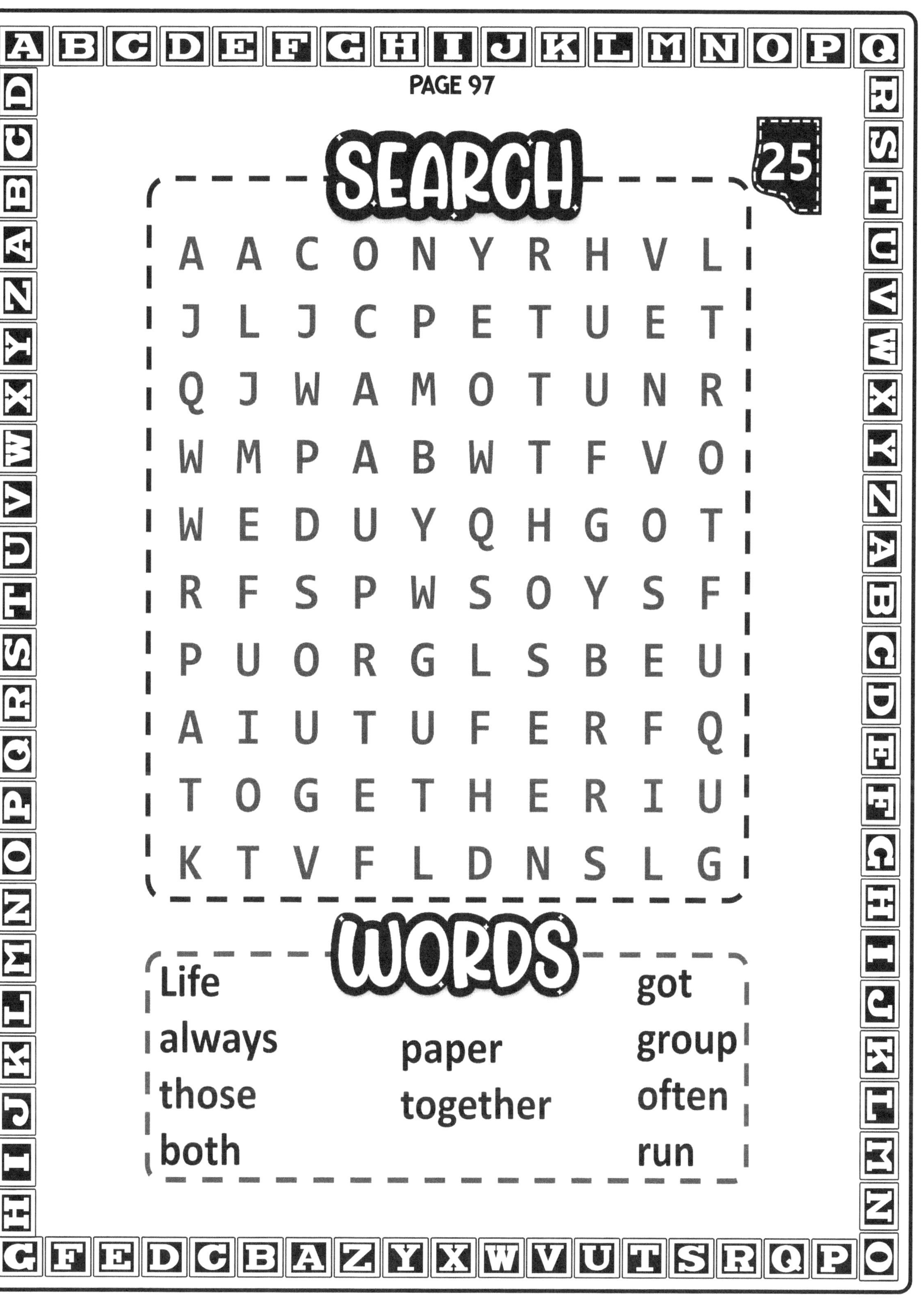


SEARCH
25

A A C O N Y R H V L
J L J C P E T U E T
Q J W A M O T U N R
W M P A B W T F V O
W E D U Y Q H G O T
R F S P W S O Y S F
P U O R G L S B E U
A I U T U F E R F Q
T O G E T H E R I U
K T V F L D N S L G

WORDS

Life
always
those
both
paper
together
got
group
often
run

26
SEARCH
N E R D L I H C A I
L E T M E I B O M T
F Q L T E D T P R H
Y W I Q T I O N G G
F H K W Z R G Y U I
W E A C T W G F O N
Y L E A S I D E M V
K O N T U R N W I S
P T W R A C Q K L T
W M Q F I V M B E B
WORDS
until
children
side
important
feet
car
mile
night
walk
white

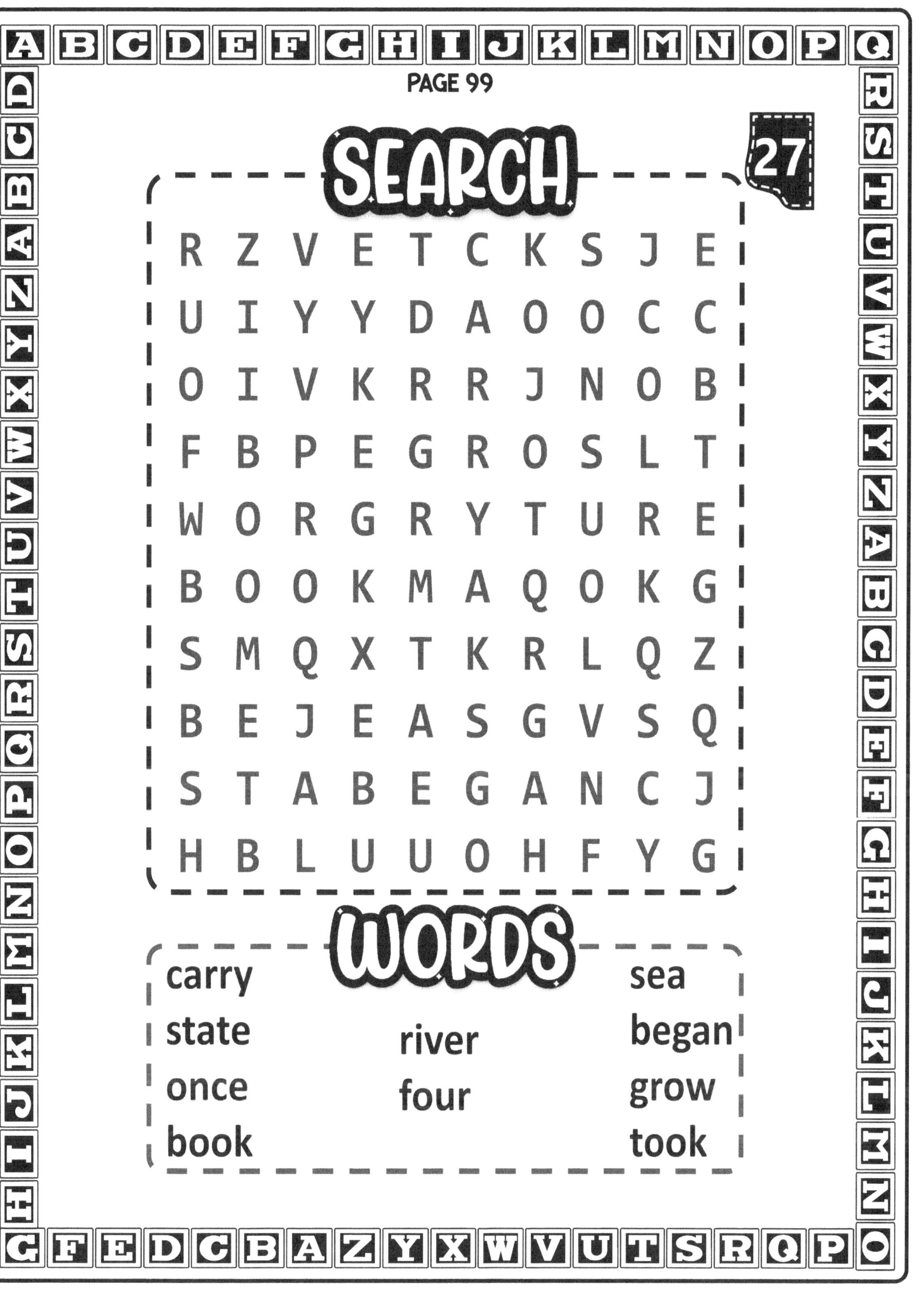

PAGE 99
SEARCH
27

R Z V E T C K S J E
U I Y Y D A O O C C
O I V K R R J N O B
F B P E G R O S L T
W O R G R Y T U R E
B O O K M A Q O K G
S M Q X T K R L Q Z
B E J E A S G V S Q
S T A B E G A N C J
H B L U U O H F Y G

WORDS
carry
state
once
book
river
four
sea
began
grow
took

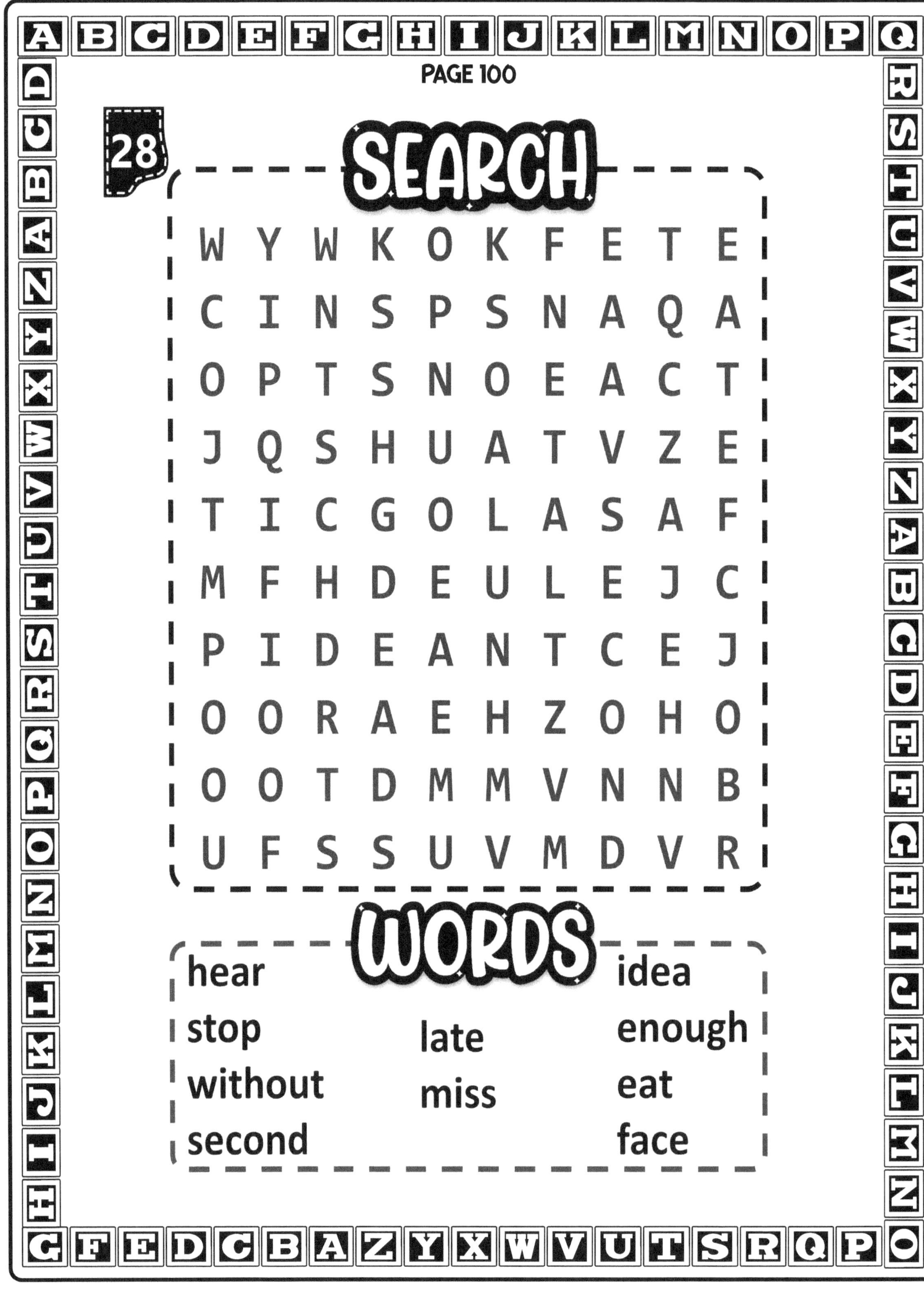




28
SEARCH

W Y W K O K F E T E
C I N S P S N A Q A
O P T S N O E A C T
J Q S H U A T V Z E
T I C G O L A S A F
M F H D E U L E J C
P I D E A N T C E J
O O R A E H Z O H O
O O T D M M V N N B
U F S S U V M D V R

WORDS

hear
stop
without
second

late
miss

idea
enough
eat
face

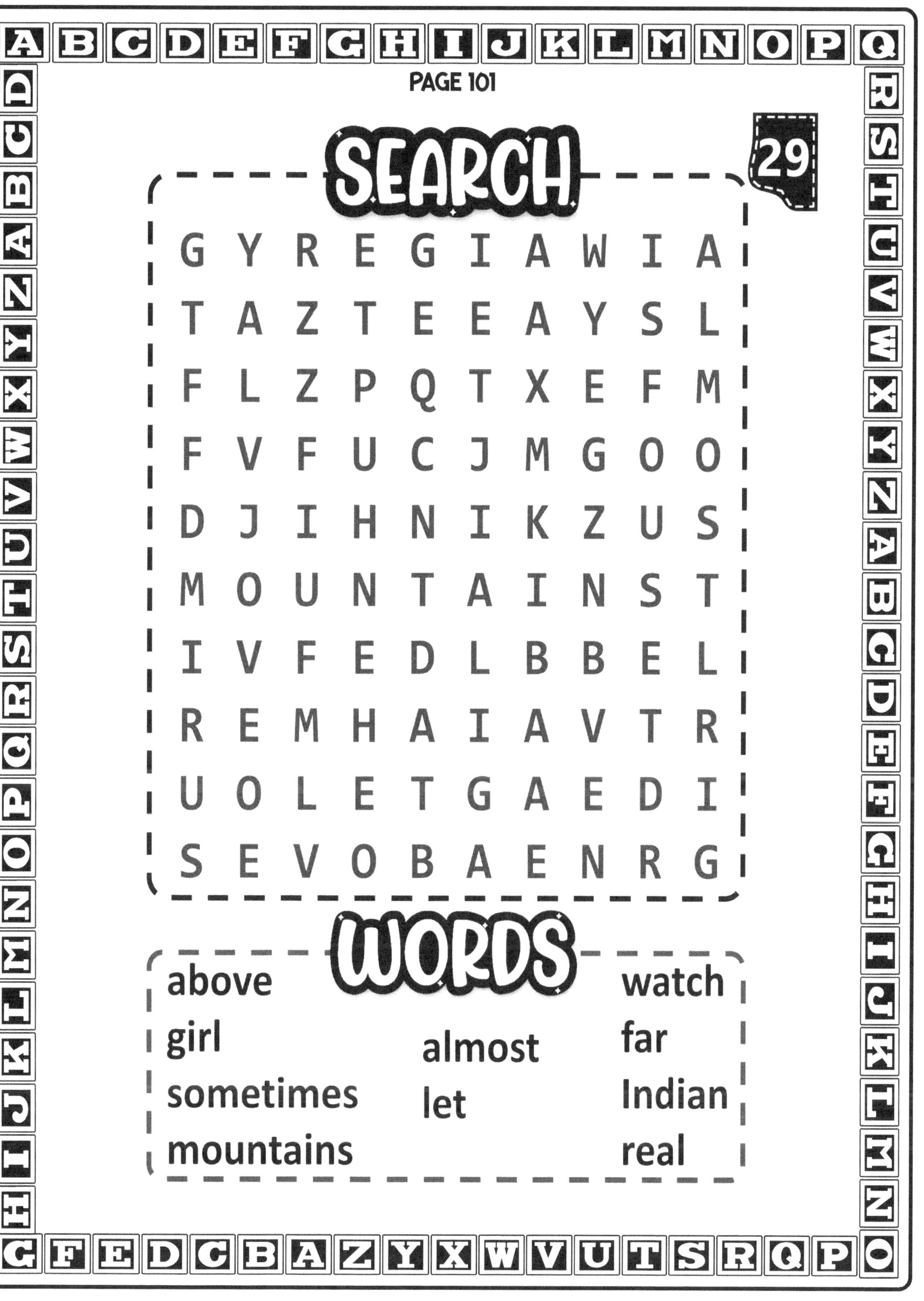


SEARCH
29

G Y R E G I A W I A
T A Z T E E A Y S L
F L Z P Q T X E F M
F V F U C J M G O O
D J I H N I K Z U S
M O U N T A I N S T
I V F E D L B B E L
R E M H A I A V T R
U O L E T G A E D I
S E V O B A E N R G

WORDS

above
girl
sometimes
mountains

almost
let

watch
far
Indian
real

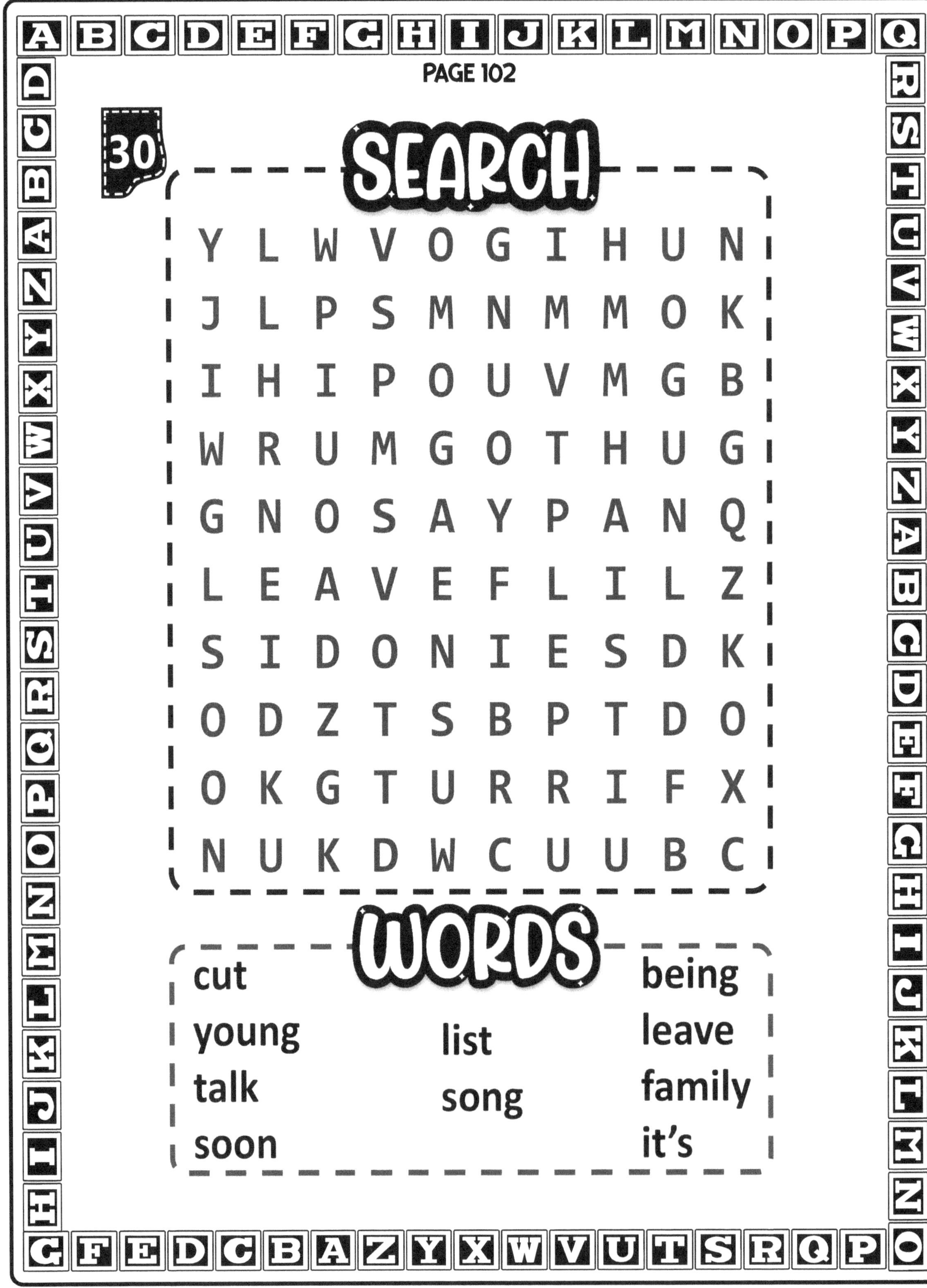
30
SEARCH

Y L W V O G I H U N
J L P S M N M M O K
I H I P O U V M G B
W R U M G O T H U G
G N O S A Y P A N Q
L E A V E F L I L Z
S I D O N I E S D K
O D Z T S B P T D O
O K G T U R R I F X
N U K D W C U U B C

WORDS

cut
young
talk
soon

list
song

being
leave
family
it's

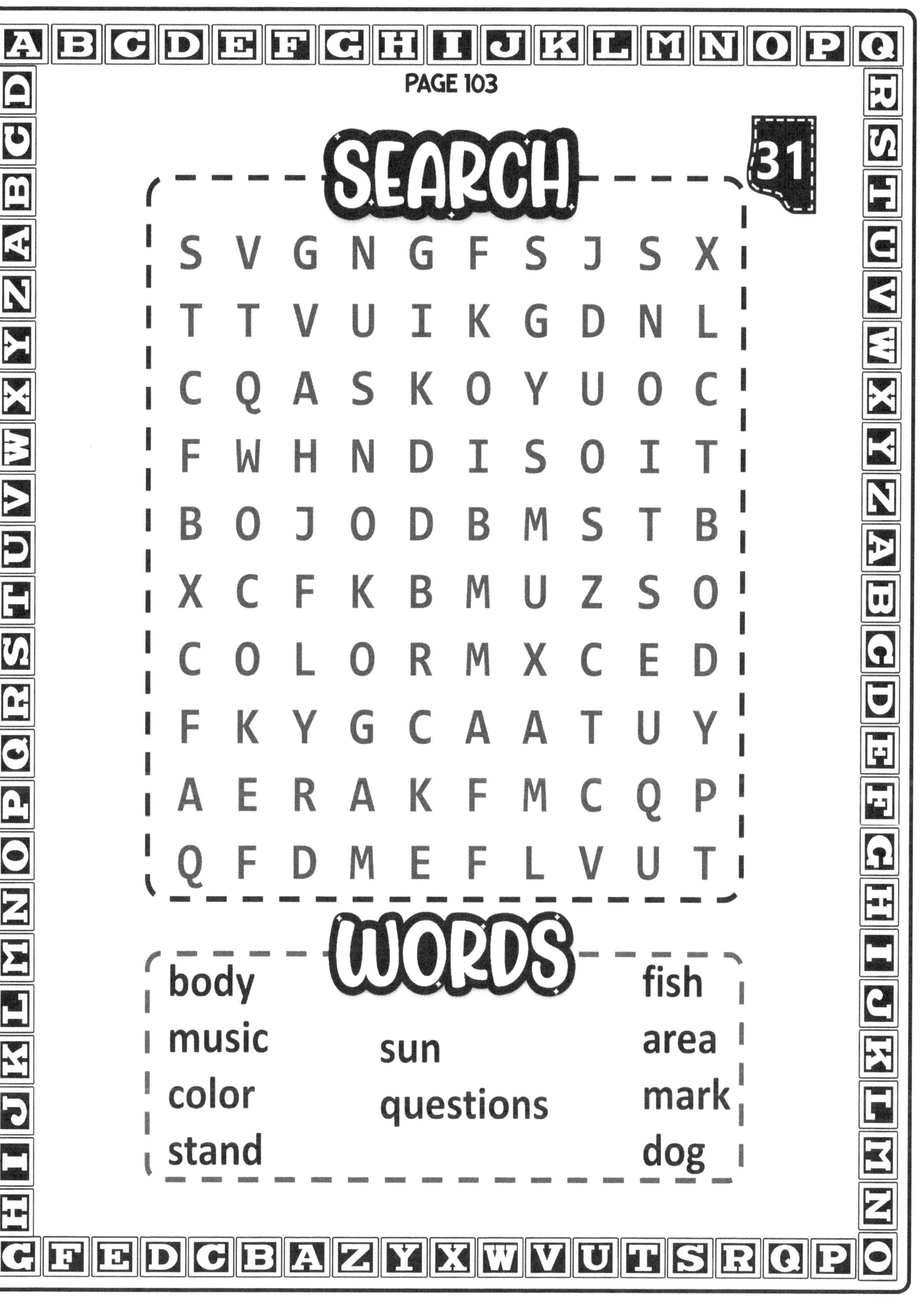
SEARCH
31

S V G N G F S J S X
T T V U I K G D N L
C Q A S K O Y U O C
F W H N D I S O I T
B O J O D B M S T B
X C F K B M U Z S O
C O L O R M X C E D
F K Y G C A A T U Y
A E R A K F M C Q P
Q F D M E F L V U T

WORDS

body
music
color
stand
sun
questions
fish
area
mark
dog

PAGE 104

32

SEARCH

N T A R U E E D J Y
H O R S E T M O O R
B M I D V E W W E E
C I L H L L S E I V
I O R B F P I I N E
T I O D I M N H T K
M R U E S O C N N H
P P C S K C E P T D
O E C V M C A Q N S
E H J C H F W W L V

WORDS

horse          since
birds    room  ever
problem  knew  piece
complete       told

# SEARCH 33

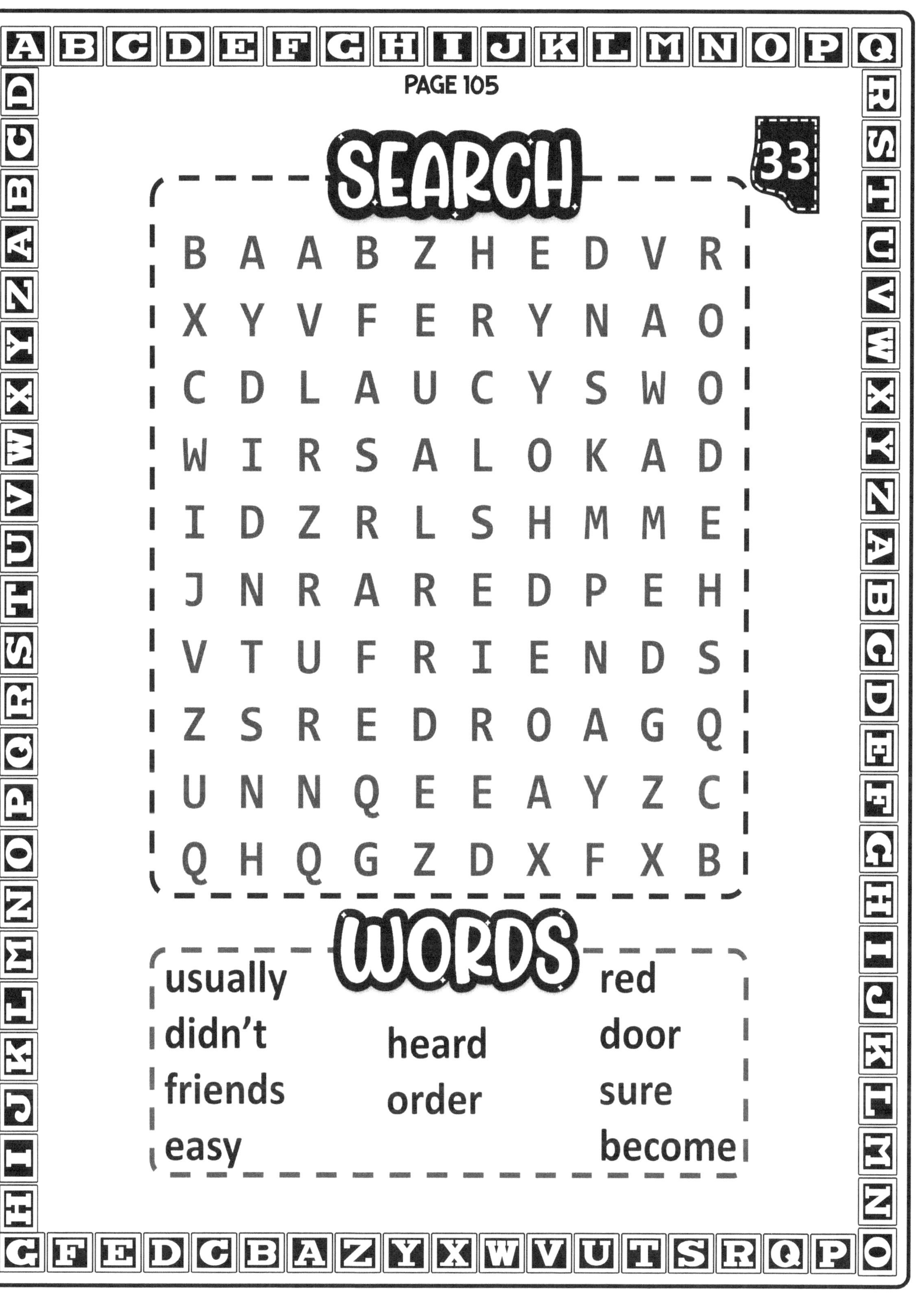



# WORDS

usually
didn't
friends
easy

heard
order

red
door
sure
become

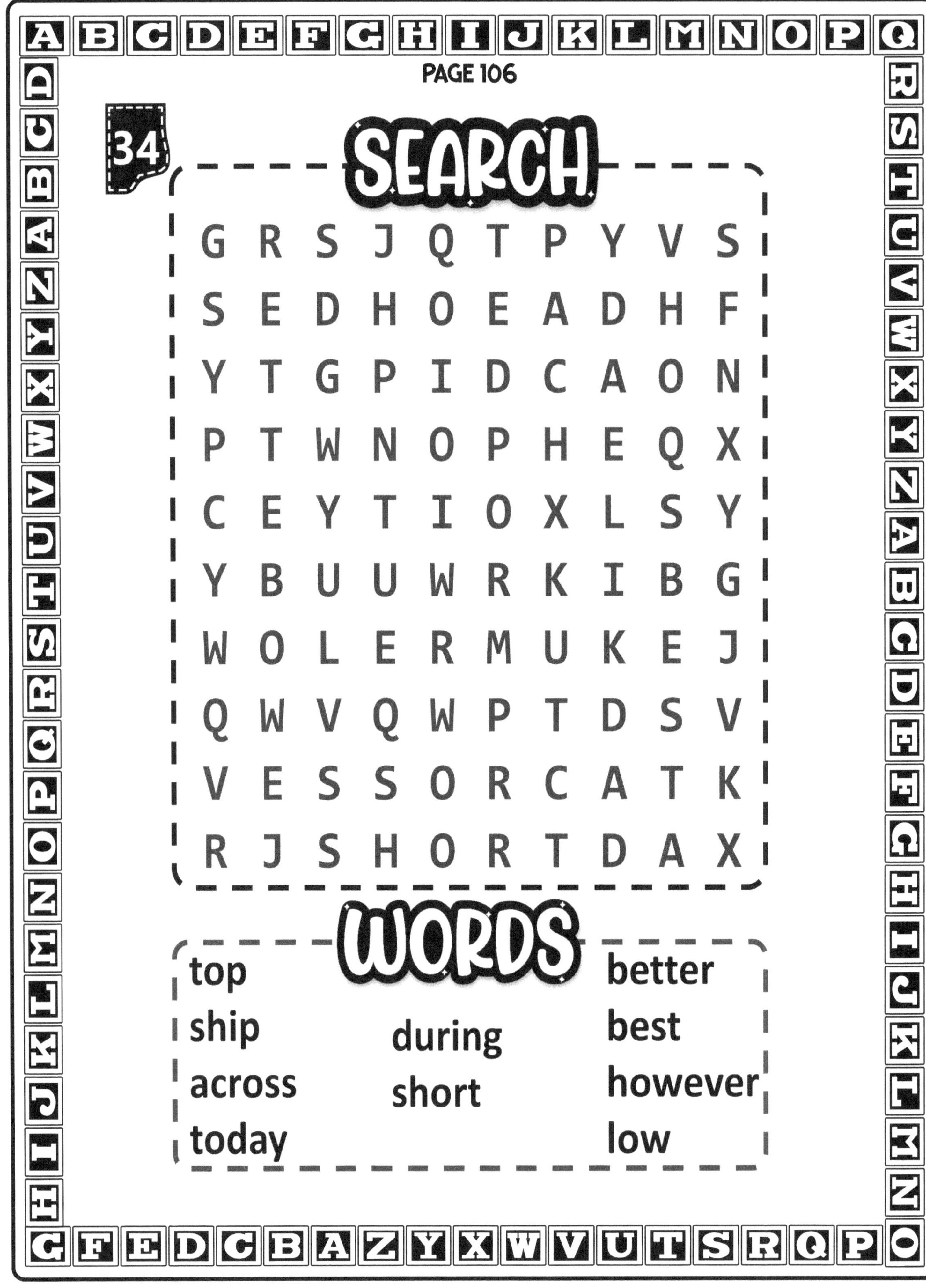
PAGE 106

34

SEARCH

G R S J Q T P Y V S
S E D H O E A D H F
Y T G P I D C A O N
P T W N O P H E Q X
C E Y T I O X L S Y
Y B U U W R K I B G
W O L E R M U K E J
Q W V Q W P T D S V
V E S S O R C A T K
R J S H O R T D A X

WORDS

top
ship
across
today
during
short
better
best
however
low

SEARCH
35

B L A C K O D H O B
P S E V A W E A O W
E R T I S S H P B S
W R O R D M C P E M
J H U D N H A E A K
A O O S U N E N R Q
H J D L A C R E L O
X V J F E E T D Y T
Z D K E B W M S J V
R E B M E M E R P D

WORDS

hours
black
products
happened
whole
measure
remember
early
waves
reached

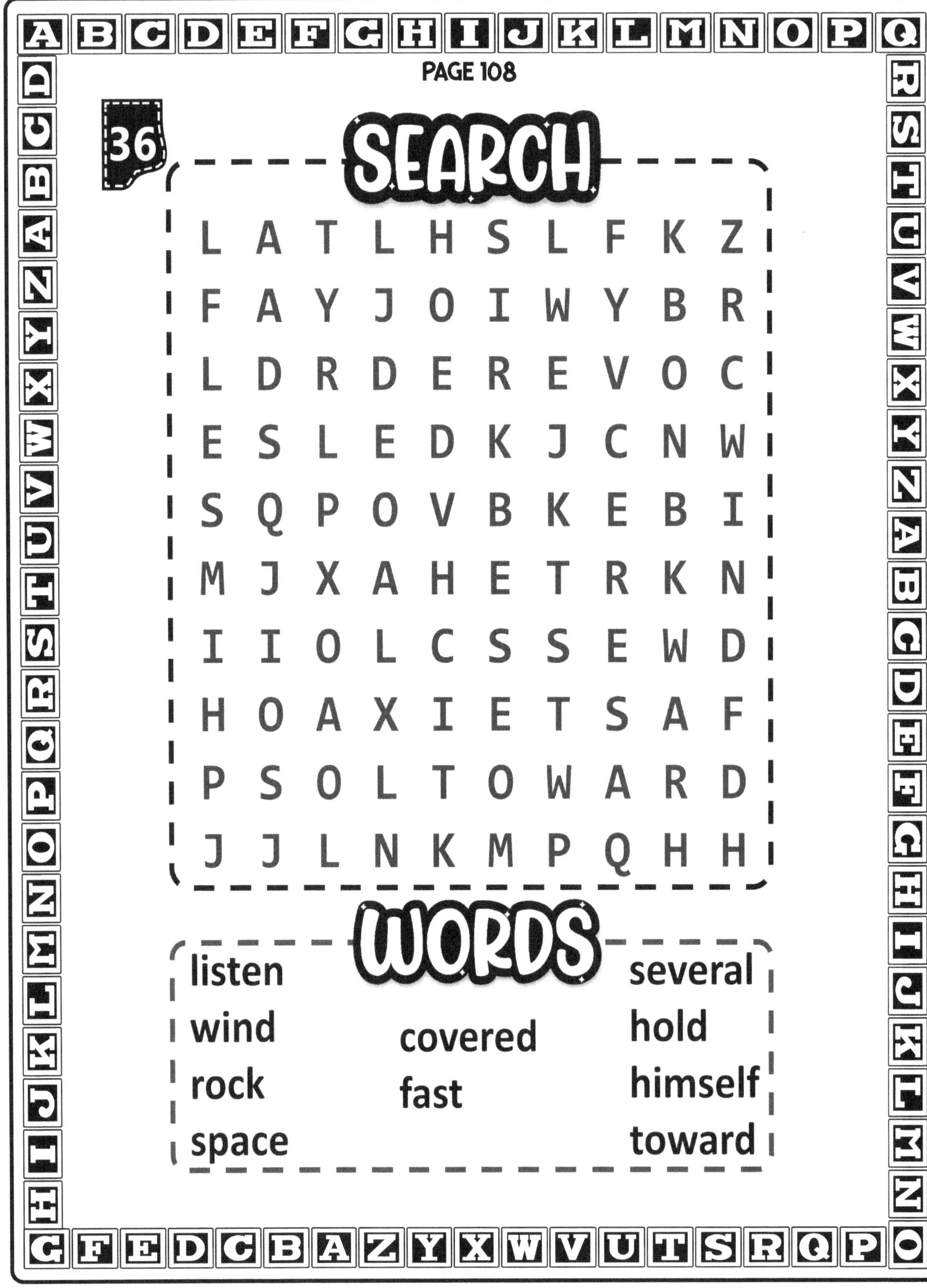
36
SEARCH

L A T L H S L F K Z
F A Y J O I W Y B R
L D R D E R E V O C
E S L E D K J C N W
S Q P O V B K E B I
M J X A H E T R K N
I I O L C S S E W D
H O A X I E T S A F
P S O L T O W A R D
J J L N K M P Q H H

WORDS

listen
wind
rock
space
covered
fast
several
hold
himself
toward

# SEARCH

37

# WORDS

five

step

morning

passed

vowel

true

hundred

against

pattern

numeral

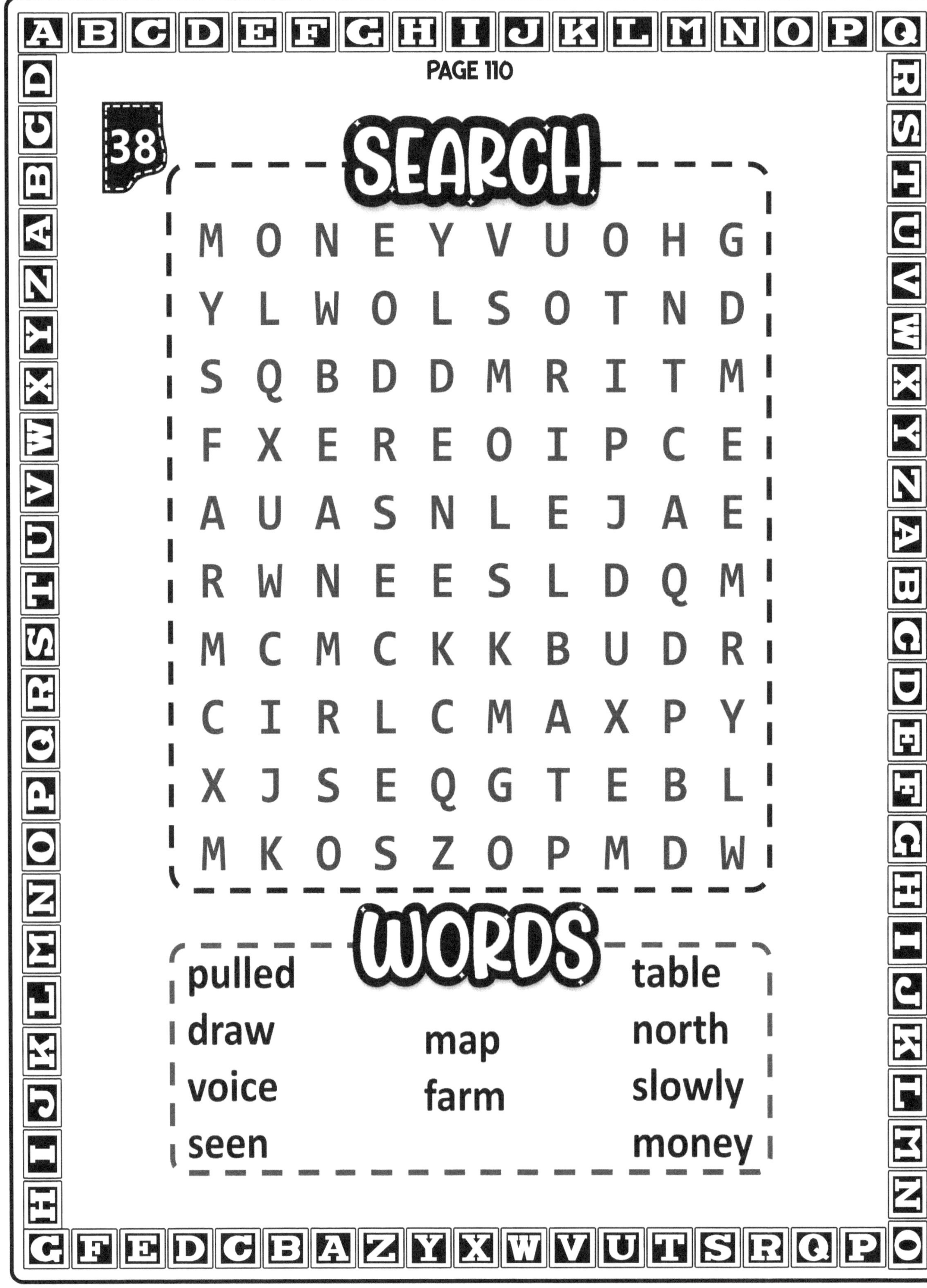


38
SEARCH

M O N E Y V U O H G
Y L W O L S O T N D
S Q B D D M R I T M
F X E R E O I P C E
A U A S N L E J A E
R W N E E S L D Q M
M C M C K K B U D R
C I R L C M A X P Y
X J S E Q G T E B L
M K O S Z O P M D W

WORDS

pulled          table
draw      map   north
voice     farm  slowly
seen            money

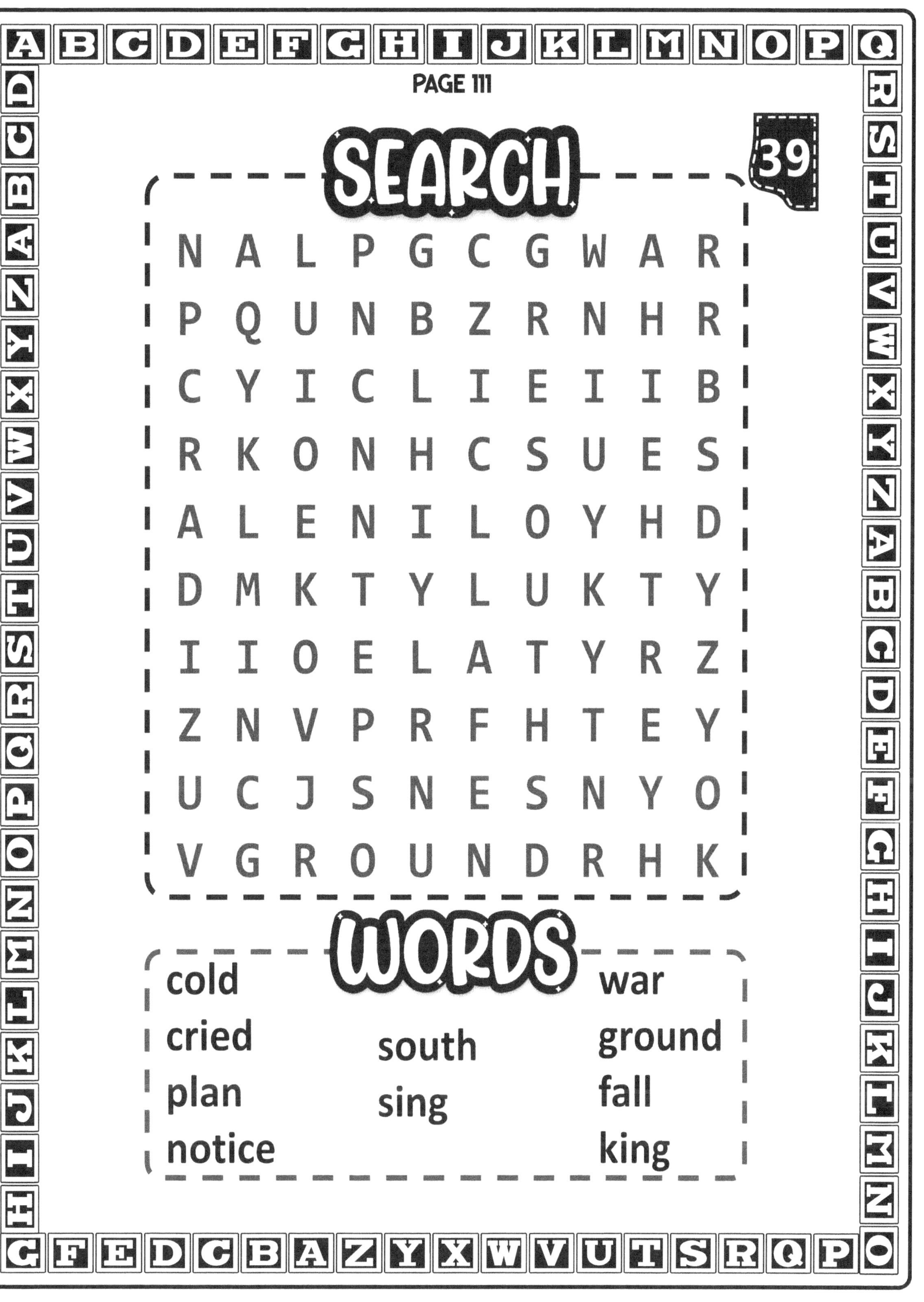


SEARCH
39

N A L P G C G W A R
P Q U N B Z R N H R
C Y I C L I E I I B
R K O N H C S U E S
A L E N I L O Y H D
D M K T Y L U K T Y
I I O E L A T Y R Z
Z N V P R F H T E Y
U C J S N E S N Y O
V G R O U N D R H K

WORDS
cold
cried
plan
notice
south
sing
war
ground
fall
king

PAGE 112

40

SEARCH

W H M Y E C Q W W D
B G B U T R F I N S
J O T F O I U H B F
N I A T R E C G A P
B P U E D L X W I R
U Q M L N E X O W F
F N E O N V N O P U
L I I Z I A C D J E
F L V T O R H Q S H
I I I Q N T O W N T

WORDS

town
I'll
unit
figure
certain
field
travel
wood
fire
upon

# Table of Contents – 150 CVC Phonics Words B – R


|  |  | |  |  | |  |  | |  |  |
|---|---|---|---|---|---|---|---|---|---|---|
| bag | – page 115 | | cot | – page 130 | | hit | – page 126 | | men | – page 120 |
| bag | – page 140 | | cow | – page 139 | | hop | – page 127 | | mom | – page 141 |
| bat | – page 136 | | cup | – page 143 | | hop | – page 136 | | mop | – page 129 |
| bat | – page 138 | | cut | – page 134 | | hot | – page 129 | | mop | – page 137 |
| bed | – page 119 | | cut | – page 142 | | hot | – page 142 | | mug | – page 133 |
| bed | – page 144 | | dad | – page 136 | | hug | – page 131 | | mug | – page 135 |
| bib | – page 124 | | dam | – page 144 | | hug | – page 138 | | nap | – page 137 |
| bib | – page 138 | | den | – page 122 | | hut | – page 140 | | net | – page 136 |
| big | – page 125 | | dig | – page 142 | | jam | – page 118 | | nun | – page 137 |
| big | – page 137 | | dip | – page 143 | | jam | – page 142 | | nut | – page 132 |
| bin | – page 126 | | dog | – page 128 | | jet | – page 120 | | pad | – page 117 |
| box | – page 136 | | dog | – page 142 | | jet | – page 141 | | pan | – page 118 |
| boy | – page 143 | | dot | – page 138 | | jog | – page 129 | | pan | – page 144 |
| bug | – page 134 | | fan | – page 143 | | jug | – page 135 | | pen | – page 122 |
| bug | – page 142 | | fig | – page 135 | | keg | – page 135 | | pen | – page 144 |
| bun | – page 133 | | fin | – page 124 | | kid | – page 140 | | pet | – page 144 |
| bun | – page 135 | | fin | – page 144 | | kit | – page 135 | | pig | – page 124 |
| bus | – page 131 | | fox | – page 141 | | lab | – page 141 | | pig | – page 140 |
| bus | – page 142 | | gem | – page 121 | | leg | – page 139 | | pin | – page 125 |
| cab | – page 137 | | gem | – page 140 | | lid | – page 143 | | pin | – page 139 |
| can | – page 141 | | gum | – page 134 | | lip | – page 142 | | pod | – page 128 |
| cap | – page 140 | | gum | – page 136 | | log | – page 130 | | pot | – page 127 |
| cat | – page 115 | | gun | – page 144 | | log | – page 144 | | pot | – page 143 |
| cat | – page 137 | | ham | – page 116 | | man | – page 115 | | pup | – page 132 |
| cob | – page 141 | | ham | – page 139 | | man | – page 139 | | rag | – page 142 |
| cog | – page 140 | | hat | – page 141 | | map | – page 116 | | ram | – page 143 |
| cop | – page 128 | | hen | – page 119 | | map | – page 144 | | rat | – page 118 |
| cop | – page 139 | | hen | – page 138 | | mat | – page 143 | | rat | – page 135 |

# R – Z  Table of Contents – 150 CVC Phonics Words

|  |  |  |  |
|---|---|---|---|
| rib | - page 125 | web | - page 137 |
| rip | - page 123 | wed | - page 122 |
| rod | - page 127 | wet | - page 121 |
| rug | - page 132 | wet | - page 136 |
| run | - page 139 | wig | - page 123 |
| sad | - page 116 | wig | - page 138 |
| sad | - page 139 | win | - page 136 |
| sip | - page 126 | yak | - page 138 |
| sit | - page 123 | yam | - page 141 |
| sit | - page 143 | zip | - page 141 |
| six | - page 136 | | |
| sun | - page 131 | | |
| sun | - page 140 | | |
| tag | - page 135 | | |
| tag | - page 117 | | |
| tap | - page 137 | | |
| ten | - page 121 | | |
| ten | - page 137 | | |
| top | - page 130 | | |
| top | - page 140 | | |
| toy | - page 135 | | |
| tub | - page 133 | | |
| tub | - page 138 | | |
| van | - page 117 | | |
| van | - page 139 | | |
| vet | - page 119 | | |
| vet | - page 138 | | |
| web | - page 120 | | |


## ~ P A R T 3 ~

- CVC Short A Phonics Worksheets &
I Can Write CVC Words Worksheets

## Teaching Kids to Read CVC Words:

1. Ensure they know the sound each letter makes and can say the sounds out loud.
2. Successive blending can make it easier for them to read CVC words by only putting together two sound chunks at a time.
3. Build reading comprehension by ensuring that they understand what the CVC word means.
4. Teach them to tie each sound in the CVC word to the letter that makes it.

### LEARNING IS FUN!

Name: ___________________________

# CVC SHORT A PHONICS

❶ Color the picture. ❷ Read the word. ❸ Find and circle the word. ❹ Trace and write the word.

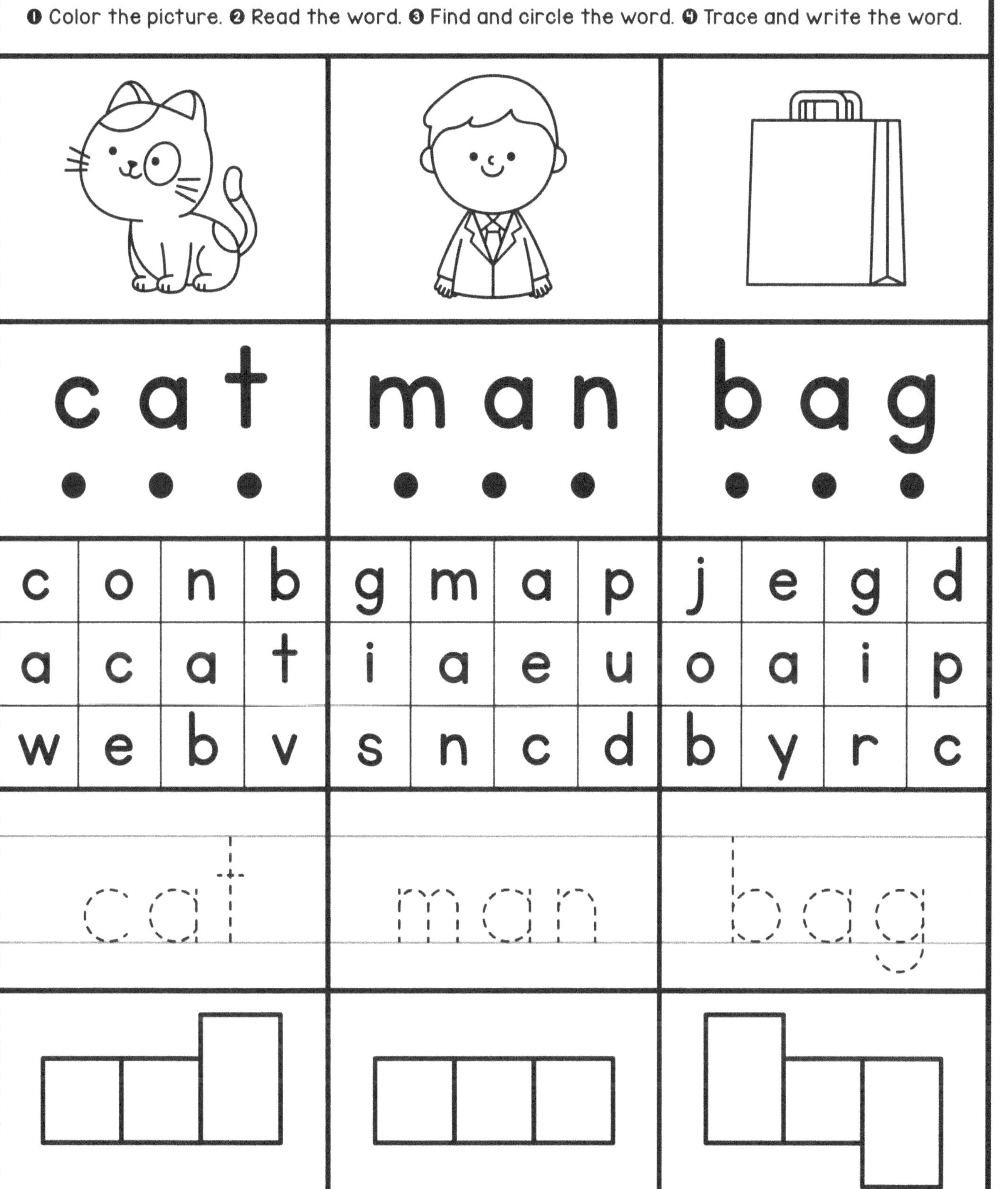

Name: ________________________

# CVC SHORT A PHONICS

❶ Color the picture. ❷ Read the word. ❸ Find and circle the word. ❹ Trace and write the word.

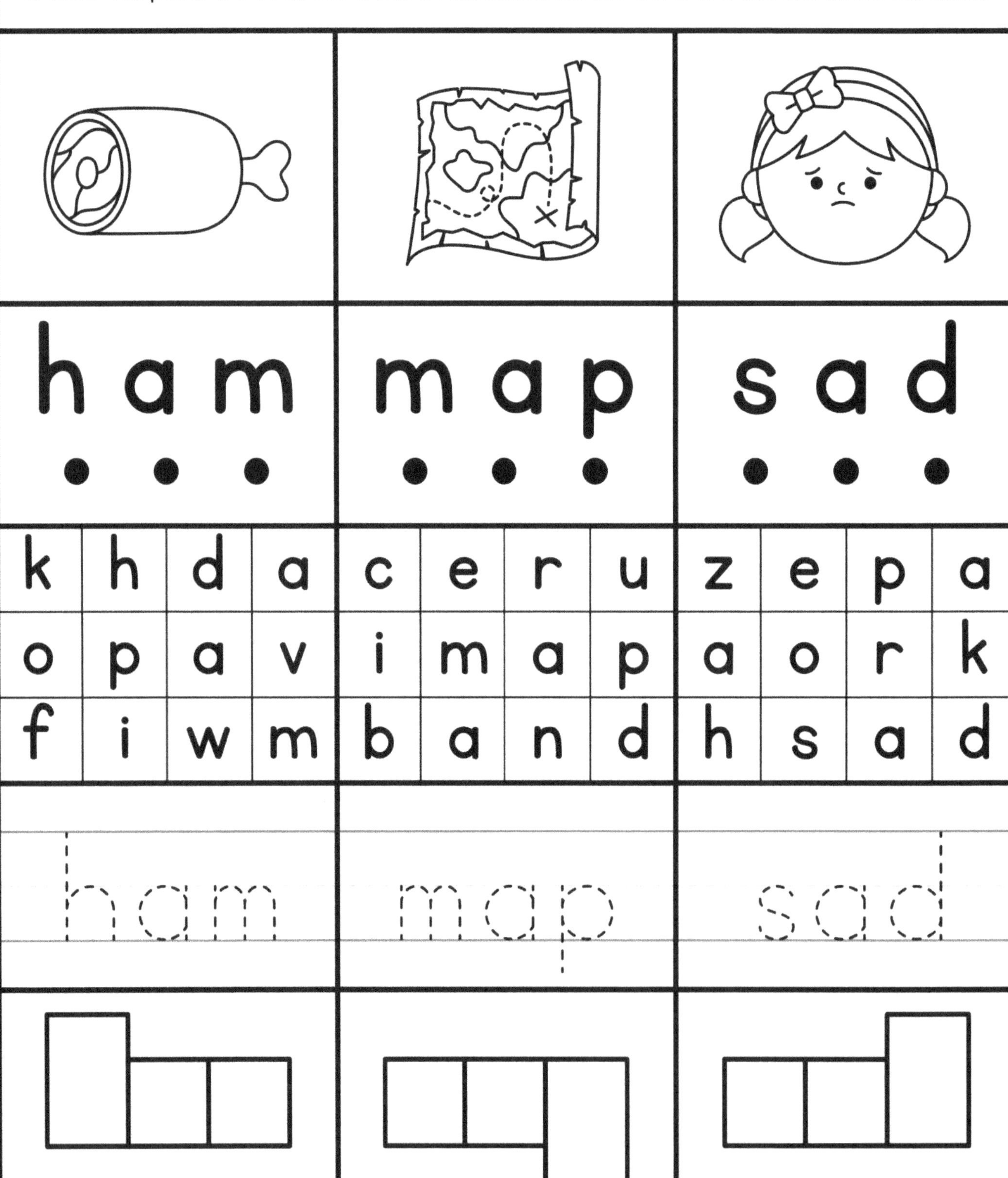

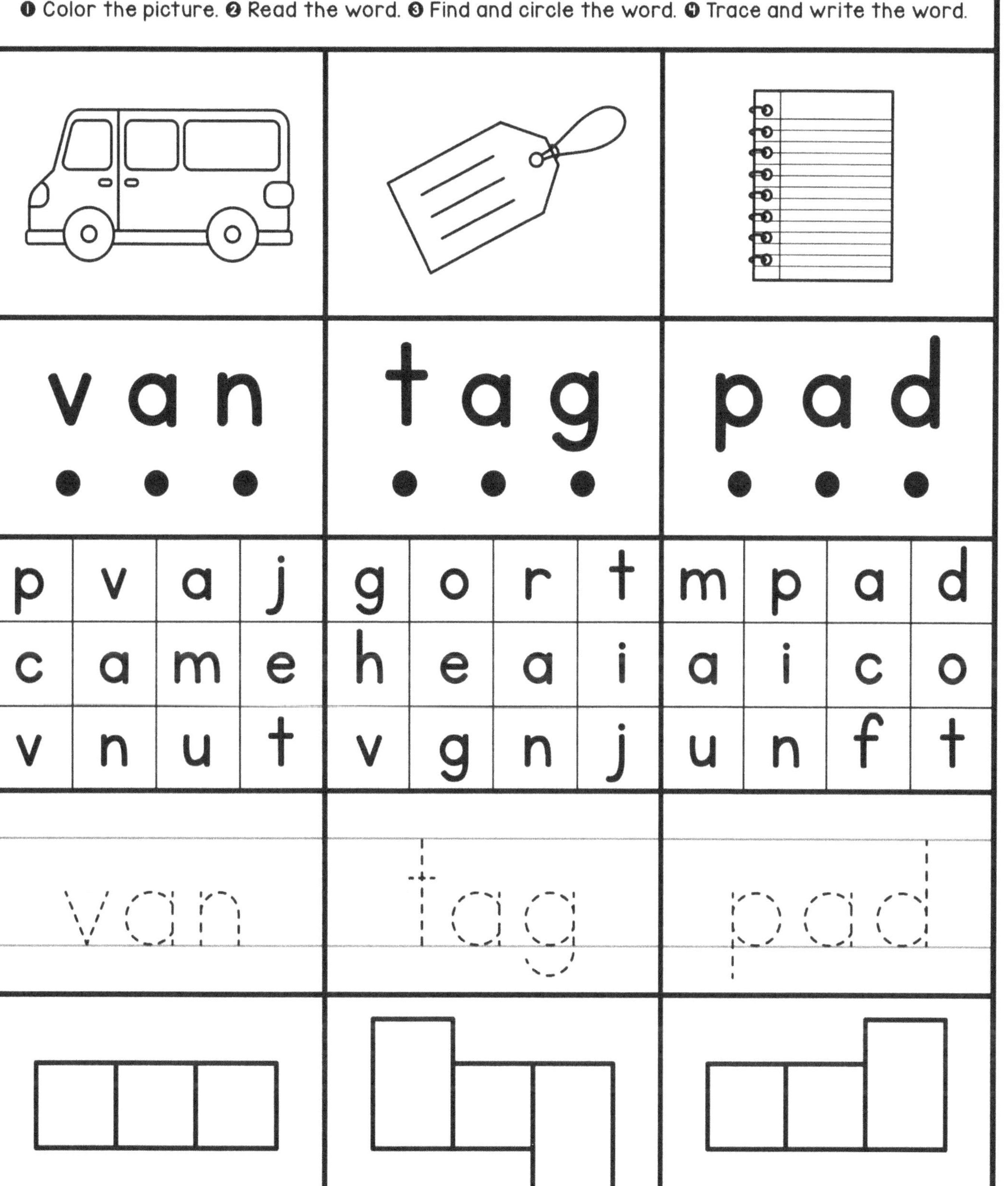



Name: _______________________________

# CVC SHORT A PHONICS

❶ Color the picture. ❷ Read the word. ❸ Find and circle the word. ❹ Trace and write the word.

van

tag

pad

| p | v | a | j |
|---|---|---|---|
| c | a | m | e |
| v | n | u | t |

| g | o | r | t |
|---|---|---|---|
| h | e | a | i |
| v | g | n | j |

| m | p | a | d |
|---|---|---|---|
| a | i | c | o |
| u | n | f | t |

Name: ___________________________

# CVC SHORT A PHONICS

❶ Color the picture. ❷ Read the word. ❸ Find and circle the word. ❹ Trace and write the word.

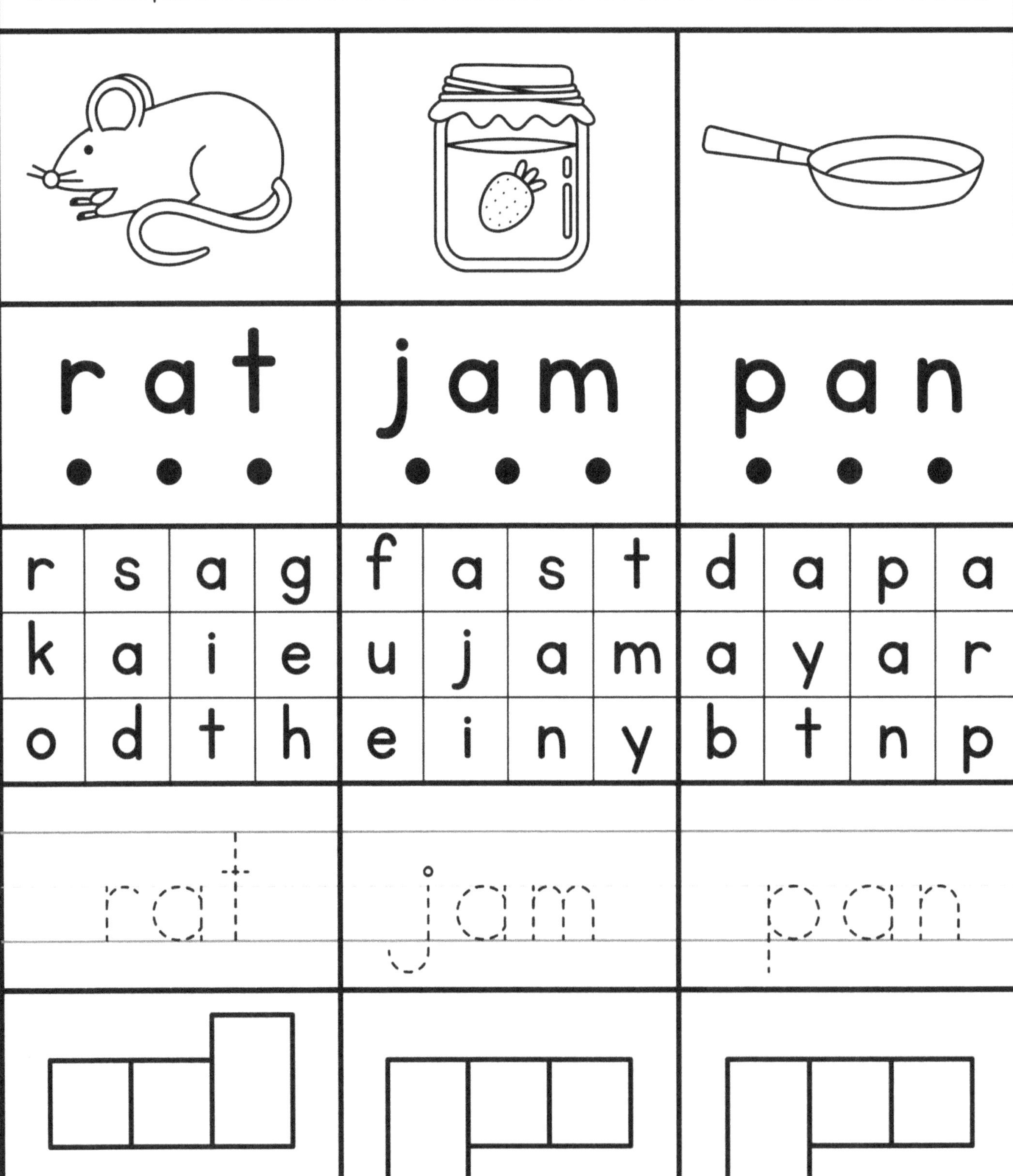

rat    jam    pan

| r | s | a | g |
|---|---|---|---|
| k | a | i | e |
| o | d | t | h |

| f | a | s | t |
|---|---|---|---|
| u | j | a | m |
| e | i | n | y |

| d | a | p | a |
|---|---|---|---|
| a | y | a | r |
| b | t | n | p |

rat    jam    pan

Name: _______________________

# CVC SHORT E PHONICS

❶ Color the picture. ❷ Read the word. ❸ Find and circle the word. ❹ Trace and write the word.

| v e t | b e d | h e n |
|---|---|---|

| y | a | c | t |
|---|---|---|---|
| b | i | e | n |
| f | v | a | s |

| g | i | b | a |
|---|---|---|---|
| a | s | e | t |
| j | o | d | w |

| k | a | p | m |
|---|---|---|---|
| b | i | t | e |
| h | e | n | c |

| vet | bed | hen |
|---|---|---|

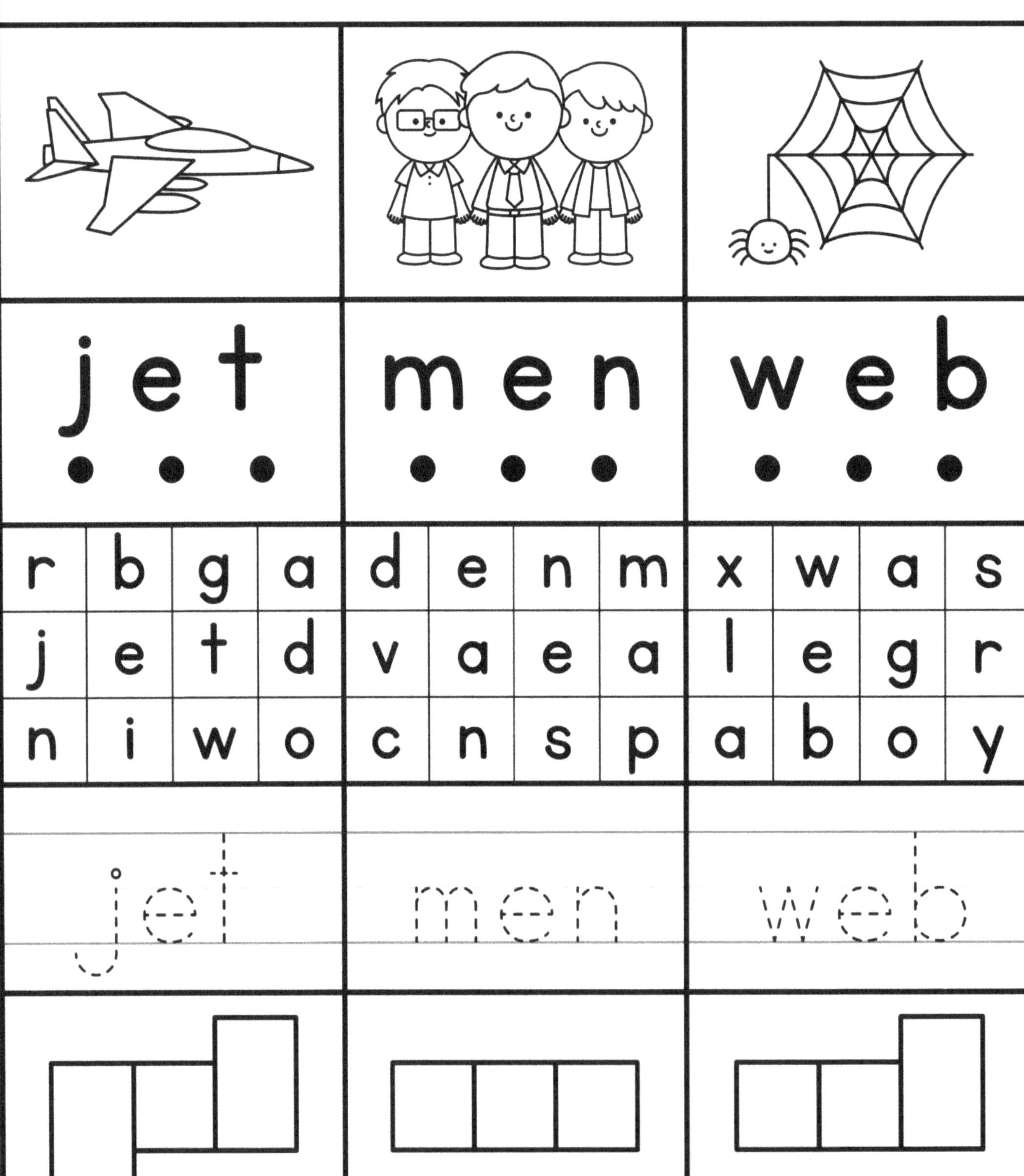



Name: ______________________________

# CVC SHORT E PHONICS

❶ Color the picture. ❷ Read the word. ❸ Find and circle the word. ❹ Trace and write the word.

Name: _______________________

# CVC SHORT E PHONICS

❶ Color the picture. ❷ Read the word. ❸ Find and circle the word. ❹ Trace and write the word.

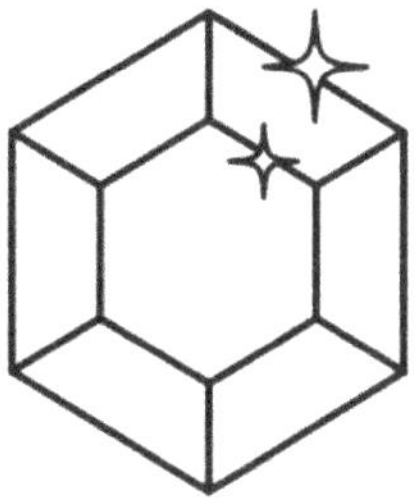

| | | |
|---|---|---|
| ten | gem | wet |

| t | e | a | m | s | n | i | g | a | m | a | t |
|---|---|---|---|---|---|---|---|---|---|---|---|
| o | a | b | h | g | a | m | e | o | v | e | a |
| p | t | e | n | k | y | u | m | l | w | f | n |

| ten | gem | wet |
|---|---|---|

Name: _______________________

# CVC SHORT E PHONICS

❶ Color the picture. ❷ Read the word. ❸ Find and circle the word. ❹ Trace and write the word.

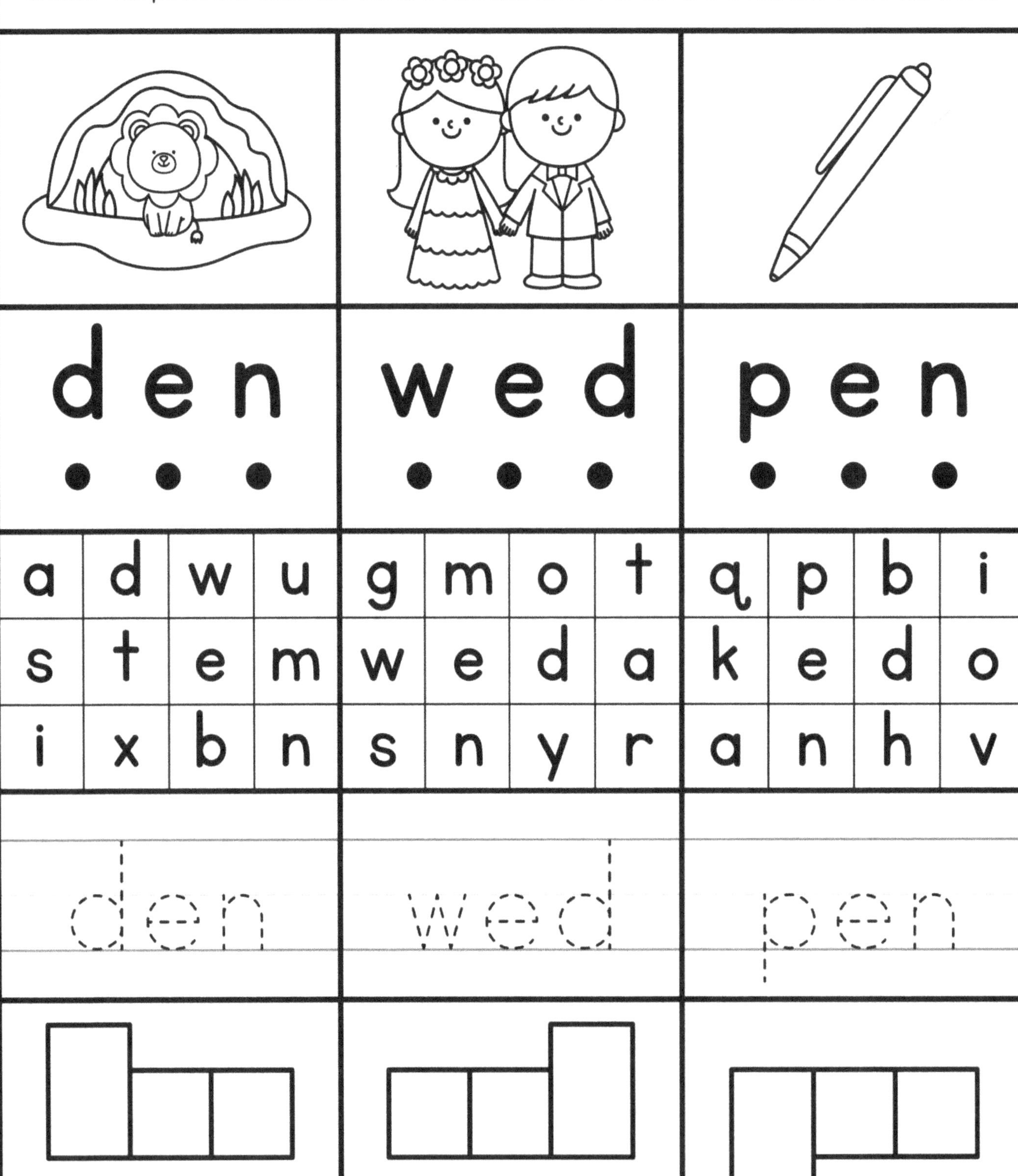

den

wed

pen

| a | d | w | u | g | m | o | t | q | p | b | i |
|---|---|---|---|---|---|---|---|---|---|---|---|
| s | t | e | m | w | e | d | a | k | e | d | o |
| i | x | b | n | s | n | y | r | a | n | h | v |

den

wed

pen

Name: _______________________

# CVC SHORT I PHONICS

❶ Color the picture. ❷ Read the word. ❸ Find and circle the word. ❹ Trace and write the word.

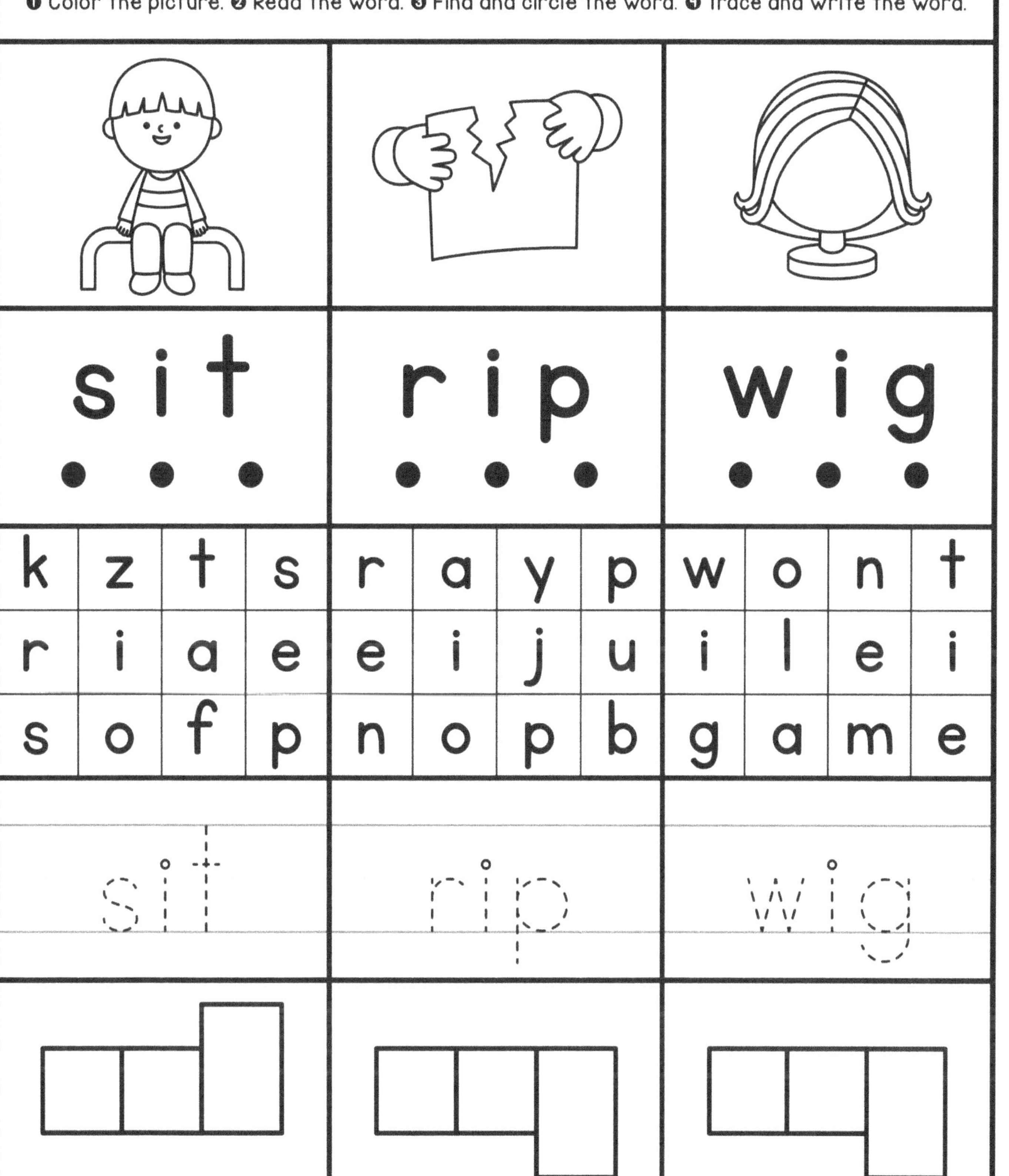

Name: _______________________

# CVC SHORT I PHONICS

❶ Color the picture. ❷ Read the word. ❸ Find and circle the word. ❹ Trace and write the word.

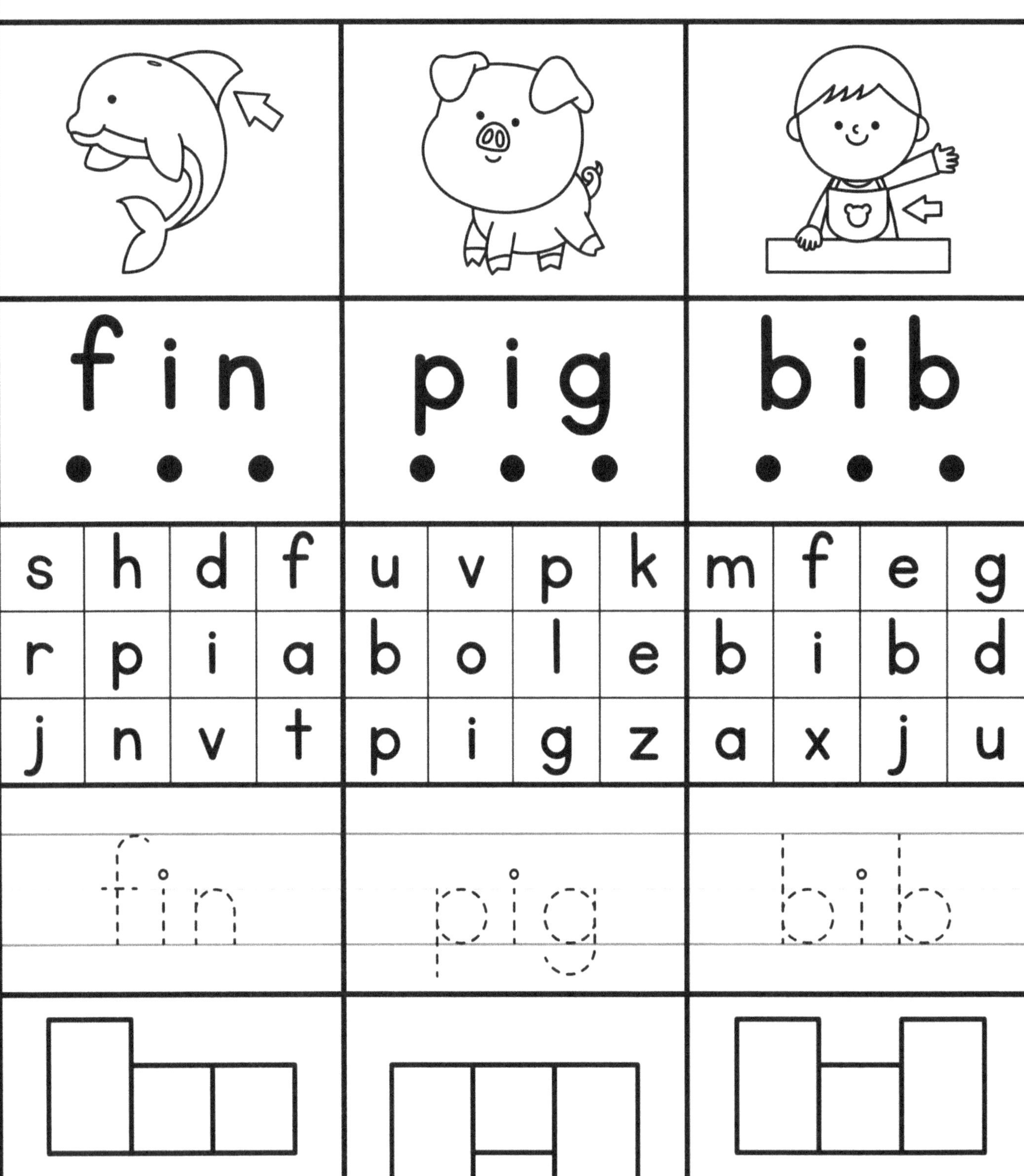

fin

pig

bib

| s | h | d | f |
|---|---|---|---|
| r | p | i | a |
| j | n | v | t |

| u | v | p | k |
|---|---|---|---|
| b | o | l | e |
| p | i | g | z |

| m | f | e | g |
|---|---|---|---|
| b | i | b | d |
| a | x | j | u |

fin

pig

bib

Name: ___________________________

# CVC SHORT I PHONICS

❶ Color the picture. ❷ Read the word. ❸ Find and circle the word. ❹ Trace and write the word.

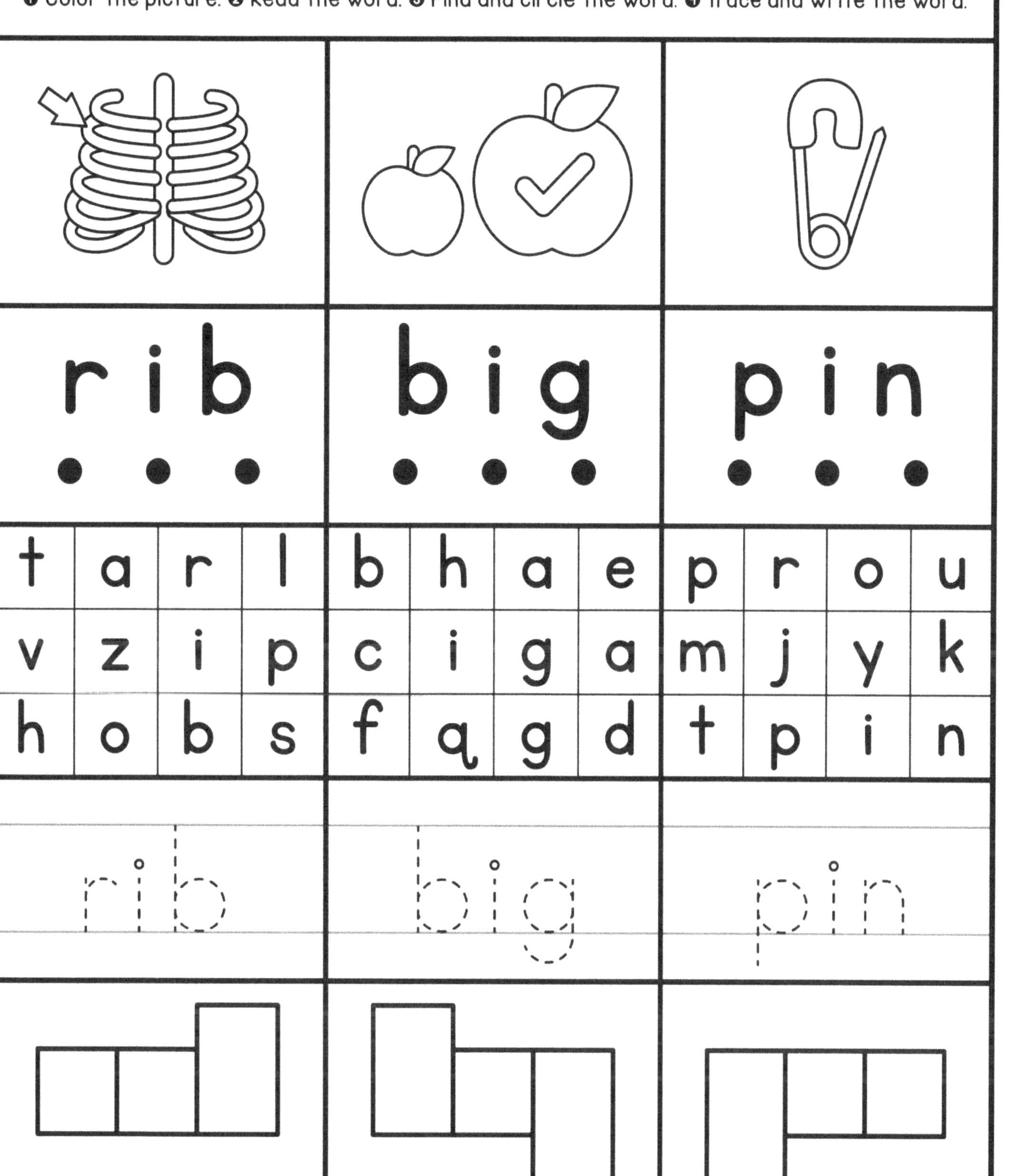

Name: ___________________________

# CVC SHORT I PHONICS

❶ Color the picture. ❷ Read the word. ❸ Find and circle the word. ❹ Trace and write the word.

## b i n

## s i p

## h i t

| d | a | w | b |
|---|---|---|---|
| f | s | i | o |
| j | n | u | g |

| z | m | k | s |
|---|---|---|---|
| s | i | p | a |
| b | o | n | d |

| p | h | e | f |
|---|---|---|---|
| k | l | i | a |
| w | y | r | t |

bin

sip

hit

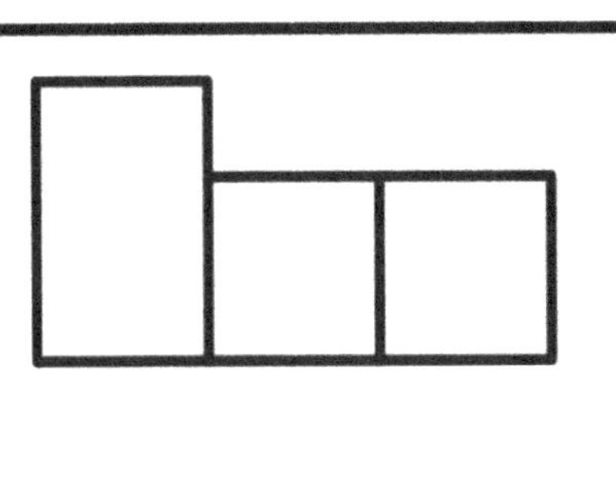

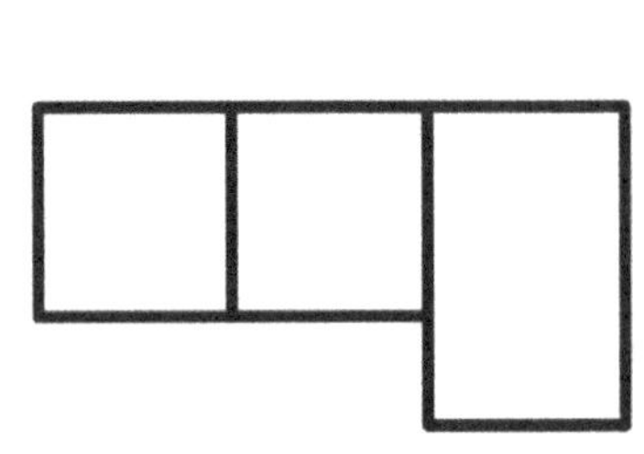

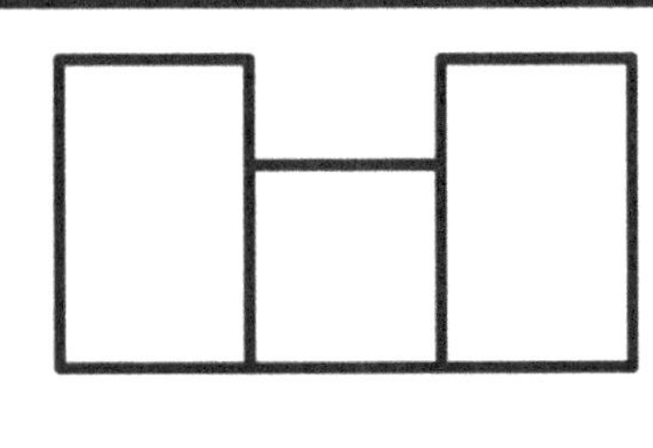

Name: ________________________

# CVC SHORT O PHONICS

❶ Color the picture. ❷ Read the word. ❸ Find and circle the word. ❹ Trace and write the word.

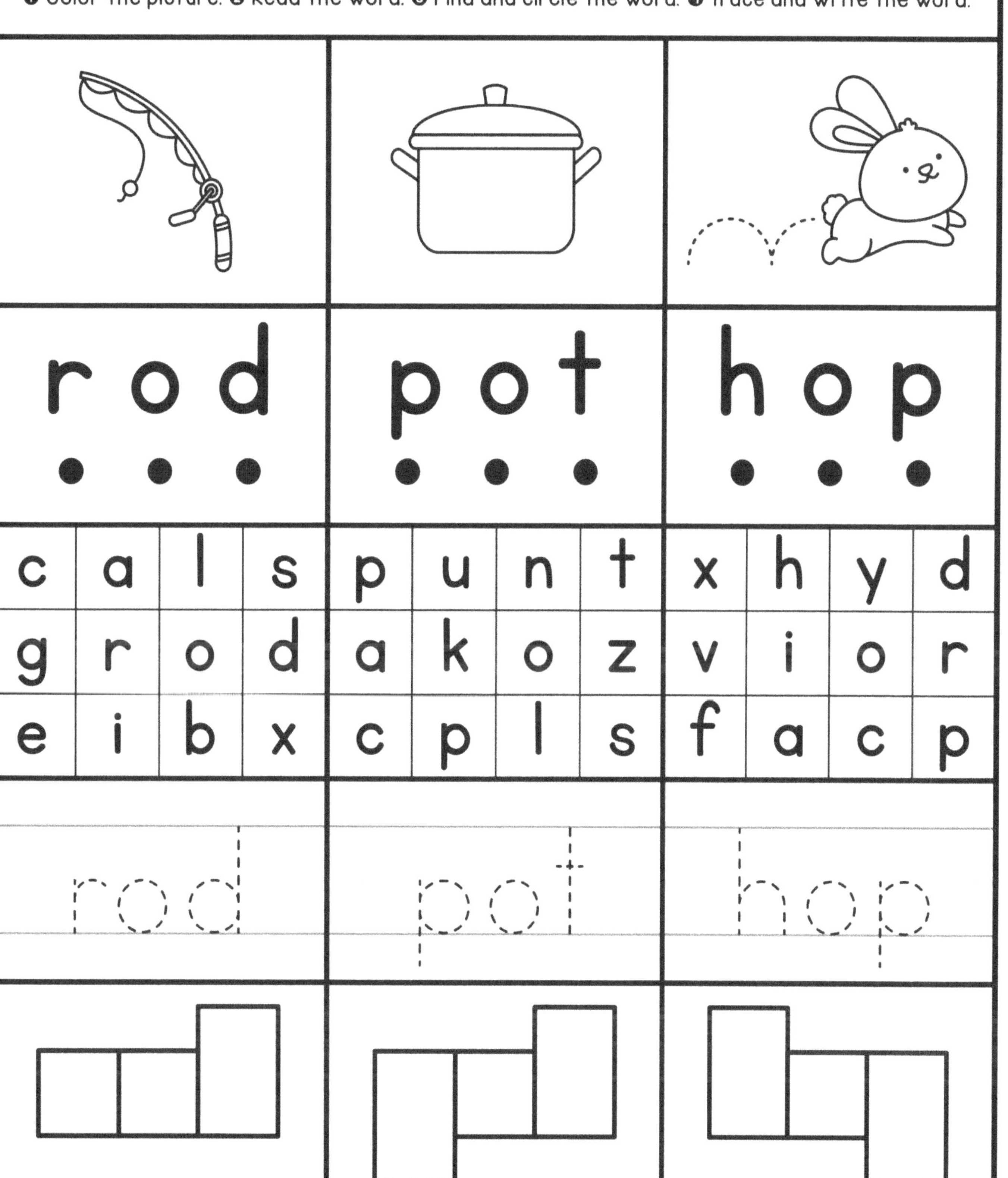

| r o d | p o t | h o p |
|:---:|:---:|:---:|

| c | a | l | s | | p | u | n | t | | x | h | y | d |
|---|---|---|---|---|---|---|---|---|---|---|---|---|---|
| g | r | o | d | | a | k | o | z | | v | i | o | r |
| e | i | b | x | | c | p | l | s | | f | a | c | p |

| rod | pot | hop |
|:---:|:---:|:---:|

Name: _______________________________

# CVC SHORT O PHONICS

❶ Color the picture. ❷ Read the word. ❸ Find and circle the word. ❹ Trace and write the word.

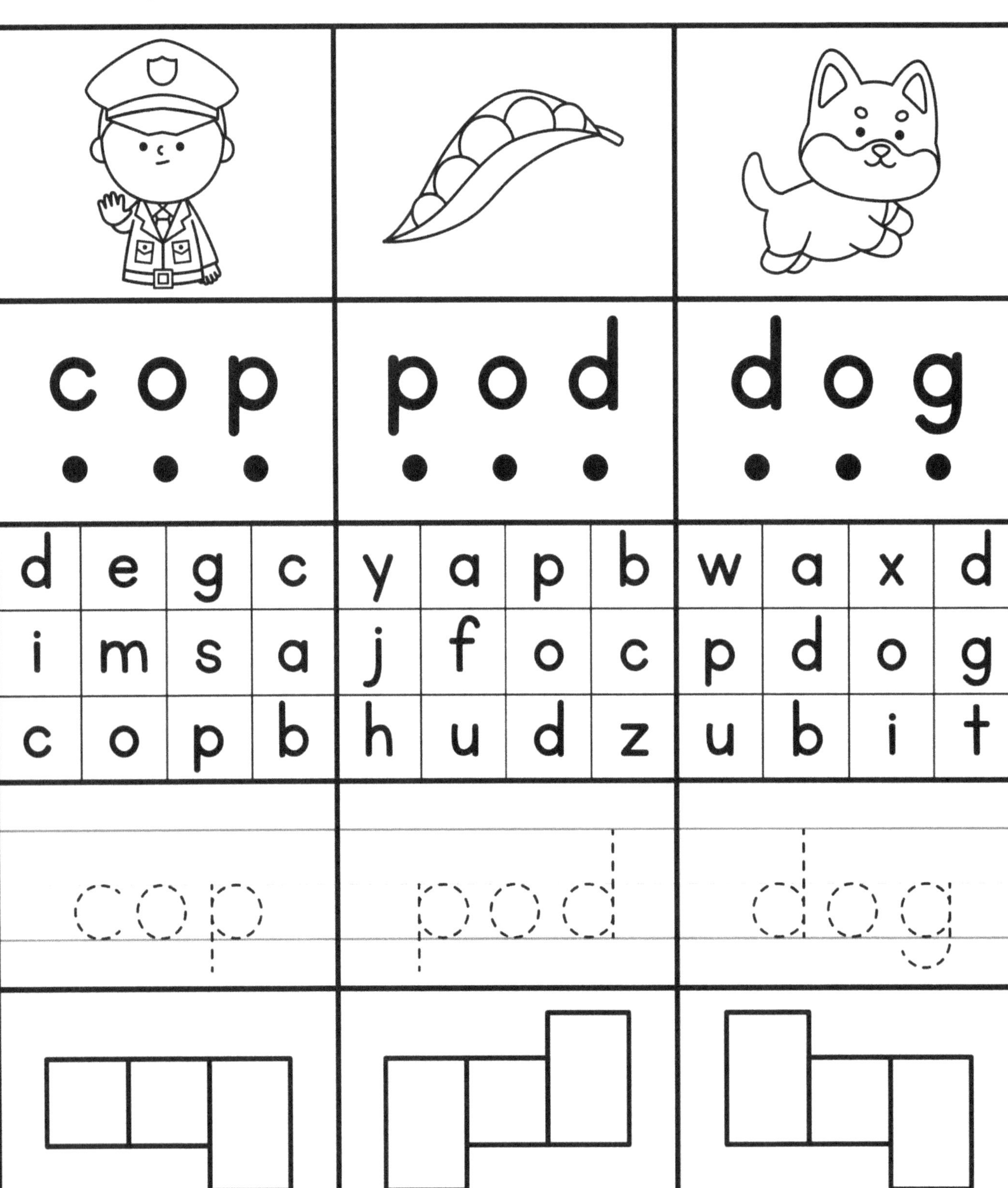

| c | o | p |
|---|---|---|

| p | o | d |
|---|---|---|

| d | o | g |
|---|---|---|

| d | e | g | c |
|---|---|---|---|
| i | m | s | a |
| c | o | p | b |

| y | a | p | b |
|---|---|---|---|
| j | f | o | c |
| h | u | d | z |

| w | a | x | d |
|---|---|---|---|
| p | d | o | g |
| u | b | i | t |

cop

pod

dog

Name: ________________________

# CVC SHORT O PHONICS

❶ Color the picture. ❷ Read the word. ❸ Find and circle the word. ❹ Trace and write the word.

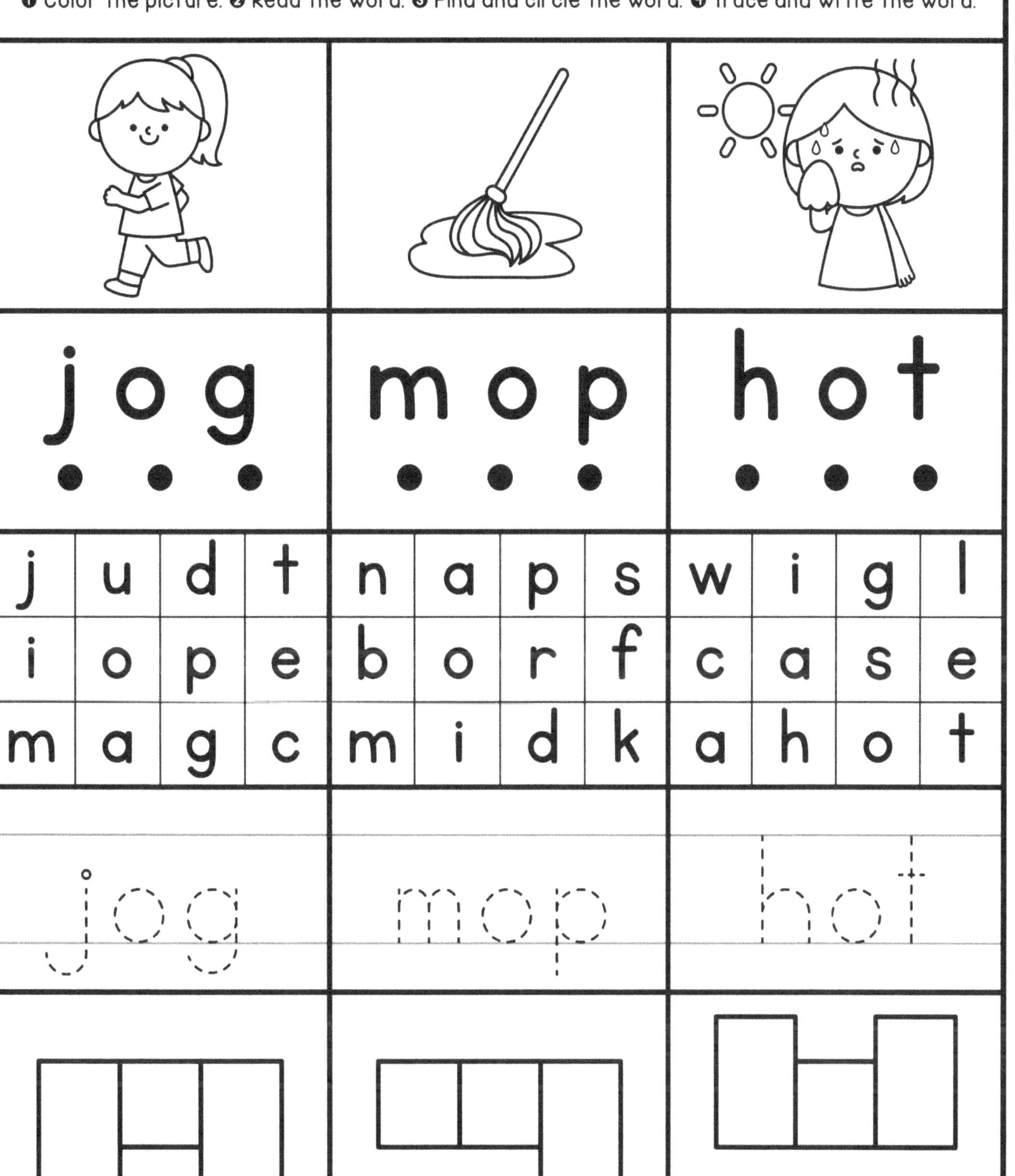

| | | |
|---|---|---|
| **j o g** | **m o p** | **h o t** |

| j | u | d | t | | n | a | p | s | | w | i | g | l |
|---|---|---|---|---|---|---|---|---|---|---|---|---|---|
| i | o | p | e | | b | o | r | f | | c | a | s | e |
| m | a | g | c | | m | i | d | k | | a | h | o | t |

jog  mop  hot

Name: ___________________________

# CVC SHORT O PHONICS

❶ Color the picture. ❷ Read the word. ❸ Find and circle the word. ❹ Trace and write the word.

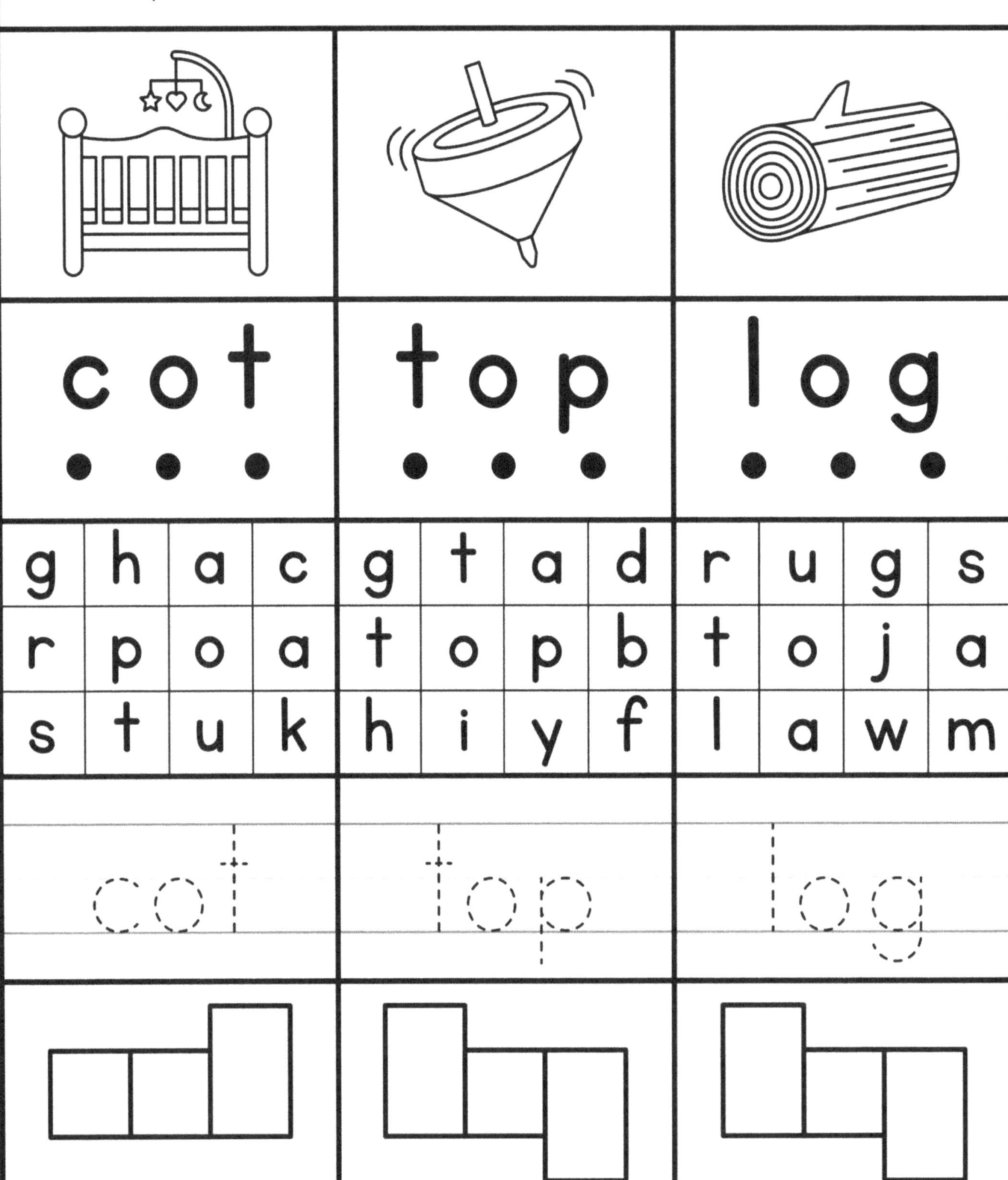

| c o t | t o p | l o g |
|---|---|---|

| g | h | a | c | g | t | a | d | r | u | g | s |
|---|---|---|---|---|---|---|---|---|---|---|---|
| r | p | o | a | t | o | p | b | t | o | j | a |
| s | t | u | k | h | i | y | f | l | a | w | m |

Name: ________________

# CVC SHORT U PHONICS

❶ Color the picture. ❷ Read the word. ❸ Find and circle the word. ❹ Trace and write the word.

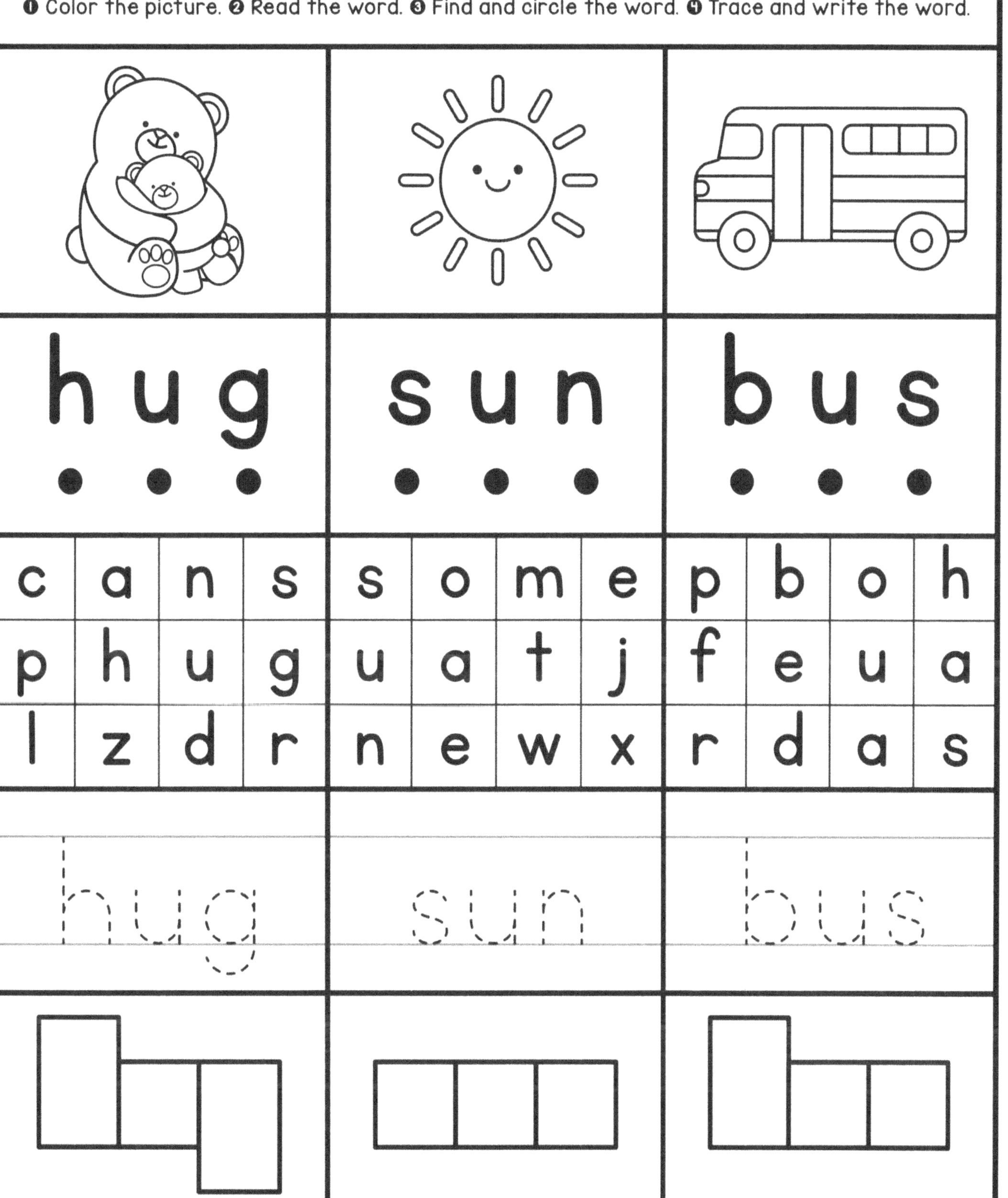

hug

sun

bus

| c | a | n | s | s | o | m | e | p | b | o | h |
| p | h | u | g | u | a | t | j | f | e | u | a |
| l | z | d | r | n | e | w | x | r | d | a | s |

hug

sun

bus

Name: _________________________________

# CVC SHORT U PHONICS

❶ Color the picture. ❷ Read the word. ❸ Find and circle the word. ❹ Trace and write the word.

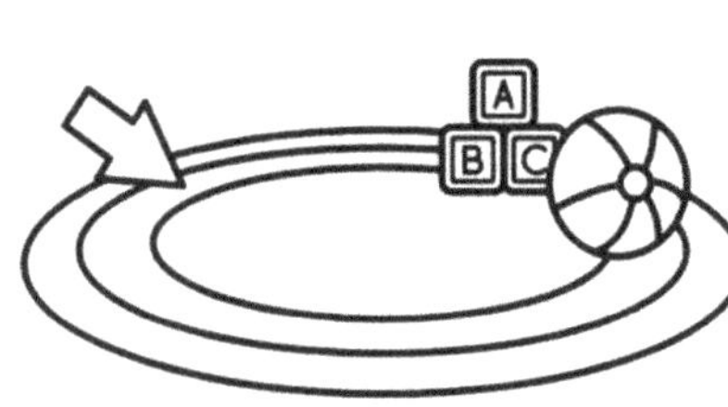

## p u p

## n u t

## r u g

| w | s | g | p |
|---|---|---|---|
| c | a | u | i |
| b | p | r | t |

| p | i | h | s |
|---|---|---|---|
| n | u | t | e |
| l | f | v | a |

| n | r | k | o |
|---|---|---|---|
| i | a | u | w |
| v | b | p | g |

pup

nut

rug

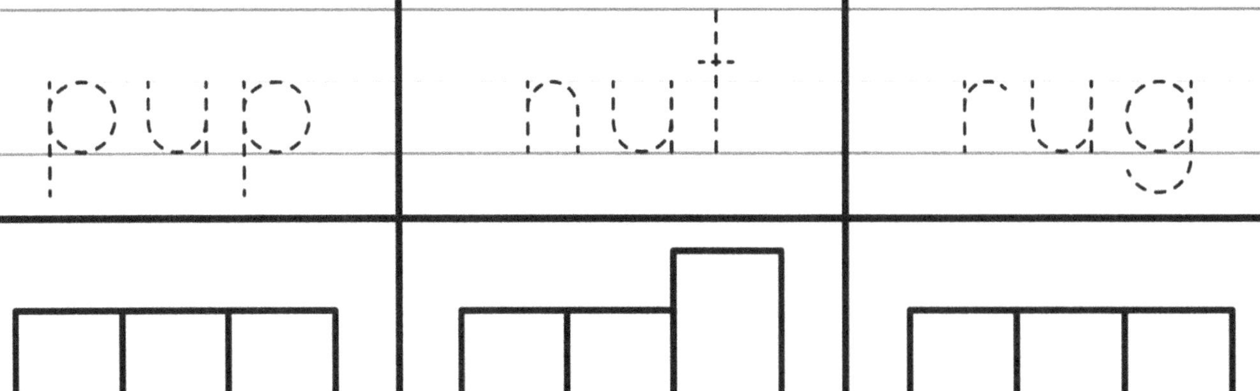

Name: _______________________

# CVC SHORT U PHONICS

❶ Color the picture. ❷ Read the word. ❸ Find and circle the word. ❹ Trace and write the word.

| | | |
|---|---|---|
| m u g | b u n | t u b |

| s | a | h | c | r | a | n | i | w | p | g | s |
|---|---|---|---|---|---|---|---|---|---|---|---|
| w | m | u | g | e | u | y | b | a | i | d | v |
| n | o | b | k | b | c | m | d | n | t | u | b |

| mug | bun | tub |
|---|---|---|

Name: _______________________________

# CVC SHORT U PHONICS

❶ Color the picture. ❷ Read the word. ❸ Find and circle the word. ❹ Trace and write the word.

|  | 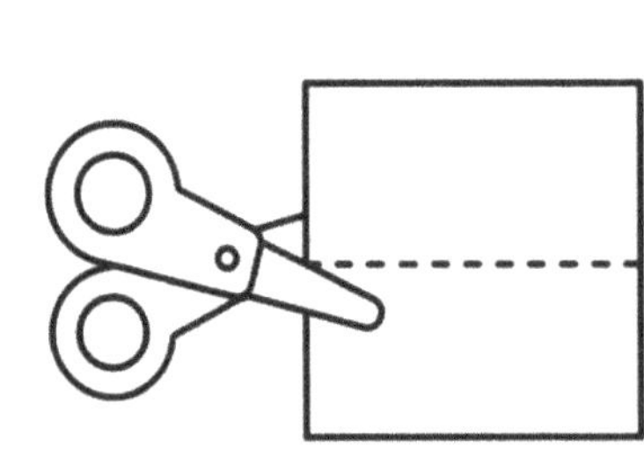 | 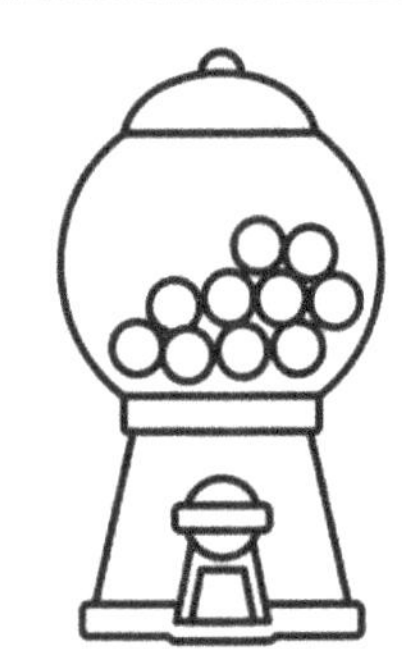 |
|---|---|---|
| b u g | c u t | g u m |

| r | i | s | d | k | c | i | p | r | e | m | t |
|---|---|---|---|---|---|---|---|---|---|---|---|
| a | h | p | u | j | a | u | o | i | u | a | n |
| b | u | g | f | w | b | a | t | g | o | d | s |

| bug | cut | gum |
|---|---|---|

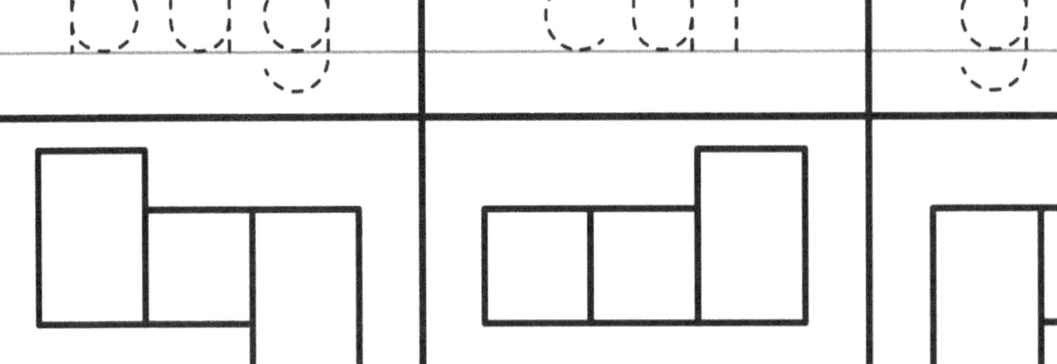

# I Can Write CVC Words

Name: _______________________________

Directions: Using the word bank, fill in the the word and color the picture.

| fig | bun | toy | mug | tag | rat | keg | jug | kit |
|-----|-----|-----|-----|-----|-----|-----|-----|-----|

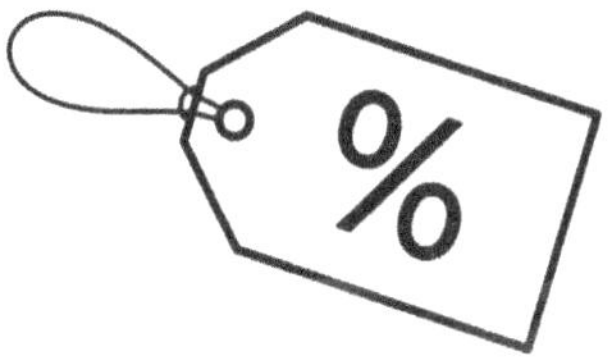

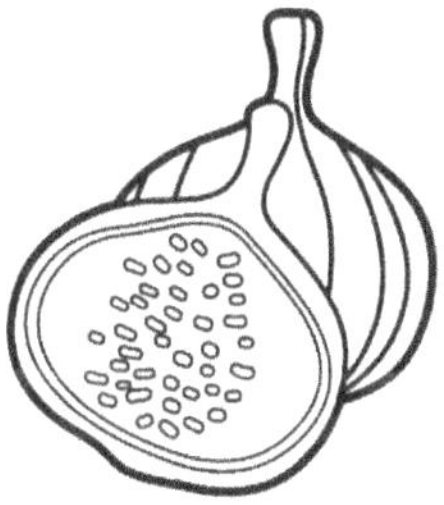

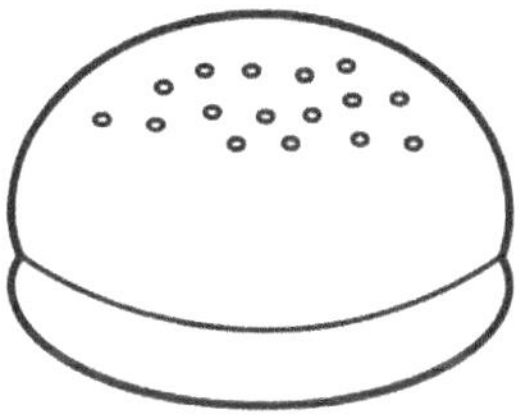

Name: ________________

# I Can Write CVC Words

Directions: Using the word bank, fill in the the word and color the picture.

| bat | hop | wet | gum | net | six | dad | win | box |

Name: ______________________

# I Can Write CVC Words

Directions: Using the word bank, fill in the the word and color the picture.

| cab | ten | cat | web | nun | nap | big | mop | tap |

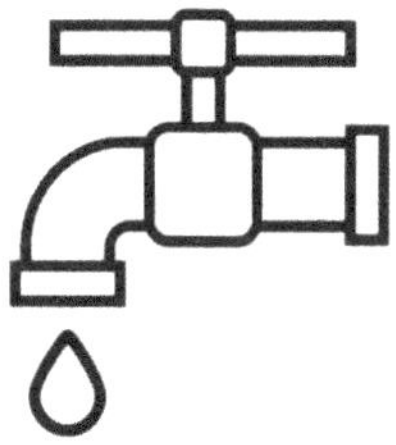

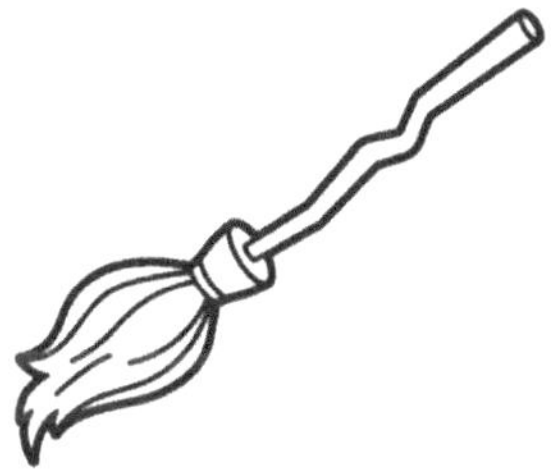

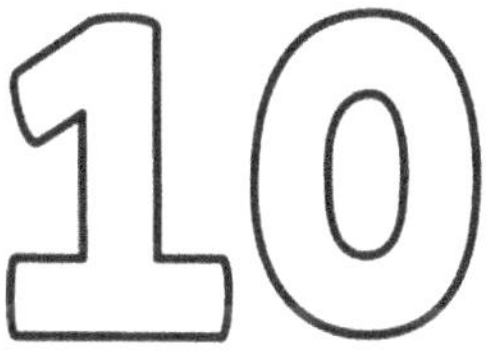

Name: _______________________

# I Can Write CVC Words

Directions: Using the word bank, fill in the the word and color the picture.

| hug | bat | bib | yak | wig | vet | tub | hen | dot |

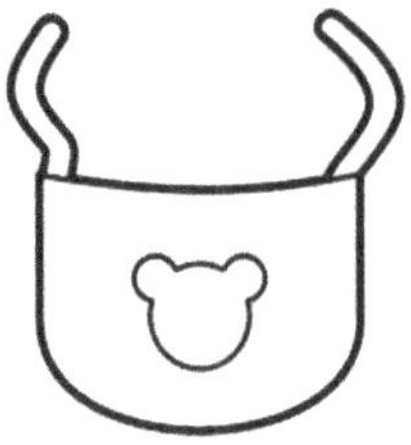

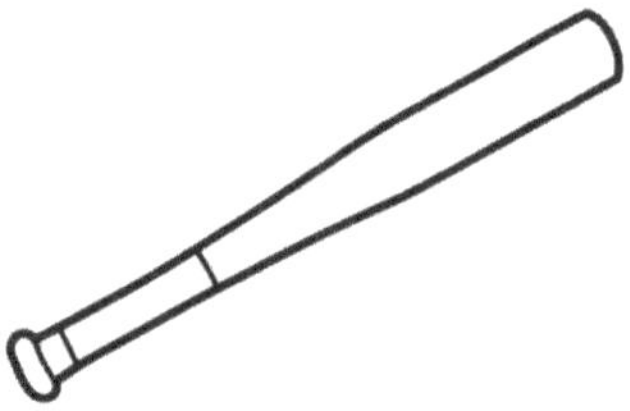

Name: ______________________

# I Can Write CVC Words

Directions: Using the word bank, fill in the the word and color the picture.

| man | pin | leg | sad | run | cop | van | cow | ham |

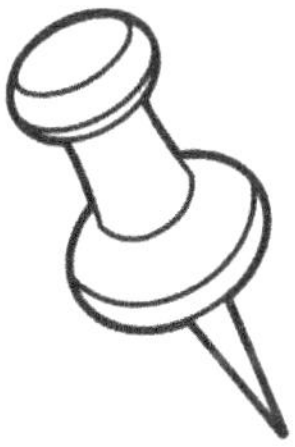

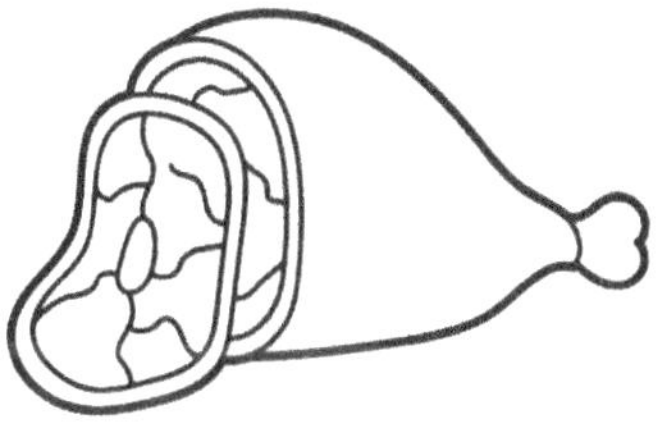

Name: _______________

# I Can Write CVC Words

Directions: Using the word bank, fill in the the word and color the picture.

| top | hut | pig | sun | cap | kid | bag | gem | cog |
|-----|-----|-----|-----|-----|-----|-----|-----|-----|

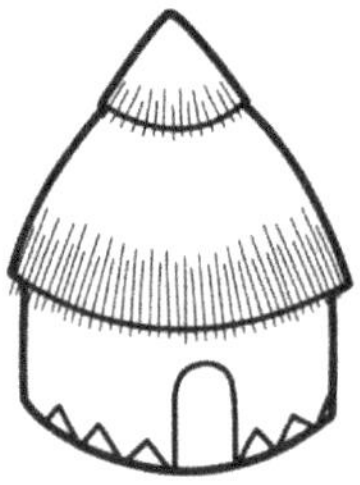

Name: _______________________

# I Can Write CVC Words

Directions: Using the word bank, fill in the the word and color the picture.

| jet | mom | lab | yam | cob | hat | fox | zip | can |

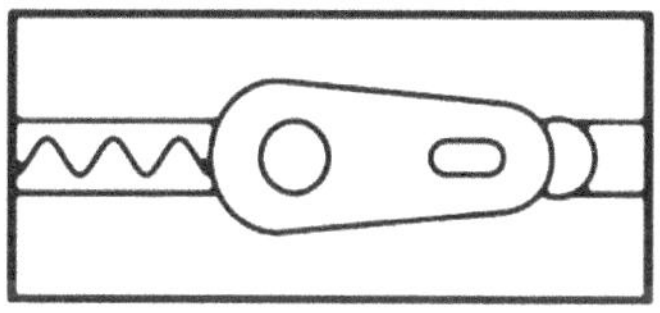

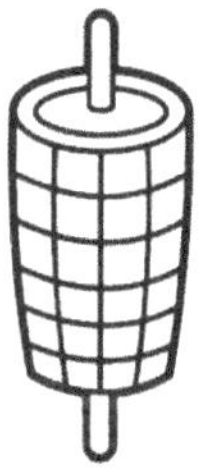

Name: _______________________

# I Can Write CVC Words

Directions: Using the word bank, fill in the the word and color the picture.

| bug | dig | cut | rag | bus | hot | lip | jam | dog |

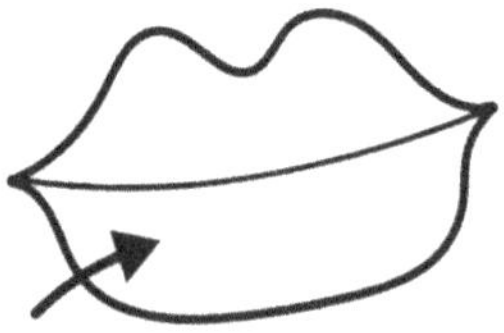

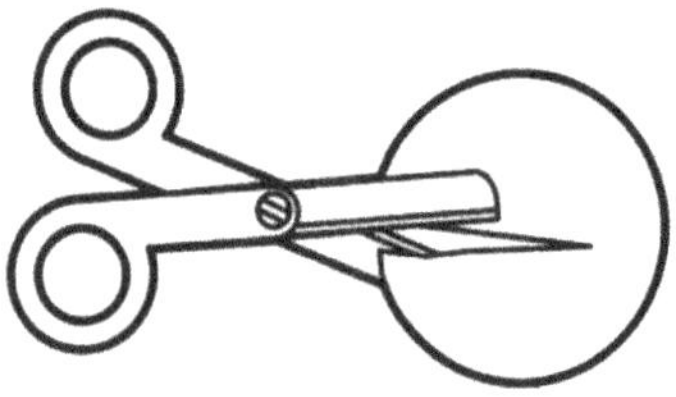

Name: ___________________

# I Can Write CVC Words

Directions: Using the word bank, fill in the the word and color the picture.

| pot | mat | sit | fan | boy | dip | ram | lid | cup |

Name: _______________________

# I Can Write CVC Words

Directions: Using the word bank, fill in the the word and color the picture.

| fin | pan | pen | map | pet | dam | log | gun | bed |

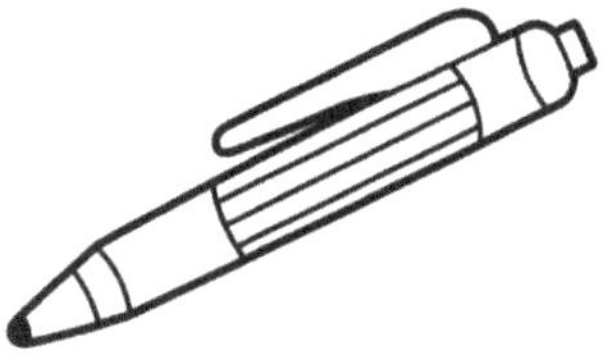

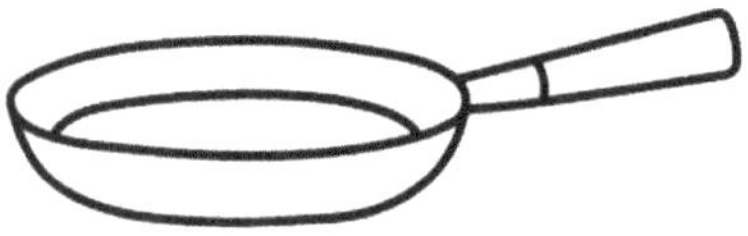

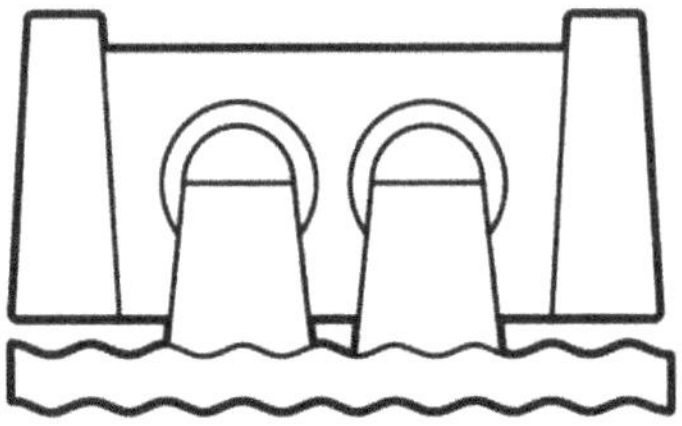

# CERTIFICATE
## Of Achievement

Proudly Presented To:

_______________________________

For Learning to Read, Write & Spell 405
Sight Words & 150 CVC Phonics Words!

CATERPILLAR KIDZ PRESS

Teacher

Date

THANK YOU!

I truly appreciate your purchase! My hope is that this Learn to Read, Sight Words & Phonics Children's Learning Book serves you and your children well. If you have a moment, would you please consider leaving me a review by using the QR code provided below?

CATERPILLAR KIDZ PRESS